ONE CHANCE

LENA HENDRIX

This is a work of fiction. Any names, characters, places, or incidents are products of the author's imagination and used in a fictitious manner. Any resemblance to actual people, places, or events is purely coincidental or fictional.

Developmental Editing by Becca Mysoor, Fairy Plot Mother

Copy editing by James Gallagher, Evident Ink

Proofreading by Julia Griffis, The Romance Bibliophile

Cover by Echo Grayce, WildHeart Graphics

Photography by Wander Aguiar

Cover Model: Peter Dockal

For the girls who were unfairly friendzoned because he was too big of an idiot to see how perfect you are.

LET'S CONNECT!

When you sign up for my newsletter, you'll stay up to date with new releases, book news, giveaways, and new book recommendations! I promise not to spam you and only email when I have something fun & exciting to share!

Also, When you sign up, you'll also get a FREE copy of Choosing You (a very steamy Chikalu Falls novella)!

Sign up at my website at www.lenahendrix.com

AUTHOR'S NOTE

This book contains contains explicit sex scenes (that's why we're all here, right?).

It also contains the death of a parent (off page/not detailed, but referenced) and a parent with early onset dementia. Oh, also butt stuff (please see above).

ABOUT THIS BOOK

Fake dating my best friend? Total disaster.

With his cocky grin and devilish charm, firefighter Lee Sullivan makes every woman in our small town swoon. Every woman except for me.

Which is why I'm shocked when he steps in at the town's Matchmakers' Gala and outbids my crush during the charity auction, committing us to six prearranged dates.

Six dates where we, *very publicly*, pretend to be falling in love.

Despite my objections and our efforts to set each other up with other people, Lee is convinced *pretending to date each other* is the perfect opportunity to get the women in town off his back (and out of his bed), while also helping to nudge my noncommittal crush in the jealousy department.

Stupidly, I agree.

After the disastrous blind dates he set me up on, what's a few months of letting Lee worship the ground I walk on? He owes me.

Trouble is—every fake kiss, every lingering

touch, every filthy word he whispers with no one around is starting to feel very, very real.

We know everything about each other—from my orphaned past to his commitment to never being committed. The only secret I have ever kept from Lee spans all the way back to his time in the Army, and it's the one thing that could ruin our friendship forever.

Because where Lee is concerned, I have learned to guard my heart. Suddenly he's asking for the opportunity to feel something real. **He's asking for the one thing he wouldn't want if he ever knew the truth: *one chance*.**

ONE
ANNIE

"Why is Lee running down Main Street with no pants on?"

My head whipped up from my vanilla oat milk latte in time to see my very fast, very *undressed* best friend running down the town's main thoroughfare.

Morning sun streamed through the trees that lined our small-town's sidewalks and everyone outside gaped at Lee hauling ass.

I tracked him as he dodged pedestrians and concrete planters with both hands cupped over his privates and wearing nothing but worn, untied work boots.

A low whistle came from my friend Emma. "God DAYUM!"

"Gross." Kate Sullivan, Lee's sister, twisted her face in disgust.

I nudged Emma, willing my eyes to not stray to the rounded muscles of Lee's butt as he ran past us.

Sitting outside the Sugar Bowl, Kate, Emma, and I watched in mild horror as Lee made impressive time streaking through town.

Kate shook her head and took a bite of a strawberries-'n'-cream scone.

"You think the Kings have something to do with it? Maybe they found out the rowdy bachelorette party at Abel's Brewery was really Lark's actor friends."

Life in Outtatowner, Michigan, was weird. It was a gorgeous coastal town in Western Michigan. Its quaint town square and walking distance from some of the world's most beautiful sand dune-lined beaches meant Outtatowner was a haven for tourists escaping Chicago and the surrounding areas. But if you were a townie, you knew the feud between the Sullivans and the Kings was generations old.

For years the families went round and round with increasingly ridiculous pranks. It wasn't just TP-ing houses or lining a yard with two thousand plastic forks. It was covering an entire car in Crisco. Wrapping every visible inch of Royal King's tattoo shop in baby shower-themed wrapping paper. Hosting a bachelorette party at a brewery . . . complete with male exotic dancers dressed as ponies.

The true beginning of the feud seemed to be lost in time, but the stakes heightened last autumn when Kate and her boyfriend Beckett discovered a hidden speakeasy when renovating her aunt Tootie's farmhouse. Hints about the early connections between the Kings and Sullivans only deepened the mystery. A few times Kate suspected someone was sneaking around their property and even had to call the police after someone tried to enter the home when she was there late at night, so the Sullivans were keeping their findings quiet for now.

It was nice to see the feud was settling down into more normal, ridiculous antics.

Or . . . maybe not.

As Lee wound his way through the busy sidewalk, a

frantic woman appeared. She was—thankfully—fully clothed but running behind him, screaming something at his back. She was also throwing things at him—pants, shoes, balled-up socks.

"Well, there's your answer." I shook my head, laughing. "This was definitely Lee's doing."

My best friend was fun, loyal, and a total playboy. His apartment was two blocks up the hill, which meant this poor woman had been at it for a while.

"Are you going to do something?" Emma asked.

I scrunched my nose at her. "What am I supposed to do?"

Truth was, cleaning up Lee's messes was something I had gotten pretty good at over the years.

Kate sighed and tipped her face to the early May sun. "I swear, he's my older brother, but he acts like a child."

Emma leaned right to continue watching the mystery woman chase Lee toward the beach. "A ridiculously hot child, maybe . . ."

When Kate and I looked at Emma, she blushed and straightened before clearing her throat. "Sorry."

I laughed and wondered what Lee had done to get himself into trouble now. "Well, I guess I should go pick up his clothes."

Kate dusted crumbs from her lap and shook her head. "You should make him do it. Serves him right for whatever he did to that poor woman. I hope he got her name this time." Dismissing her brother, she looked at me and wiggled her eyebrows. "Will you be at book club tomorrow night? We're supposed to be finalizing details for the Matchmakers' Gala."

I cringed.

Ah, yes. The dreaded Matchmakers' Gala.

Outtatowner's annual ball where they attempt to pair up local singles through an old-fashioned date auction. To make matters worse, the women who organize the event make it for charity, so you're a real asshole if you bail.

Emma beamed. "I'll be there. I can't wait for the gala. Dress shopping is my *favorite*!"

I sighed. "I'll see you there." I placed a cash tip on the table and looked down the roadway for any signs of Lee, then directed my attention back at my friends. "But I'm only going so I can sabotage the planning and find a way out of it. I am *not* spending another year getting humiliated or being auctioned off to Stumpy Larson again."

A small snort shot out of Emma's nose.

Stumpy Larson was a townie with one leg visibly shorter than the other. I didn't care about his condition, or the fact that in Outtatowner we often got painful nicknames for the sake of humor. No, my issue with Stumpy was that he was known for whipping out his dick to show you just how *inadequate* he thought the nickname was.

I shuddered just thinking about it. One night after too much wine, I'd told Charles Attwater, our local sommelier and object of my current crush, about it, and he'd turned as red as a tomato and quickly changed the subject.

Now Charles I wouldn't mind getting paired up with . . .

"Hey, Kate, think we can bribe Tootie to nudge Charles to bid on me for the dates?"

Kate grinned and lifted a shoulder. "It's possible. She has mentioned she could use a new set of coffee cups."

My smile widened and hope bloomed in my chest. "Consider it done!"

Kate smiled at me. "Don't skip tonight. I want your input in planning your birthday too."

Heat crept up my neck, like it did any time excess attention was thrown my way. Over the years, birthdays leaned more painful than celebratory. If it weren't for the Sullivans, I'm not sure anyone would remember them at all.

I offered Kate a small smile when she wrapped me in a hug. I hugged her back, then looked at Emma. "Okay, we need to get to the shop before the rush."

Kate's bright smile was locked in place as she looked down the path where her older brother had run and shook her head. "Well, I'm headed home to bleach my eyeballs. Beckett and I have a new place to scope out for our next *Home Again* renovation. See you tonight."

After a quick goodbye, Emma and I crossed the street to head toward my small Main Street storefront. Along the way, I scooped up Lee's T-shirt, jeans, and one sock. He'd have to deal with finding the other.

After unlocking the glass door to my shop, I flipped on the light and looked into the small space. It was cramped, and every available area was piled with art. As a creative, my artwork was often chaotic. Ceramics were my specialty, so in addition to the small trinkets tourists loved, I had artfully arranged sets of plates, cups, and bowls—in various sizes to mix and match. All were hand-painted, beautifully glazed and fired.

"Can you open the register? I need to check on the kiln."

Emma nodded as she flipped on the radio and began humming to the song that flowed from the small speaker. She was a loyal customer turned friend and an extra set of hands I needed during the busy summer season. She also didn't mind getting shit for pay and bonuses in the form of finished artwork. Emma was a saint.

In the back room, the gentle hum of the kiln greeted me. It had taken a long time to save up for it, but the moment I could afford it, the kiln took my artwork from hobby to actual business. I was bursting with ideas to expand, but, unfortunately, in a tourist town tchotchkes were a dime a dozen.

I just need to find something that helps me stand out.

With a sigh, I dumped the armful of Lee's clothing on my desk in the back. I took a moment to stare at the rumpled pile and willed away the lump that caught in my throat.

AFTER A GRUELING DAY of ninety-seven customers and a measly five purchases, I was done. As I stepped up to Lee's apartment, I knocked twice. After accidentally walking in on him balls deep in some woman on his couch, I had learned the hard way to never, *ever* use my key without knocking.

I can never unsee that.

I knocked again and slipped my key into the lock. Lee was on shift at the fire station, so I didn't expect him to be home.

Still, I only cracked the door before I called out to him. "It's me! I'm coming in. I would prefer not to see your bare ass again today."

Greeted by silence, I pushed the door open. Lee's scent punched me square in the chest as soon as I opened the door. Earthy, yet floral, the clean scent was citrusy and at the same time hypermasculine.

I swallowed hard and walked into his space, gently closing the door behind me. The entryway table was bare except for a small bowl Lee used to deposit his keys and pocket change. The riot of reds and purples on the bowl had turned into a gorgeous melding of color, but one edge had sagged in the kiln. I had intended to throw the ruined dish away, but Lee refused to let me and stole it before I could toss it into the trash.

His apartment was meticulously neat, unlike my own organized chaos. I suspected it was partly because of his time in the Army, but also because his mother, June Sullivan, had been the most beautifully put-together woman I had ever known.

A painful ache bloomed in my chest when her smiling face filled my memory. June Sullivan never forgot a birthday.

I placed the folded pile of Lee's discarded clothing on his kitchen countertop. Glancing at a notepad, I ripped out a fresh sheet and scribbled a note on top:

You're an idiot. ♥

Looking around his tidy apartment, I slipped my hand into my large satchel. Grinning, I pulled out a small handmade trinket. It was a ceramic cat face, intended for Lee's niece, Penny. I had molded it out of discarded clay and fired it along with the rest of my pieces. It had wonky eyes and a lolling tongue. Originally it was intended to be cute and quirky, but somehow during the firing process it had morphed into a horrifying mess of frightening catlike features.

It was perfect.

I looked around, searching for the right place to hide the hideous cat. My eyes scanned the apartment and landed on the light jacket hanging on a hook. With a smile, I slipped the quarter-size monstrosity into the inner chest pocket. It might take weeks, maybe even until next fall, for Lee to find it. The thought sent a happy giggle dancing through me.

Lee had been the one to start the unspoken game between us. One night after drinking too much at the Grudge Holder, our local bar, I'd found that he'd hidden a jar of spaghetti sauce in my shower. Lee thought it was hilarious. I retaliated by hiding the same jar in his sock drawer a few weeks later. We went back and forth with that same jar of spaghetti sauce for nearly a year, until one hot day it rolled around and burst in the trunk of my car.

I was not happy.

Since then we had taken to hiding other ridiculous items for each other to find. It had been years of back and forth—a creepy bunny painting hung in my bathroom, a crab flipping the middle finger, a broken key chain from Sheboygan—a town neither of us had ever visited.

The best part was knowing something was hidden and just *waiting* for it to be found.

Satisfied that Lee would find the one-eyed cat in time, I quietly slipped out of his apartment and went in search of Charles.

TWO
LEE

"I HEARD you had a wildcat on your hands." My friend and fellow firefighter, Connor, clamped a hand on my shoulder as I hit the button to brew my fifth cup of coffee.

The corner of my mouth tipped up. "Yeah, something like that."

He shouldered next to me to pull down his own mug as we waited for the coffee to brew.

"I swear, man, I don't know how you do it." He looked at me with an eager smile. "You meet her last night?"

I nodded once. "Took her for a spin around the dance floor at the Grudge Holder. She's not local—from a few towns over. Allegan, I think."

"Well, what the hell happened?" Connor asked. "How do you go from moving her around the dance floor to running bare-assed through the streets while she throws your own clothes at you?"

I planted my hands on the countertop, shook my head, and sighed as I let the weight of my head hang between my arms. "I don't know. It's a long story."

Connor was a good friend, but he *really* didn't need to know.

"Yeah, you dog." Connor shoved my shoulder. "I bet you did some freaky shit and she didn't like it."

I shook my head but didn't respond. He may be a good friend, but what he didn't need to know was that, in fact, Marissa was pissed off, but not because I gave her the business. I was a considerate and thorough lover, after all. No freaky shit unless we were both into it.

No, she was pissed because after she sank to her knees and smiled up at me from the floor, I'd put my hands under her arms and lifted her back to her feet.

I had suggested maybe we make breakfast instead.

I was dog-fucking-tired, and Marissa was not pleased.

After leaving the bar, we had passed out naked before either of us could do anything stupid—and, for that, I was also a little relieved.

At my perceived rejection, she had started screaming, and when a glass went flying, I ran out of my apartment.

I didn't need some out-of-control woman trashing my place. Trouble was, I had only managed to slip on my boots before she had come after me.

I turned around and leaned against the counter. "I don't know, man. I'm getting kind of tired of unpredictable women."

Connor let out a low whistle. "Who would have thought the playboy of Remington County would get tired of drowning in pussy? We both know you're full of shit."

"I'm serious, man." I shook my head again. "Sometimes it's exhausting. I go to the gym, I eat right. I mean, I know I look good, and I like sex, like the rest of them. But sometimes I wonder what it'd be like to be with someone, I don't know . . . Normal."

Maybe someone who gave a shit about me.

Connor tipped his head at me in a smirk. "You mean normal like Little Orphan Annie?"

I straightened to my full height. "Don't fucking call her that."

Connor lifted both hands. "Dude, I'm kidding. You know I love Annie. Besides, if you haven't hit it by now, you're never going to. It amazes me you two are even friends. Poor girl can't even get groceries without running into one of your conquests."

I cleared my throat and snatched the coffeepot to fill my cup with hot, black sludge. I let out a breath, ignoring the matter-of-fact way he'd categorized my relationship with Annie. *As if he had any fucking clue.* "I'm sorry. I'm just edgy and tired. Hoping for a slow day around here."

Working at OFD as a firefighter and EMT meant most of our calls were either medically related or the occasional fender bender. Actual fires were rare, but they happened, and we were all trained and ready to go at a moment's notice.

Whenever the alarm sounded, it never ceased to make my shoulders bunch and dread pool in my stomach. I hadn't felt normal since that awful call that changed everything. Before that, my military training in the Army meant I was unshakable. Now every time the alarm sounded, flashes of *her* face went through my mind.

Most times I had to swallow back the bile and remind myself that it was over.

Margo was gone.

Determined to change the subject, I scanned the room and called out: "Hey, Brooklyn, are you on dinner duty tonight?"

She turned and smiled, both palms facing upward. "Dude, it's Taco Tuesday, of course I'm cooking."

Brooklyn had been on the fire department with me for the past few years. She was tough and reliable. Someone I could count on when things got messy. She also made the best tacos in Remington County. I was about to bust her balls about her rice being dry last time—it wasn't—when Whip King came into the fire station day room.

His real name was William, but like many of the townies, he had acquired a nickname and was known solely as Whip around Outtatowner. The Kings and Sullivans had a long-standing tradition of fucking with each other, and the rivalry wasn't just a series of silly pranks. It meant something, and I took my role seriously.

Whip was an arrogant prick like the rest of the Kings, but thankfully, when it came to the job, we were able to put our feelings aside and just be firefighters.

In the break room, however, anything goes.

I nodded in his direction. "Bill." I strode past Whip, enjoying the scowl that marred his pretty-boy face as I shouldered past him. His thick arms crossed, showing off the tattoos that covered both forearms. His brother Royal owned the local tattoo shop, so it wasn't uncommon for him to be sporting fresh ink. Annie had once noted it was a funny juxtaposition from the sharp angles and clean lines of his face. She said he looked like a *GQ* model with hot biker tattoos.

Fucking guy . . .

After my phone pinged with a text message, I slipped it from my pocket.

CATFISH KATE

Annie picked up after you and apologized to Ms. Tiny for the sock that hit her in the face. YOU BETTER THANK HER.

I scoffed at the image of poor little Ms. Tiny getting a sweaty sock to the face and fired off a reply in the form of a salute emoji to my little sister. Kate had been back in Outta-towner for only a year, but things felt more complete with my little sister home.

She had even found her groove with a wildly successful Instagram page after renovating our family's one-hundred-year-old farmhouse. Aunt Tootie lived there now, but it would always be our family home. For the renovation, my brothers, Duke and Wyatt, and I hired Duke's best friend to do the contract work. Everyone was surprised when Beckett fell head over heels in love with our little sister.

Well . . . everyone but me. Kate was the best.

I frowned down at her message.

Annie cleaned up my mess again.

A low throb formed at the base of my skull.

Fantastic. Yet another check mark in the *Lee Did Stupid Shit and Annie Cleaned Up His Mess* column.

I checked my watch and noted I still had eighteen hours left on this shift, so I sighed and settled into the worn recliner in the TV room. It wasn't nearly as comfortable as the green recliner in the apartment above the barn at my family's Highfield House, but it would do for a few rounds of some mindless video game to pass the time.

THE NEXT MORNING, the bell to Sand Dune Studio tinkled, as the buzzy rush of entering Annie's space coursed through me. In the years I had known her, she had always been creative—doodling and crafting, usually covered in some sort of glitter or glue since we were kids. When I had signed up for the Army, I had come back to find Annie had found her groove as Outtatowner's resident artist. Despite her grumblings about cheap art flooding the tourist market, people flocked to her store for her creative and original designs.

I moved around the patrons milling in her store, examining her beautiful ceramics and the trinkets that lined the shelves. I caught the eye of a cute brunette but offered her only a tight smile and curt nod.

I was a man on a mission.

I spotted Annie in the back, talking with a customer and gesturing wildly. Her unruly red curls bounced as she talked, and her animated gestures lit up her bright-blue eyes. She answered the man's question and pointed him in the right direction. As she moved past him, she gave his arm a gentle squeeze.

Annie was affectionate by nature, always offering a friendly hug or a gentle pat to everyone in her circle.

Everyone but me, of course, which was a fact that seemed to irk me more and more.

Annie had grown up in a foster home and, being the same age, she and Margo were more like sisters than not. Margo and I had dated in high school, so Annie was always around. After Margo's accident, my relationship with Annie had morphed into something . . . *different.*

Something more.

We had both been careful never to cross the line into anything more than friends, but calling her my *friend* was somehow grossly inadequate.

Annie was a part of me.

As I approached her, I plopped down the box of her favorite pastry—Junkers. The small scraps of homemade biscuit-dough discards were rolled in cinnamon sugar, then baked. They were the brainchild of Huck, owner and pastry genius behind the Sugar Bowl, the only bakery and coffee shop in town.

I had to practically beg him to sell me the last batch.

I leaned my elbow on the counter and gave Annie my most charming grin. A peace offering.

Annie lowered her chin and looked at me with bored eyes, but I could tell by the way the shades of aqua and navy twinkled in her eyes that she wasn't truly mad at me—probably just annoyed that she'd had to collect my clothes scattered down Main Street.

"You are a man-whore."

My grin widened. "I may be a man-whore, Annette, but I'm *your* man-whore."

It was easier to joke about than to admit to my best friend that despite my playboy reputation, I hadn't had sex in months.

Not since I had been banging a redhead and Annie's face flashed in my mind.

"I see you got my note," she said, pulling me back to the present. A smile tugged at her lips.

My chest thunked with a comfortable familiarity, as it always did whenever Annie was nearby.

"I did and you are correct. I am an idiot."

She flipped open the top to the white bakery box, and her smirk grew a fraction wider. "You are forgiven."

I turned to look out into her small shop and leaned my elbows against the counter as Annie sat on the high stool next to the register. She pulled out a small piece of sugared biscuit and popped it into her mouth.

"So who was she?" she asked around the sugary treat.

Annie and I kept no secrets. She knew about my dating history, and I knew hers. Probably better than she knew her own. But it also felt weird talking to her about it sometimes. I certainly didn't need her knowing about the random intrusive thought I'd had with the redhead.

I reached over and tugged at one of her curls, but she slapped my hand away. "Ugh, cut it out. You know you really owe your sister apology biscuits, not me. She's the one who had to see"—Annie waved her hand between us—"all of that."

It took a lot to embarrass me, but even I could admit that my sister seeing me in nothing but a pair of old work boots holding my dick as I ran down the street was not my finest moment.

"Don't worry, she's next on my Lee Fucked Up Apology Tour." I smiled at my best friend.

"That tour has been going strong for a while now, hasn't it?" she teased.

I laughed at her playful dig. The door chime sounded again, drawing our attention to the woman who walked in.

Bug King was the matriarch of the King family—the Kings' version of our very own aunt Tootie.

She barely gave a sideways glance down her nose at Annie's shop as she beelined straight toward us. She held out a paper poster, and Annie grabbed it.

"With all of the details finalized, these should be hung in the storefront windows. The charity this year will be the Remington County Child Protective Services."

Annie smiled brightly at Bug. "Great!"

Bug's eyes raked down me, and she made no attempt to hide the obvious disapproval in her scowl. "I take it you'll be there?"

My back tightened. I hated the annual Outtatowner Matchmakers' Gala. Sure, it was for charity, but really it was an opportunity for the biddies in town to play matchmaker and pair off the singles in town through a ridiculous date auction. I had no trouble finding my own dates and learned early on that dating women from town usually ended in an uncomfortable disaster.

Heat prickled at the base of my neck under her hard stare. I swallowed thickly, willing the words to leave my throat.

Say something.

Say anything.

I willed myself to give any reason, any reason at all, why I couldn't attend this year's gala.

"It is for charity, you know," Bug added.

Annie looked between us, and I caught her eyes narrowing a fraction.

Oh shit.

Annie gently cleared her throat. "Actually, Miss Bug, Lee might not be able to be in the auction this year." Annie beamed her brightest, albeit fakest, smile at the woman.

Her delicate fingers trailed a burning path on my forearm, and my eyes locked on the spot where our skin connected.

"He won't be attending solo."

The subtle gesture did not go unnoticed, and Bug's eyes held the spot where Annie's fingertips danced along the fine hairs of my forearm.

My jaw was locked tight. The words, any words at all, still clogged in my throat.

Annie blinked her wide, crystal-blue eyes at me. "You're all set for our dinner, right?"

"Uh . . ." I glanced between the two women. "Yeah. Yes. Just swinging by to finalize plans."

Bug's eyes grew wide. "Oh . . . oh well, that's . . ." She cleared her throat. "That is interesting. I'm sure we'll hear hearts breaking all throughout Remington County."

With her final remark, Bug turned on her heels and sailed out of Annie's shop.

With a playful laugh, my best friend turned to speak with another customer, taking her hand with her and the heat of her touch, but the warmth of her fingertips spread up my arm and across my chest.

It's not like that between us.

Jesus Christ.

"Hey, I gotta run," I called to Annie's back, and she lifted her hand in a two-finger salute.

Gathering my thoughts and the last shreds of my dignity, I shook my head and left, wondering what the hell that was all about.

THREE
ANNIE

Howdy, Charles! I was hoping to take you up on your offer to try the new wine varietals that came in. Just let me know when you're free!

Hi! Me again 🙂 Does Friday work?

SITTING IN MY SHOP, I stared down at the text messages. *Howdy? Oh my god . . .*

My stomach dropped. The last message had been sent six days ago, which, in small-town time, felt like twenty years.

Slumping my shoulders, I called out to the universe: "Why am I such a loser?"

"Annette." I recognized Lee's deep, gravelly voice and immediately whipped around on my stool. "You better not be talking about my best friend like that."

A cheesy grin split my face. Everyone called me Annie, except for Lee, who occasionally called me by my real name. *Annette* sounded different when it rolled off his tongue. My stomach flipped every time, and I tried not to think too hard about why I liked the fact it was only him who used it.

Friends. Friends. Friends.

I made a face at Lee and swatted the air. "I *am* a loser. It's fine."

"Okay, if you say so." He shrugged. "So what's the problem, loser?" His smirk was boyish and charming. It made me want to punch him in his handsome face.

I gestured toward my phone. "It's Charles. He got some fancy new wines for his shop and offered to sample them together. Like a date." I shrugged and frowned down at my phone. "I was trying to nail down a day, but he hasn't texted me back."

Lee frowned and crossed his arms. "How many follow-up texts did you send him?"

I scrunched up my face and closed my eyes. "Four?" I peeked through my lashes to see him cringe.

"Ooofff. Okay. Yeah, that's a lot."

I let out a huff. "I know! But *he* asked *me* out." I lifted my palms and let them smack my thighs as my lower lip jutted out.

Lee leveled me with his gaze and shrugged. "If he wanted to, he would."

I had to remind myself Lee was talking about Charles and not himself. I pushed down the little pang of hurt every time I was reminded that Lee had never once made a move on me. Instead, I rolled my eyes. "What, did you learn that on TikTok? Shut up." I gestured between us. "We're wallowing here."

Lee's rumbling laugh filled the small space of my art shop. It was a warm, happy sound, and since I was already in a *mood*, I had zero patience for it.

Lee sighed. "It's the truth, whether or not you want to hear it. What kind of friend would I be if I lied to you?"

"The good kind?" Frustrated, I started arranging, then rearranging, pottery along one shelf. When Lee made himself comfortable, I turned to him. "Don't you work?"

A smile tipped up the corner of his mouth. "Day off. You know that."

I did know that.

I knew Lee's schedule backward and forward. It was one of those things that was ingrained into my mind. His schedule, along with a host of random tidbits of useless information. Diamonds can have other gemstones as inclusions, like garnets, and they're ridiculously rare and stunning. Cats can be allergic to humans, which was why I have never rescued one for fear of that particularly pathetic rejection. Competitive art used to be in the Olympics. *I would have slayed, by the way.*

"Well, you're going to be bored here."

"Slow day?" Lee took to absently spinning a pen next to the register.

"Slow *every* day." I sighed. "I think I'm going to have to move."

That got his attention, and he straightened on the stool he'd settled in. "Move? Where? What the hell are you talking about?"

I looked around Sand Dune Studio and tried not to let the swell of emotions get to me. "JP King bought three more storefronts, this one included. He's raising the rent for the shop *and* my upstairs apartment. I have thirty days."

"He can't do that." Anger simmered beneath his words. Whether or not my last name was the same, I had been claimed by the Sullivans a long time ago, and when you slight one, you slighted them all.

"He can, and he did." I picked up the notification letter off the countertop and flipped it in front of him.

Lee grabbed the note and began scanning it, shaking his head.

"It's fine, really. Sand Dune Studio has been quietly struggling for a while. Quirky, high-end ceramics are just not working in a tourist town. People want cheap knick-knacks from their vacations." I shrugged. "I get it."

Lee tipped a dark eyebrow upward. "What about the other idea?"

I frowned at him. A few too many glasses of wine and I'd spilled an idea for a space that I truly believed would be amazing for Outtatowner. The idea really came from his niece. Wyatt had been struggling to come up with a birthday party idea, so his girlfriend Lark and I had suggested throwing an art party. I had molded and fired cutesy shapes—beehive mugs, piggy banks shaped like unicorns, a goofy-looking cobra with googly eyes—and the kids had a blast decorating them with various colors of glaze. At the party I taught them different techniques and reveled in the laughter and the mess. Afterward, I finished the pieces in the kiln and, within a few days, each little guest had his or her own unique piece of art.

Penny had beamed and made the comment, "I would do this every day if I could!" It was then my wheels had started turning.

I envisioned a large open-air space. Soaring ceilings with a vintage charm. An art studio where anyone, regardless of age or artistic talent, could come and explore art and crafting. Tourists and townies alike could spend hours—a whole day—painting their own pottery, stringing beads, and mosaicking. I envisioned a space where I could share my passion for art, but let artists of all ages explore it at their own pace. They could leave with unique, custom art created with love by the artists themselves.

But it was a pipe dream that required money.

"I can barely afford this place." I gestured toward the paper he held. "Definitely can't afford it now. Plus, I would need a space for tables and unfinished pottery. Paints, mosaic tiles, kilns—plural. It's just too much."

Lee frowned at the paper. He knew I was right.

I tipped my head toward Lee and sighed. "This is depressing. Can we please talk about something else?"

Lee rubbed his hands up his jean-clad thighs. "Yep. Let's talk about our date."

My mind sputtered to a halt, and I choked on absolutely nothing. "Date?"

His eyebrows lifted up. "Yeah. Date. You told Bug we had dinner plans so . . . pick you up at seven thirty?"

"Lee. Come on. You didn't think I was serious, did you? I was just helping you out." I laughed and turned away to keep him from seeing the color flood my pale cheeks.

"Oh, I am serious. And you *are* going to help me out."

I painted on a smile but could feel the tension wobble at the corners. "You know I only said that to keep her off your back about the gala."

"I'm aware, and it was genius. But it's out there now. I already got, like, four calls about us going out, and I haven't heard another word about who I plan to bid on at the Matchmakers' Gala."

I stared at my best friend. In the years we'd known each other, we'd never *once* been on anything remotely close to a date.

"Come on. We eat together all the time. Only this time I'll pull your chair out, politely nod, and say, *Oh, that is so interesting, Annette,* to whatever it is you're talking about."

Right. Only . . . not *like a real date because this is Lee and he is never serious about anything, especially relationships.*

I laughed. "You're a real charmer. You know as well as I do, girls like me and guys like you never work out. But look at us—we're proof why friends are better."

Instead of laughing at the joke, a small muscle in Lee's jaw flexed, my smile slightly wobbling at the corner under his unwavering gaze.

He stood from the stool and crossed his arms. "Fine. You don't want to do it, help me find someone else."

I rolled my eyes with a snort. "Like you need any help getting a date."

Lee paused and stopped me with his suddenly serious stare. My breath hitched at his intensity. "I really can't go through the gala this year. It's humiliation disguised as charity. Please."

It was the sad way that *please* tangled with a sigh that did me in.

"I know." I frowned as I considered what he was saying. My own dating life was totally lackluster, but I knew plenty of women who would find Lee absolutely charming. Girls who came from nice families and had smooth straight hair and didn't fill awkward silences with random internet facts.

I sighed. "You know, everyone is always saying there are plenty of fish in the sea, and somehow I got hung up on one specific emotionally distant salmon with commitment issues."

Lee laughed. "Charles is an idiot." He lifted his hands after I shot him a dirty look. "What? He is. *You* are the catch. Maybe you just need to show him what he's missing."

I had been talking about Charles, hadn't I?

I cast a wary gaze his way. "I don't even know where to look anymore."

Lee snapped his fingers and my eyes flew to his. "That's why this is perfect."

"What is?"

He spread his arms, his thick biceps testing the limits of his T-shirt. "I'll set you up."

My heart thrummed as a strange humming coiled in my belly.

"You have to admit—we know *a lot* about each other. Clearly we're both doing a shit job picking someone for ourselves, so why not do it for each other? I find someone for you, and you find someone for me." Lee's excitement grew as his idea developed before us. "Consider it an early birthday present."

I thought for the tiniest moment about his proposition. "Why does this feel vaguely like a sixteenth-century arranged marriage?"

The full wattage of Lee's irresistible smile was aimed my way. "I would happily provide my prized goat if it meant your happiness, Annette."

I laughed at how effortlessly charming he could be. "If we do this—*if*"—I paused so he could take in just how serious I was—"you realize this is going to be infinitely harder for me than for you, right? You've already dated the entire population of Remington County."

"Very funny." Visible energy thrummed through Lee as his knee bounced. "But I'm not going to lie—I have a feeling I can do a better job of finding you a date than you can."

"Just so we're clear—I'm not looking for Mr. Right. I'm looking for Mr. Annie Doesn't Have to See Stumpy's . . . stumpy."

Lee's face twisted in disgust, and a laugh burst from me.

I chewed my lip as I considered Lee finding a guy for me to date. "No weirdos . . . and no Kings."

Lee's eyes rolled. "Obviously. No redheads." His eyes quickly swooped up to mine, and he had the sense to look sheepish. "No offense."

"None taken." A thousand jumbled thoughts ran through my mind as I pushed down the immediate pang of hurt his comment caused. "No sex." I pointed my finger before Lee could interrupt. "I'm serious. If I set you up with any of my friends, I don't need you making it weird after you break it off. Keep it in your pants."

A smirk tugged at his lips. "I think I can handle that, but same for you."

I breathed a small, strange sigh of relief. "Obviously. So how many dates are we talking?"

Lee considered. "As many as it takes, I guess. We have four weeks until the gala." He nodded confidently. "Worst-case scenario, we can always pretend to date each other." He winked as he stuck out his hand.

I swallowed hard. *Worst-case scenario.*

I pressed my palm into his and squeezed my eyes closed. "Deal."

FOUR
LEE

"SO YOU'RE *NOT* DATING ANNIE?"

My jaw clenched as I looked at my brother, who was perched on a stool next to me at the Grudge. "Sorry, bro. Just a rumor."

Wyatt shook his head and took a sip of his beer. "Lark is going to be pissed. She was pretty excited, even if she was pretending to not be hurt that Annie hadn't told her herself."

"Annie and I are . . . friends." The word was bitter in my mouth, and I quickly washed it away with a deep gulp of beer.

"If you say so." Wyatt shook his head. "Probably for the best. Annie's a good person."

"What the hell is that supposed to mean?" I pinned Wyatt with a look.

He rolled his eyes. "Look, I love you, man, but we both know how she is." His eyes flicked over me. "And how you are. You really want to hurt that girl?"

I scowled at my brother, hating the fact he wasn't entirely wrong. "Of course not." I waved my hand in dismissal. "It doesn't matter. In fact, Annie set me up with a friend of hers. I'm taking her out for coffee tomorrow."

He grunted a response, and I decided not to try to decipher what that meant. "From what I've seen, Annie doesn't really seem to date. Wasn't she going out with that Charles guy?"

My eyes stopped on Charles Attwater, sitting in a circle of people and laughing. My jaw tensed. Wyatt's eyes tracked my glare.

"Charles is a tool," I grumbled.

Wyatt shrugged. "Seemed like a decent guy to me."

I shot a look at my brother. "Have you seen the way he smiles? So many teeth."

My brother shook his head and focused on his beer while I scanned the crowd, considering who I could fix her up with. Someone who *wasn't* Charles Attwater.

Deacon Malroy? Too boring.

Josiah Richardson? Still into Legos.

Randy Feldman? Too . . . pretty.

The truth was, any one of those idiots would come clamoring for a chance to take Annie out, but I just couldn't see her being happy with any of them. None of them even came close to being good enough for her.

Wyatt took the last sip of his beer before stretching and releasing an audible sigh as he stood. "I'm outta here. Tootie has Pickle for the night, and I've got plans for my wife. Have fun on your date."

My jaw worked, and nerves bunched the muscles in my back when the words slipped out. "I kind of agreed to fix her up with someone too."

Wyatt flipped out a few bills and barked out a laugh before clamping a hand on my shoulder. "Good luck with that."

~

I WALKED into the Sugar Bowl and smoothed down my shirt. I'd opted for a hunter-green waffle-knit Henley, sleeves rolled, and a pair of jeans with boots. Casual but still nice for a morning coffee date. With a fresh shave and light touch of cologne, I thought I looked pretty damn good for a first date.

Sammy was already here, seated on a soft bench near the entrance. She popped up when I walked in and lifted a hand in greeting. I breathed out a sigh of relief. She was pretty, even vaguely familiar, with a bright and friendly smile. For some reason I'd worried that Annie would try to play a joke on me and set me up with one of my aunt Tootie's septuagenarian knitting friends.

I smiled and waved back. Sammy was cute. Really cute. Long blonde hair. Bright-green eyes.

I walked up and held out my hand. "Hi there. Lee Sullivan."

"Samantha." She smiled. "But you can call me Sammy —er, or Sam! Samantha! Whatever you like is fine."

O . . . kay.

"It's great to meet you, Sammy." The Sugar Bowl was unusually quiet. We stood in a slightly uncomfortable silence as the teenage hostess gathered menus and guided us to the table.

As we approached, I pulled out a chair for Sammy. She smiled again as she took her seat across from me, and thinly veiled excitement radiated from her. I took a steadying breath. Something was just *off*, and I couldn't figure out what the hell it was. Deep down I hoped I hadn't slept with her and forgotten about it. A slimy trickle of shame slid down my spine.

"It was so nice of Annie to set us up," Sammy said.

I could manage only a polite nod before Sammy reached for her water and bumped into the table. The plates and silverware rattled as water sloshed out of the top of her glass. "Sorry. I guess I'm a little nervous."

I smiled at her. "Don't be. There's nothing to be nervous about."

The server came, and we ordered coffee along with an apple fritter for me and a coconut maple donut for her.

Sammy fluffed her hair and rubbed her palms on the tops of her thighs.

"So," I tried, "Annie said you two met in design school? You're an artist too?"

"I am! Though I'm not nearly as talented as Annie. In school, she could do *anything* she set her mind to. I found my niche in dolls."

I blinked and angled forward. "Excuse me?"

She nodded eagerly, her eyes growing wider. "Dolls. Lifelike miniatures, really."

I managed a slow nod as her words sank in. Before I knew it, Sammy was leaning over to reach down into her very large purse. From beneath the table, she produced the most horrifying, lifelike doll I had ever seen.

When its cold, dead eyes moved in my direction, I jumped, my knee banging into the underside of the table, and splashing even more water onto the surface. "Oh, Jesus."

Sammy laughed as she bounced the doll, pretending to walk it toward me. "Hi, Lee. I'm Elsa. My mommy thinks you're cute!" Sammy giggled as I did my best not to recoil and scream like a baby.

What. The. Fuck.

"Oh, wow. Sammy. That's . . ."

Sammy sighed wistfully as she looked at her unholy creation. "I use silicone to mold the faces. Even the skin feels real. Isn't she darling?"

"Sure. Yeah, she's . . ." I swallowed hard. "Great."

"And you're a firefighter." Sammy rocked the doll back and forth and took on a high-pitched, doll-like voice. "Mommy hopes that means you're good with your hose!"

A laugh burst out of me. I looked around, fully expecting to see Annie hiding somewhere in the corner, laughing her ass off. There was no way this chick was for real.

When the server came to deliver our coffee and pastries, my eyes pleaded for help as he made a horrified face at Sammy and her doll.

"You are very handsome, Lee. We both think so."

We?

Sammy pulled out her phone and scooted from her side of the booth and into mine. "Do you mind if we take a quick selfie?"

"Um." I was still trying to get over the shock of Sammy producing that horrifying doll. "Sure."

She leaned in close, squishing the doll between us as she held out her phone. The dark, beady eyes of the doll seared into my soul, but Sammy's sweet face was smiling, so I leaned in slightly and tried not to wince as its silicone skin brushed my arm.

"Thanks! I have the perfect frame for this."

Frame? What in the hell?

"So, Lee . . ." Sammy inched closer, and I was acutely aware of the fact a doll, which was more than likely possessed, was touching me. "Should we go to your place? Or mine?"

I blinked once. *Wasn't that my line?* "I'm sorry. What?"

Her big green eyes blinked up at me. “I’m only a few towns over, but your place is probably closer.”

Was I having a stroke, or had this completely unassuming, doll-loving woman just propositioned me in the middle of the morning on a Thursday? I blinked my eyes—*no double vision.* Twitched my face—*no paralysis.* I inhaled a deep breath—*oh shit. Is that burned toast?*

“Uh, okay. Somebody’s a little shy.” Using her doll voice, Sammy cooed as she moved the doll’s tiny hand to stroke my arm.

“Okay.” I gently muscled my way out of the booth, shoving Sammy and her creepy doll across the bench until we were both standing. “It’s been . . . interesting. Unfortunately, I don’t think this is going to work out.” I pulled a pile of bills from my wallet and dumped it on the table without bothering to count it.

With a pout, Sammy waved the doll’s arm goodbye as I turned and beelined toward the door. Once outside, I hustled down the street until I could duck into an alleyway and pull out my phone.

Me: *I’m coming over. You better be there.*

I didn’t bother waiting for a response. I knew Annie would be working at her shop, talking with customers or starting a new project. I stomped up the sidewalk toward the lake, where her shop was tucked next to King Tattoo.

Just outside, Royal King was unlocking his tattoo parlor. When we caught eyes, his narrowed. He knew us Sullivans were lying in wait, and he was anticipating a comeback for the latest prank they’d pulled—delivering seventy-two pizzas over the course of two days to me, Kate, Duke, and even Dad at Haven Pines.

Joke’s on them. I fucking love pizza.

But Royal was right to be suspicious. I already knew

how I was planning to get back at them, but I hadn't found the right opportunity to exact my revenge quite yet.

While I didn't love that Annie's shop was next door to Royal's, I also knew that with his imposing stature and extensive tattoos, most people were too afraid to fuck with him. The Kings were known to be ruthless in business and in a fight.

I had stormed past him, fully intending to ignore him, when he caught my attention. "You finally got the balls to shoot your shot with her, then?"

My glance sliced to the painted front door of Sand Dune Studio. *Fucking small-town rumors.* I eyed the cocky smirk on his face. "Mind your business, King."

He grunted a response. "Well, if you won't, I'd be happy to."

Barely contained rage simmered through my veins at the thought of Royal King *shooting his shot* with Annie. I stepped forward, locking eyes with him as he raised his chin. "You stay the fuck away from her."

The asshole had the balls to *laugh*. "If you're not staking a claim, someone else will." He gestured toward Annie's shop. "And she looks good. *Real* good."

I shook my head, reminding myself that Royal liked to stir up trouble, and Annie was a Sullivan—by association, at least.

I scoffed. "That woman would gnaw her own arm off before ever being with you."

I had turned to leave him when his comment shot over my shoulder. "You sure about that?"

My jaw clenched as I tore open the door to the studio. The little silver bell rattled angrily against the glass.

"Well hello to you too." Annie looked up from the small corner of her studio, her hands and forearms covered in wet clay. A streak of gray fanned across her cheek where she must have scratched an itch. The annoyance running through me was replaced with something different.

Darker.

Hungrier.

Annie's wild hair was piled high on her head in a riot of loose curls. She'd wrapped a scarf around her head and the bow at the top was slightly off-center. Her blue eyes widened as I stormed into her studio.

I looked around to find a few tourists stopping to stare at me. I nodded in their direction. "Morning."

Annie's soft hands continued to work the clay despite my intrusion. My eyes snagged on the way her fingers slid and tangled with the wet clay, and it immediately sent my thoughts spiraling.

I wanted to smooth my hands over hers. Feel the wet softness slip between my fingers. Run my nose up the side of her neck and have a full-on Patrick Swayze–in–*Ghost* moment behind her pottery wheel. Her disheveled beauty hit me like a ton of bricks, and I struggled to remember why I'd stormed into her place to begin with.

Oh, right.

Dolls.

"A doll maker? Seriously?" I shoved my hands into my pockets to hide the fact my errant thoughts of her had gotten me hard.

Annie snorted. "She did not." She flipped off the wheel and dipped her hands into water before starting to wipe them clean. "Damn it! I told her no dolls until at least the fourth date."

A bubble of her laughter filled the studio as I frowned down at her. "You're cackling."

She sighed and laughed again. "Of course I am."

The sight of Annie laughing, her wild red curls bouncing, her head thrown back, was almost enough to make me forgive her.

Almost.

"If you're not going to take this seriously, then just forget it."

Annie stepped closer, wiping her hands dry on a towel. I slid her the bottle of lotion I knew she used after working with clay. She scooped it up and began working it into her hands.

"I am taking it seriously. Sammy is a little quirky, but she's so sweet. I thought you were over the whole fear-of-dolls thing."

"It had *skin*, Annie."

She swallowed down another laugh. "I'm sorry. I'll do better next time, I swear. Emma has a cousin I think might be great. A real sweetheart."

I looked down at my best friend. Her pink lips tipped up in the tiniest smile, and I wanted to call the whole thing off. Tell her that we should just skip ahead to the part where I give in to this gnawing feeling and kiss her already.

And chase away the only woman who's ever seen the real me and not run.

Instead, I doubled down on my promise to find her a date.

FIVE
ANNIE

AGREEING to find someone for Lee to date had been a mistake. I had worked so hard to put our friendship neatly into a little box and shove down all the inappropriate, very *not-friendly* feelings I once harbored for him.

Suddenly all I could think about were things like: *What would Lee like in a girlfriend? She should be funny and sweet and adventurous. Pretty. Strong enough to uncover and accept the deep emotions he works so hard to hide. I bet that man fucks like a god.*

Heat pooled low in my belly at the thought I had no right thinking.

No redheads.

I frowned down as I fluffed my soft, bouncy red curls and waited for my date, Timothy, to arrive. *Someone's got to love red, right?*

I'd been excited when Timothy said he had reservations at Etoile Brasserie. It was fancy for a first date, but I'd always wanted to try it, so I eagerly agreed. Only a few miles up Blue Star Highway, the French restaurant was popular among tourists in the area. Dinner here was on my wish list.

When he arrived, Timothy was dressed in a charcoal sport coat with a red ascot and dark trousers that fit his slim body perfectly. The white shirt beneath the suit jacket was subtly striped with horizontal navy lines. *How very French of him.* His dark-blond hair was neatly trimmed and slicked back. Smooth jaw. It was a good look on him.

When he stepped up to me, he clicked his heels together and dipped in a deep bow, brushing his lips across my knuckles. "Mademoiselle."

I chuckled and bent my knees in a gentle but awkward curtsy. As he straightened, his nose twitched, and he lifted a knuckle to stifle a sneeze.

"Pardon me." Timothy grinned and gestured toward the entrance of the restaurant. "Shall we?"

After being guided by the hostess, we took our seats and I crossed my ankles. I'd chosen a little navy dress with a subtle sweetheart neckline and enough fabric that I felt pretty, but not too exposed. My hair was half-up, and I was wearing the adorable yellow peep-toe heels I'd splurged on recently.

"You are stunning." Timothy's mouth hooked in a soft smile.

"Thank you. And thanks for . . . this." I gestured to our sophisticated surroundings. Soft lighting and plush leather seats. Glittering candlelight on white linens. Gentle French music in the background. The whole place felt opulent and romantic.

"It's very close to the real thing. Have you been?" Timothy gently cleared his throat, but leaned in to listen.

"To France?" I asked. "No, I haven't really traveled."

My small-town roots and growing up in the foster care system meant opportunities abroad had been slim.

I picked up the menu and scanned through the selections. Etoile Brasserie was upscale—and very pricey. My eyes scanned the menu, a slight panic prickling at the base of my hairline as I mentally calculated the cost of dinner. It had been several, *several* dates since anyone had treated me to a meal, and this dinner alone was going to put a hefty dent into my checking account.

Timothy leaned forward. It was nice to have the attention of a man as put together as Timothy. He tugged his collar and scratched at the base of his jaw, a glittery gold band twinkling on his wrist. "So how do you know Lee?"

"Oh, I . . ." *Shit.* In my experience, the minute a man found out Lee and I were close, the questions started. Jealous questions. *How close? How long have you been friends? Have you ever slept together? Have you ever wanted to?*

It was infuriating. And insulting. Except for maybe the last question . . . I'd lied through my teeth every single time I had been asked.

"Oh, well . . . we grew up in the same hometown. I've known him forever. Lee dated my foster sister all through high school."

"Dated? As in past tense?" Timothy leaned forward, giving me his full attention. "I'm surprised you and Lee stayed friends after the breakup."

I swallowed hard. "She, um . . . she passed away."

Timothy's hand covered mine, and his eyes went soft. "I am so sorry."

I resisted the urge to pull my hand away as a sinking feeling filled my stomach. "Thank you. Yes, it was very hard on all of us. Especially Lee."

Timothy nodded and lifted his napkin to sneeze. “I am so sorry.” He delicately wiped his nose before smiling. “We were stationed together in the Army. We only recently reconnected, but I remember he was head over heels for his girl back home.” A gentle laugh rolled out of him. “Lee stalked the mail carrier every time we had postage come through. He lived for those letters.” He shook his head and sniffed again. “That’s a real shame.”

Bile rose in my stomach, and tears burned behind my eyes. Timothy’s eyes raked over me, seeing my discomfort on full display.

He straightened and cleared his throat. “I am so sorry. I shouldn’t have said anything.”

I used the linen napkin to blot at the corners of my eyes. “No, it’s fine. Really. It was a long time ago.” *And a long time for buried secrets to come to light.*

Timothy leaned back in his seat and blew out a breath. “I am really blowing this.” He looked around. “Do you just want to get out of here?”

I looked at him with a watery smile. “Yeah.”

With a nod, he signaled to our server, dropped money on the table, and held out a hand for me. I stood, walking through the restaurant as Timothy followed behind me. Once outside, I sucked in a deep breath of warm May air.

Beside me, Timothy’s hand brushed the small of my back. A loud sneeze erupted from him, and I jumped with a small yelp.

“I apologize.” He wiped under his nose with a tissue. “I’m not sure what’s happening here.”

I placed my hand on his elbow. “Are you sure you’re okay?”

Timothy sneezed again and took a step back. “I think . . . I’m sorry, but I think it’s you.”

My back went straight. "Me?"

He took a tentative step forward and, sure enough, as soon as he got within breathing distance, he let out another loud, wet sneeze.

I recoiled. *Are you freaking kidding me?* My hands hung limply at my sides. "Maybe let's just call this one, huh?"

His sad, watery eyes raked over me. "I do think it's for the best."

"Thank you, Timothy, for the almost-date." I extended my hand and immediately snatched it back after he sneezed again and small, wet droplets dappled my face. "Yep. Good night."

I turned on my heels and reached into my purse to slather myself in antibacterial gel. As I sullenly walked toward my car, I opened my phone to text Lee.

Oh for one . . . turns out it's not just cats that can be allergic to humans.

Three bubbles immediately popped up, and my tummy did a little flip.

LEE

I've got Chinese takeout and Benadryl. Come on over.

"So you are, in fact, *not* better at this than I am." Sitting cross-legged on Lee's apartment floor, I dipped my chopsticks into the open container of lo mein noodles. Before heading to his apartment, I stopped by my own to change out of my adorable date-night dress and heels and into ratty gray sweatpants. They were my comfort pants when I wanted to wallow and eat shitty takeout.

Lee had seen me in worse, anyway.

He absent-mindedly pushed a shrimp to my side while I nudged the slimy bell peppers his way. "Actually allergic?"

"He sneezed *in my face.*"

Lee stifled a laugh. "I'm sorry, really. Tim's a nice guy."

I nodded. "He was. Until my mere physical being nearly sent him into anaphylaxis."

Lee shook his head in disbelief, then sighed. "It's probably for the best anyway. Tim's *really* into the whole French thing. On the weekends he's a mime."

I coughed. "Excuse me?"

"A mime. You know . . ." Lee lifted his hands to silently perform a hilariously poor imitation of a mime in a box. "A mime."

"I know what a mime is. Why in the world would you think I'd want to date a *mime*?"

He twirled his chopsticks in dismissal. "It's not like that's his full-time job. It's just something he does on the weekends."

My eyes bugged at him. "You are unbelievable."

He pinned me with his dark stare and pointed his chopsticks in my direction. "Dolls."

I laughed and ate another bite. "What about Connor from the fire station? He's cute."

Lee's back straightened, and I tried not to focus on the ripple of his pecs beneath his T-shirt. "You think he's cute?"

I shrugged and peeked at him from under my lashes. "Sure. Everyone does."

He huffed. "Everyone?"

I narrowed my eyes and grinned. Truthfully, the thought of Lee being jealous had never occurred to me, since he and I were careful to avoid all conversations regarding the opposite sex unless it was me teasing him about being a playboy.

The possibility of him being jealous formed a scratchy ball in my throat. "Wait. You're not *jealous*, are you?"

Lee blew a breath through his lips. "Jealous? Hell no." He chewed and paused. "But I think he might have a thing for Emma. Besides, I know a guy from the gym. Aaron. A real rugged manly type. Just like you like." He waggled his eyebrows at me.

I rolled my eyes playfully and laughed. "That's great, because I also have a date for you. She's from Chicago, one of Lark's friends, but apparently she's not that picky and *definitely* pretty. Right up your alley," I teased back.

He tapped his chopsticks against mine. "Fine."

I grinned. "Fine."

SIX
LEE

"You know, if you want me to pretend to be your fake girlfriend, I'd be up for it." My date, Renee, cocked her head and smiled a sweet smile in my direction. There was no malice or hint of anything other than genuine kindness.

"Oh, I, um . . ." I pressed my lips together and cocked my head, looking at the beautiful brunette in front of me. I cleared my throat. "Yeah, that's, I don't know . . ."

Renee laughed, and her hand grazed against the back of mine as we stood near the bar in the Grudge, looking out onto the dance floor.

She leaned in closer. "Lark told me all about why Annie is setting you up on dates, and honestly, the thought of a Matchmakers' Gala is horrible."

I laughed into my beer as I took a sip and nodded. "Yeah, no shit."

"But really, if you need help"—she spread her hands wide—"I'm available." Renee's warm brown eyes looked at me as she smiled. "No charge, of course. Consider it a favor to a friend."

I stalled. *What the hell is wrong with you?*

It was the perfect out, yet I couldn't bring myself to agree to it. I drained my beer and looked out onto the dance floor, then looked down at Renee.

"Hey, you wanna go for a spin?" I grinned at her, and she smiled back up at me, but there was . . . *nothing*.

"I'd love to." She wove her hand into the nook of my elbow as I guided her to the dance floor.

I had danced hundreds of miles on that beat-up old oak floor with countless different women. Some had two left feet, and I found it a particularly fun challenge to show them how fun it could be to dance with a partner who knew what he was doing. Others knew a lot of the steps, and we could go through a dance or two without fumbling too much.

But it was never quite the same. It never had the ease and comfort or *fun* it was with Annie.

I shook my head to rattle loose the thoughts I was having about my best friend. It was weird to start having her pop up in the most unexpected ways when I thought I had gotten a handle on that a long, long time ago.

Back in high school, when I'd started dating Margo, I had to put a stop to the inappropriate thoughts that would pop into my head from time to time.

I hated myself for even going back there. It was a disgrace to Margo's memory. Besides, *Girls like me and guys like you never work out. But look at us—we're proof why friends are better.* Annie's words from earlier bounced around in my skull, settling as a twitch behind my right eyeball.

Renee popped back into my vision. "Hey, are you okay?"

I looked down at her and blinked.

She smiled. "I thought I lost you there for a minute."

I swallowed back my feelings and gave her my best smile. "All good. Let's do this."

Renee was actually a decent dancer. Her body moved with the grace and comfort of somebody who was used to being on display. The curious eyes that tracked our dancing didn't seem to rattle her. She didn't shrink back against the whoops and hollers when I spun her and dipped her low. When I led her around the dance floor, she would move her body in a way that drew her own attention.

We ended the song with a dramatic spin, and her leg hiked high on my hip. Claps erupted around us, and she drank it up.

When the song faded and one of Annie's favorites came on, I dropped my arms and—*shit*—there she was walking through the door of the Grudge with Aaron right behind her.

I tipped my head in their direction. "Hey, there's Annie and her date. Let's grab a drink."

Renee smiled, breathless. "Sounds great."

We headed off the crowded dance floor, and as we approached, I tipped my chin to Aaron. "Hey, man, what's up?"

He grinned, his eyes flicking toward Annie. "It's great, man. Really good."

My eyes shifted to Annie. "Hey."

Her smile lit up, and her lashes swooped over her high cheekbones. "Hi." She looked around the Grudge. "I love this song."

I tipped my head toward the dance floor. "You want to?"

She looked toward her date, and Aaron shrugged. "Fine by me."

Her gentle eyes shifted back to mine. "Thanks."

We walked to the dance floor, a walk we'd done a thousand times before. Confident. Comfortable and familiar.

Back in middle school, we had been forced to learn two-step and line dance in PE. Annie and I had been partnered up, and we quickly found out that we were a great match when it came to dancing.

I appreciated her subtle flair, but she could also read my cues, like when I wanted to shift sides or pull her into a spin or change it up a bit.

Annie was always right there with me.

The song played on around us as I stopped and held my arms out for her. She slipped in like we were two lonely planets pulled into each other's orbit.

Without a word, we started moving. The twangy chords of the song flowed over us, and my heart thunked beneath my ribs. I looked down at her, her eyes sparkling with familiar joy as we swayed together.

I pulled her close to me, wrapping my arm around her waist. The heat of her body radiated against me, and her breath tickled my neck, sending shivers down my spine. I lost myself in the music and the moment, and everything around me dulled and faded away.

I closed my eyes and let myself sink into the sensation of holding her. Reveling in her in a way I had never allowed myself before. The silkiness of her hair brushed against my cheek, and the subtle, delicate fragrance of her shampoo filled my nose as we moved in perfect rhythm. Her laughter blended with the song as I led her around the floor. Her soft voice hummed along to the music.

I twirled and she spun. We laughed and sang the bridge aloud. Her curves molded to my hands. Her breasts pressed into my chest, and it hit me that, tonight, dancing with her felt entirely new.

Different.

I dipped her low, my arms supporting her upper back. And she beamed a smile at me as I righted her. Like always, we maneuvered around the other couples on the dance floor. Some as skilled as us and others simply swaying back and forth to the music. But together we moved, owning the entire dance floor as if there were no other people out there.

When the song ended and slowed to a moody country ballad, I held her in my arms. I looked down at her sea-blue eyes, unable to break the connection. Annie's breaths came out in pants from the exertion, and my mind wandered to dark and devious places of what those pants would sound like under different circumstances.

"Renee seems nice." I watched as Annie swallowed and the muscles in her neck worked. "Lark said she was pretty, but wow, she's really stunning."

Yeah, well, she's not you.

"Yup. She's really nice."

"Nice." Annie squeezed my biceps but made no move to leave my embrace. "Come on, Lee. This is me you're talking to."

Oh, I knew who I was talking to. That was the fucking problem.

I looked over the top of her head back toward the bar to see Renee and Aaron watching us, but they were engaged in a friendly conversation of their own.

"How about the big guy? Things go okay with him?"

She let out a small chuckle. "He's really nice, but I don't know . . ."

"So you get to say your date is *nice*, but I can't? Come on, Annette." I frowned down at her. "What's the problem?"

Her cheeks went pink. "Did you know that he's into raw food?"

My brows pinched together. "Raw food. Like sushi?"

She smiled and blinked up at me. "Raw food as in *everything*. Sure, sushi. But also broccoli, carrots, oats. He doesn't eat anything that's cooked. *Nothing*. It's . . . weird."

I let out a laugh. "I did not know that. I guess that means Momma Faye's Barbecue is out."

Annie swatted at my arm. "Oh my god, I didn't even think about it. Yeah, that . . ." She shook her head, sending her curls bouncing. "That's it. It's not going to work out. There's no way I could live a life without Momma's."

For heavy moments, I stared down into her cerulean eyes. Our bodies continued to sway to the music of their own accord. Years and years of practice moving together and dancing. It was like muscle memory in the most torturous, painfully amazing way.

Her attention caught on our dates again. "I think maybe we should go rescue them."

I reluctantly stepped back and released her from my embrace. But even then I could still feel her presence, like an echo of her body still imprinted on mine.

I dropped my arms and wiped my palms on the sides of my jeans. "Yeah, you're probably right."

Annie led the way, and my hand found the small of her back. A gesture that was far too friendly, too intimate—something I had always been careful *not* to do. I didn't miss the tiny way her shoulders jumped and bunched at the contact. I let my hand fall and tucked it into my pocket.

My fist clenched, and I could feel the heat of her skin radiating across my palm and up my arm.

"Wow," Renee beamed. "You two were amazing out there."

Annie pushed back a curl. "Oh, thanks. Lee and I have been dancing together a long time. It's just fun." The dismissal irked me, but I couldn't pin down exactly why. Dancing with Annie *was* always just fun, but it bugged the shit out of me how easily she could dismiss it. Something was off.

Changing.

I scanned the crowded bar, my eyes landing on an empty four-top that had opened up. "How about that drink?" I focused on Annie and Aaron. "Would you like to join us?"

Annie nodded and smiled, and the four of us made our way toward the table. When we sat, a server swooped in, taking our orders and scurrying away. Renee and Annie looked out onto the dance floor as an awkward silence fell over the table.

Annie gently cleared her throat. "Lee, did you know Renee once played an EMT on that TV show *Chicago Medics*?"

My eyebrows lifted. That show was a joke, known for taking many, *many* liberties when it came to anything close to medical facts. "Oh, no kidding?"

Renee beamed and cleared her throat. "He's in supraventricular tachycardia. Beginning ALS measures now!"

I could only blink.

"Whoa . . ." Aaron was in awe.

Renee preened and smiled at him. "It means 'advanced life saving measures.'"

Advanced life support, actually.

Aaron nodded, clearly impressed, his grin widening. "Killer."

Oh boy. We all fell back into polite, tense smiles.

Annie picked up the small plastic menu nestled between the napkins and drink menu. "Anyone up for a snack?"

I looked over her shoulder to see if anything new had been added to the Grudge's ever-evolving menu. My eyes lost focus every time she shifted and a waft of her hair caught in the air. "The fried pickle chips with spicy mayo are a must."

Annie's blue eyes rolled playfully. "Obviously." I ordered them almost every time they rotated back onto the menu.

"No can do." Aaron patted his stomach. "I have Hero WODs in the morning."

I looked at Annie, whose confused expression matched my own.

"Now *those* are killers. It's a metcon day for me." Renee flashed her smile toward Aaron, and her dimple deepened.

"Metcon?" Annie asked, her nose scrunching.

Renee lifted a shoulder. "It's a CrossFit thing. Do you work out?"

I didn't miss the subtle way Renee's eyes raked down Annie's lush curves.

"Hey, how do you know if someone's into CrossFit?" All eyes turned my way. I could barely contain my shit-eating grin. "Don't worry, they'll tell you."

Annie's barking laugh sent pleasure dancing over my skin. Her curls bounced as she planted a hand over her chest and continued to giggle at my ridiculously weak joke.

The line down Aaron's mammoth forehead deepened. "I don't get it."

His response sent Annie into another fit of snorting laughter. Renee leaned closer to Aaron, engaging him in a peppering of questions regarding his upcoming workout. I risked a glance at Annie, seeing that humor danced in her eyes, and I shot her a wink.

As a foursome, we had struggled through one round of drinks when Annie sighed and stood. "Are you about ready, Aaron? I'm beat."

He glanced toward Renee and frowned. "Oh, sure. Yes."

We all stood, Annie reached for her purse, and I gave her a bored look. "Don't even try it."

Aaron patted his chest and back pocket but made no move to actually pull out his wallet.

I held out a hand to stop him. "Don't worry about it. This one's on me."

He smiled. "Thanks, bro."

I quickly paid for the drinks, and we walked toward the exit. As the music and laughter from the Grudge spilled out into the night air, I paused on the sidewalk. Renee's arm was hooked with Annie's as they slowly walked up the sidewalk.

"Hey, bro. If you don't think you're into Renee, do you mind if I call her?"

I watched the women quietly chat as Aaron and I meandered behind them. My eyes stayed trained on their backs, though it was a battle to not lower my gaze to watch the way Annie's ass moved beneath her tight jeans.

"No. Fine by me. But maybe wait a few days. Let Annie down gently, ya know?"

"Good. Great!" He cleared his throat to hide his obvious enthusiasm. "Of course."

"This is me." Renee stopped by her bright-red car and pulled her keys from her purse.

"My car is a few blocks up that way." Aaron pointed in the opposite direction of where we had walked.

Annie glanced up at her upstairs apartment only a few storefronts down. "I'm close. I'll let myself in."

"Do you want a ride to your car?" Renee leaned over the driver's door and smiled at Aaron.

Without missing a beat, he nearly shouted, "Yes!"

So much for subtlety. I covered my laugh with a cough. "'Night, you two."

Annie gave Aaron a waving salute, and within seconds Renee and Aaron were driving away.

I looked at my best friend. "Well."

"Oh for two?" Annie asked with a smile.

"Big ol' goose egg."

Her laugh floated above us in the night air. "Come on. Let's go back and get those pickle chips to go."

Annie stepped toward me and smiled as we made our way back toward the Grudge.

SEVEN
ANNIE

"How is it that you can eat those in the most unladylike way possible?"

I grinned, my cheeks puffed out. "I simply do my best."

I plucked the last fried pickle from the Styrofoam take-out container and swiped it through the spicy mayo.

Sitting at the edge of a water tower with your legs dangling 130 feet in the air was like being transported to a different world. Our quaint town stretched out in front of us. Our roads wound around each other, and you could track the line of Main Street all the way down to the lake. The rolling waves of Lake Michigan sprawled out for as far as the eye could see.

It was years ago, right after Margo's accident, that Lee had found access to the landing high atop the water tower.

He had sneaked up there to spray-paint a childlike rendition of a cow wearing a crown.

In the years since, no amount of new locks nor a fancy new gate had kept the water tower from becoming a quiet place to sit and think.

Our place.

"All right, so Aaron was a wash," Lee said as he sighed and licked the remnants of the spicy mayo from his thumb. I swallowed hard and forced my eyes to look away from where his tongue darted out.

His hand slapped gently against his thigh. "Okay, I'll do it."

I looked at him as my eyebrows crept up my forehead. Lee sighed and wiped his palms together. "I'll talk to Connor. You're right—he's good looking, he's a decent guy, and a good friend."

I continued to stare at Lee, unsure of how to tell him I didn't need him to set me up.

He misread my silence and immediately added, "It's not like a pity date or anything."

That elicited a laugh, and I shook my head. "It's not that. I don't need you to set me up with him."

"Well, what do you mean? I thought we were helping each other out so that we had a date to the gala and wouldn't be lined up like cattle at auction."

I laughed at the image because, in reality, that was a lot like what it felt like. "This morning, Charles messaged me back. I would have said something, but I didn't want to cancel on Aaron with such short notice. I thought that might be rude." I shrugged but couldn't seem to look Lee in the eye. "I think we're going to go out again." I offered him a sheepish smile. "I'm hoping that he might take pity on me and bid for dates at the auction. Maybe even go as my date so I can get around the whole thing."

Lee scoffed, and his annoyance surprised me.

"What?" I asked, unable to read the curious expression that marred his handsome face.

"It's nothing. I just . . ." Lee sighed and looked down

across our town. "I think relationships should come naturally. It just seems weird. Forcing someone into six dates."

"Forcing?" My voice came out much more shrill than I had intended, but Lee had hit a nerve.

"I didn't mean forcing. It's just that . . . shit, Annie, I don't know. You agreed that the whole premise of the auction is ridiculous."

"Of course I think it's ridiculous, but I also don't want to be forced into six dates with Stumpy Larson again just for the sake of charity. I'm not going to force Charles into anything, but he's also newish to town, and maybe he doesn't realize how the auction works." I shrugged. "Maybe if he knew he'd —I don't know—*want* to bid on me." I picked at invisible lint on the hem of my skirt and couldn't dare look Lee in the eyes.

"Hey." His voice lowered a degree to a timbre that sent shivers dancing down my back. "Of course he would want to. I'm sorry I said anything."

"What about Emma?" I needed something, anything, to get the focus off me so that I could collect my fraying nerves.

"Emma?"

"Yeah, she saw everything on display when you were running through town, and she wasn't mad at it." I laughed softly at my slightly obnoxious friend. "Why don't you go on a date with her? You could even take her to the gala. She's *really* excited about going. And then you wouldn't have to worry about being put up and bid on, since you're there with someone."

The solution was simple, and I knew Emma would be up for it even though I hadn't asked her about it beforehand.

Lee sighed and looked down onto our quiet streets. Cars moved in and out of town, but they were so far down and removed it was like we were the only two in the world. Our breaths were in opposite rhythm, a soft breeze through the trees the only sound.

"Yeah, okay," Lee finally said. "Talk to Emma and see if she's interested. I'd be happy to take her out. And listen"—his elbow nudged me, and I finally met his gaze, his green-gray eyes soft but intense—"Charles is a lucky guy. He'd be stupid to let you slip away."

I lowered my lashes and smiled. "Thank you."

I looked around as the night sky grew inky and hundreds of stars twinkled above us. I sighed with contentment.

"Doesn't get much better than this, does it?" Lee asked beside me, looking out onto the vast waters of Lake Michigan.

"No, I guess it doesn't." I wanted so badly to lean my head against him, to sigh deeply and let the world melt away as I enjoyed this moment with Lee.

Instead, my feet kicked out, and I focused on my upcoming date with Charles and how it might finally be the one to help him see us as more than just occasional make-out buddies.

"You know," Lee finally broke the silence. "This is the best day of my life."

I snorted a laugh and leaned into my best friend. "You always say that."

"Yeah." He sighed. "I know."

"This pinot noir is from the Burgundy region." Charles smiled at me. "Bring the glass to your face. Inhale deeply from your lungs, hold the aroma."

I did as Charles instructed and tried not to cough as the burn from the alcohol tickled my lungs.

"Tell me what you smell."

I thought hard, trying to think of fancy words or smells I might be experiencing. My mind blanked.

This is not off to a great start.

"It smells . . . sharp, maybe?"

Charles flattened his lips and shook his head. "No, deeper than that. Search for the subtleties underneath."

"Okay." I tipped the glass toward my nose and inhaled again. "Like maybe caramel or something?"

That earned me a tight smile. "This particular varietal is redolent with upturned forest floor, subtle rot, morning dew. It has an excellently executed sous-bois characteristic with hints of burned sugar on the nose." He tipped his glass toward me and saluted. "Which could be what you're accurately describing as caramel."

Charles stuck his nose deep into the glass and inhaled deeply with a gentle, appreciative moan.

Subtle. Rot.

I sniffed again to try to see if I could pinpoint what the hell he was talking about, but the wine pretty much just smelled like booze to me.

He held his glass up in the air and swirled it. "This also has nice legs on it."

I smoothed the skirt over my knees as we sat on a blanket on the beach. "Oh, well, thank you," I teased with a laugh.

His eyes whipped to my legs. "Oh, I meant . . . I wasn't insinuating that I . . ."

"Oh, I know. I'm sorry, I was just teasing. It was a joke." Heat flooded my cheeks, but then Charles's wide palm smoothed over my knee.

"I do appreciate those legs as well."

I smiled and relaxed. There were times when it felt like Charles and I had nothing in common. Case in point: me trying to figure out how something that smelled like morning dew and rot was supposed to be an expensive glass of fancy French wine.

But then there were other times we could both relax and just be ourselves, and it felt much easier. Natural. I knew Charles was attracted to me, and I was certainly attracted to him. We had even kissed once in the back of his storeroom, and at the time it had felt really good. But since then there always seemed to be something between us. A barrier we couldn't get past.

Around date five, which this impromptu beach date was, men got very prickly about my relationship with Lee. Charles had never mentioned Lee, which I also found a bit odd. It was no secret that Lee and I were close friends, but Charles seemed to always tactfully avoid the conversation regarding my friendship with the town's playboy.

"So the Bluebird Book Club is finalizing details about the Matchmakers' Gala. Will you be attending?" I took another sip of the wine in an attempt to hide the nerves that tickled my belly.

"Of course. One of your lovely members reached out to see if I could sponsor some of the alcohol sales. I believe the hope is to offer a bit more variety than Abel King's brewery. It seems that Outtatowner's tastes have been slightly elevated." Charles offered me a smile.

My fingertips twirled around the rim of my glass. "So you're going, then?"

I was hoping he would pick up on the fact that I was quite literally *dying* for him to ask me to go as his date. "Did they also explain to you that a part of the gala is an auction?"

"She did." He smiled. "In fact, I'm donating a few cases from my reserve for the auction. It's a write-off for the business, and I'm always happy to extend money to charity."

"That's very generous of you. I'm sure they will earn a lot from that." I looked down at the hemline of my skirt. "There's also a date auction that you might not know about." My eyes flicked up to his, and I willed myself to keep going. "Anyone who attends the gala without a date is entered into the date auction. So, for example, if I were to go without a date and someone like, say, you, bid on dates with me and won, then that money goes to the selected charity, and we have a set of prearranged dates."

"That's a bit archaic, isn't it?" Charles frowned.

"It is, and trust me, some of us have been trying to get rid of it for years, but in reality, it makes a ton of money for the year's selected charity, and there have been several marriage proposals as a direct result. In a grand finale, one couple is announced as 'Top Couple.' They get to present the funds raised to the charity, *and* receive $10,000." More times than not, that money went toward a pretty engagement ring, but I carefully left that tidbit out.

My thoughts immediately ran to my impending housing situation and how helpful that money would be to get my business idea up and running. It was well known that the majority, if not all, of the Top Couple prize money was a donation from the Kings, but pride be damned—I was desperate.

I looked at Charles. I could *definitely* make six dates with him work and convince the town that we were the top couple.

I shrugged, hoping to sound nonchalant and not the

wound-up mess I was. "I think it's just one of those things about Outtatowner that's going to be around forever."

Charles took what I shared about our quirky community. "These dates are put on by the Bluebirds?"

I smiled, proud to be a part of an exclusive club of women who essentially run the town under the guise of a book club. "We do. They're usually really fun, quirky dates that bring everyone together. It's a town spectacle more than anything." I smiled, thinking about how I had seen more romantic marriage proposals in my lifetime than I ever thought possible. "But in the past it has always been a good time. Well . . . if you get matched with someone good. Not Stumpy Larson."

I gave him the abridged version of my series of unfortunate dates with Stumpy, and he shuddered.

"Exactly." I laughed, finishing off the glass of wine. When I lowered it, I noticed Charles's eyes taking in my empty glass. His glass was still half-full.

Shit.

I giggled. "It's delicious."

He lifted a new bottle. "Try this one. There are notes of seashell and pear. This wine is made from Melon de Bourgogne grapes grown on the Atlantic coast."

I raised the glass to my lips and took a sip.

Still just tastes like wine.

Conversation flowed, and Charles went on about the region in which those particular grapes originated, and the topic of the Matchmakers' Gala seemed to fade away.

I only hoped I'd planted a seed and Charles would be willing to take a chance on me at the auction.

All I needed were six dates.

EIGHT
LEE

"My lord. My lady. Please, after me." Our host, dressed as a medieval page boy, swooped low into a bow before leading Emma and me into Outtatowner's local theater.

The latest production wasn't a play but rather dinner and a tournament, including a madrigal dinner, knights' tournament, and revelry.

It was Emma's idea, and who was I to deny a woman her pleasures?

That was, until she also insisted we dress up for it. Emma's outfit was a long, flowing gown made of what looked like silk and velvet. It was fitted at the waist and flared out at the bottom, creating a dramatic silhouette on her petite frame. The sleeves of the dress were long and fitted, with a slit down the middle that showed off a silky undershirt with puffy sleeves.

The neckline of her dress was square, with fancy embroidery around the edges. Emma also wore a small crown-like headpiece with jewels and embroidery that matched the dress and dipped into the middle of her forehead.

It was clear she was taking this very, very seriously.

I leaned down to whisper in her ear. "You look nice."

Emma smiled. "Thank you! I'm a ho for a good costume party." She held her smile, but her eyes drifted over my outfit. I couldn't blame her. Assuming my jeans and work boots wouldn't be medieval-era appropriate, I'd enlisted the help of Wyatt's fiancée, Lark, and my niece, Pickle.

Big mistake.

Thanks to those two, I wore an oversize blouse of Lark's that was nearly skintight on me and a pair of black trousers. Pickle insisted on using safety pins to attach a chenille blanket to my shoulders as a cape, and I looked more like a drunk pirate than a medieval lord.

The lights dimmed, and Emma clapped her hands together. Her voice was soft and low. "This is so exciting, isn't it?"

Our local theater had been transformed. The company had added castle-like elements to the stage and seating area. Large stone walls had been crafted and tapestries had been hung around the theater to create the feeling of a dark castle. The small stage was decorated with wooden benches, crates, and barrels.

Flickering bulbs had been added to the sconces lining the perimeter of the theater. Fake candles and torches were everywhere. Through the dim lighting, we were led to our seats.

"Welcome to the knights' table. I'll be your server, Marcus. May I get you something from the barkeep?"

Emma was practically dancing out of her seat as she looked over the small paper menu in front of her. "One mug of Maiden's Mead for me, please!"

I looked down the menu, without a clue what any of the drinks were. "Do you have Dr Pepper?"

Marcus scoffed. "I'm afraid I have never heard of such an ale, my lord."

He and Emma burst into a tittering round of laughter. It was too ridiculous not to join them, and I chuckled. "I, uh . . . I'll take a Knight's Nectar then."

Marcus winked. "Of course, my lord."

As he walked away, I took in the scene in front of me. Despite the insistence the audience stay in character, apparently iPhones were okay. Several of the actors leading guests to their seats were illuminating the dim walkway with their phones.

I leaned back into my seat, trying to relax. "So, Emma, I—"

"Hear ye! Hear ye! Attention in the hall!" A loud voice boomed and crackled over the speakers. "On behalf of our royal cousins and kin, I bid thee great welcome to our humble hall. Hail and welcome, good lords and ladies, neighbors and kindred to this—a celebration of a madrigal feast. We are privileged this evening to have in our presence royalty and nobility from lands far and wide. Let the announcements and procession begin!"

I leaned closer. "Emma, thanks for coming out tonight."

"Shh!" Emma swatted my arm. "And call me Lady Emmaline."

I relaxed back into my chair and laughed. I knew Emma from around town, and she was a bit of a nut, but a good time.

And I loved a good time.

The show and feast made it difficult to have a real conversation with Emma, particularly because of how into the show she was, and honestly, by the time the actors were performing a sword fight, I was hooked.

We'd eaten half a chicken with our hands—apparently

silverware had yet to be invented—slurped soup from a goblet, and washed it all down with Knight's Nectar, which I was pretty sure was Squirt mixed with melted grape Popsicles.

By the end of the show, soft lighting illuminated the space, and we stood.

"So what's your deal anyway?" Emma's eyes raked up and down my torso as though she was trying to figure me out.

"My deal?"

"Yeah, your deal. Word around town is you're desperate for a date." She laughed. "Who would have thought? Lee Sullivan, desperate." Another snort escaped her nose.

"I'm not desperate."

She stifled a laugh. "If you say so," she singsonged. When I wouldn't give her any more information, she rolled her eyes. "Fine, have your secrets. Annie wouldn't tell me why she was setting us up either."

As we wound our way out of the theater, Emma took time to bow dramatically at the other patrons, and I couldn't help but feel it was like taking an older version of Pickle out on the town. She was fun and good for a laugh, but as far as a romantic connection—zero.

Not happening.

Still, Emma was quirky, and we got along great. If I wanted to get out of the gala's date auction, enduring one more night with her wouldn't be a hardship. We could go as friends.

Thoughts of Annie swirled in my mind. We'd done plenty of *friendly* activities together, but somehow attending the gala with her on my arm felt too close. Too real. The growing, decidedly *not-friendly* thoughts I'd been battling would be too much, combined with the inevitable spark to Outtatowner's gossip mill.

Outside the theater, the cool coastal breeze fluttered Emma's dress. I reached for her hand. "Lady Emmaline, would thou do me the honor of attending the Matchmakers' Gala?"

I lifted my mouth into a smirk and brought her hand to my lips. Her other hand moved to her chest.

That's right. Good ol' Lee Sullivan charm.

"Oh, Lee."

I straightened and smiled.

Emma frowned. "No."

My brain stopped. It wasn't often I was turned down for a date. "No?"

Emma's laughter filled the night air. "*Hell* no."

I looked down at her and she laughed again. "I'm sorry. That was rude. No, thank you, good sir." She paused. "Wait. You're not actually taking this date seriously, are you?" She looked up at me with pity. "Oh, honey, this is just a favor for Annie. You slept with my sister . . . and my friend Tina."

I dragged a hand through my hair, the familiar prickle of shame washing over me. "I don't know what to say. I'm not really like that anymore."

Was I?

"Well, I sure hope not." She waved a hand between us. "But don't stress about it. They had nothing but wonderful, *amazing* things to say about you. In fact, my sister called you the perfect gentleman, which is saying something, because she is a notorious man-hater."

I smiled. "Thanks, I guess."

Together we made our way toward Emma's car. "So tell me why Annie insisted I go on a date with you?"

I looked at Emma and really took her in. She was cute and smart and funny—and also a little bit wild, which would always keep things interesting. She was Annie's friend, and that meant something to me.

Why the hell not?

"Annie and I are trying to get out of the auction, which was why I was kind of hoping that you'd be my date to the gala. That way I wouldn't be up for bidding. I can show you a nice time." I put both hands in the air. "No expectations, no funny business. I'd love to take you out again, as friends."

Emma snorted and laughed. "Still no. I'm sorry, I can't." Emma reached forward and dropped her hand on my forearm. "It's nothing personal, I swear. It's just—I don't know—I *love* the auction." Her voice grew wistful. "Yes, it's old fashioned, and yeah, there's a chance that Stumpy Larson might outbid someone for me, but I don't know." She lifted a shoulder. "I'm hopeful this year. I like the idea of the dating battlefield being taken out of my hands." She raised both of her palms to the night sky. "I'm leaving this one up to the universe." Emma grimaced as she looked at me. "And the Universe is telling me I shouldn't go with you."

I pressed my lips together and nodded, trying not to laugh. "Fair enough." I looked around, unsure of what to do or say after such a thorough rejection. "Is there anything I can do to help? Anyone in particular you've got your eye on? I can put in a good word for you."

"You think Royal King will be there?" She batted her lashes.

"Not funny."

"What? I've been thinking of asking him out after he gave me this." Emma pulled up the sleeve of her shirt, revealing a fresh mini-line-drawing tattoo of a dainty floral bouquet.

I was stunned. "You know the Kings are nothing but trouble, right?"

Emma shrugged. "I'm an equal-opportunity ogler." She smiled as she swished her skirt from side to side. *A townie would know you had to pick sides.*

Emma smiled, and her brown eyes lit up. "You know, I wouldn't mind a good word put in for your friend Connor."

I nodded. Maybe Annie was right—everyone did seem to have a thing for Connor. Good for him. "I'll see what I can do."

Emma brightened. "What about Annie? Just take her."

I frowned. "No can do. I already tried that, and she turned me down too."

Emma toyed with the inside of her lip. "Yeah, I think she's hoping Charles will bid on her."

I shook my head. "What is with that dude? Annie *never* dates, and now this guy comes along and somehow he's got a hold on her?"

She scoffed. "Yeah, he's charming and cultured and a business owner. What's the appeal?" Sarcasm dripped from Emma's words.

I leaned back against Emma's car and crossed my arms. "There's just something about him. I don't think he's right for Annie."

Emma laughed. "Why are the hot ones always so dumb?"

"What?"

"You're an idiot, but never mind." She flapped a hand in dismissal. "I think I know what it is." She pursed her lips. "You've got this whole charming, rakish appeal thing going on, and it bugs you that you can't find a date."

"It's fine," I lied.

"Well, how did it start?" She circled her hands between us. "The whole man-whoring thing."

I shot her a bland look, and she smiled. "No offense. But seriously, tell me your last girlfriend that lasted longer than . . . four dates."

I sighed. "Well, it was probably . . ."

I dragged my hand through my hair.

Shit.

Emma laughed. "Exactly what I thought."

"I guess my last serious girlfriend would have been Margo, in high school."

Her eyes widened. "Crap. I'm sorry. I didn't mean to, you know, bring that up."

I shrugged. I was used to pushing away uncomfortable feelings, and there was just something about Emma, like she didn't take things too seriously, and maybe I shouldn't either.

Emma's voice was soft. "Annie doesn't really talk about her, but she had mentioned her foster sister was in an accident."

I swallowed hard and willed my emotions to stay at bay. "Yeah, it was pretty bad."

"I heard it was a drunk driver."

I nodded. "Yep, hit and run, but they found the guy, so that's something." I shrugged as if that night hadn't completely changed the path of my life. What no one knew was that earlier that night, Margo and I had been on the phone while she was at a wedding reception at Palomino Stables. We'd gotten into some bullshit argument, and she had been drinking, so she took off walking down a dark country road. The guy who struck her had the decency to call 911, but he'd fled the scene.

When a call came in at the fire station for a person-versus-vehicle accident, I jumped in the ambulance without a second thought. What no one ever talked about was the fact that when a firefighter answers a call in a small town, it was your friends. Neighbors. Your girlfriend.

I was the first on the scene, and Margo died in my arms.

Emma sighed as silence stretched between us. "You two dated in high school and then through your time in the service?" she finally asked.

I nodded. "Junior and senior year, yeah, we were pretty hot and heavy. So when I enlisted, we stayed together. I really only saw her on the rare occasion I was back home, but we wrote letters back and forth a lot." I thought back to that time, when those letters were the only things keeping me sane through my time overseas. "It wasn't until I was away that we figured it out. Those letters are what made me fall so head over heels for her. Before that, it was your typical high school kid drama. Young kids too dumb to know what they were doing. But in those letters something changed. I think we both matured."

Tears were thick in Emma's voice. "That's so romantic."

"It didn't last. We were back to bickering and drama the minute I was home. It wasn't even two months after I was back that she was gone." A cynical laugh escaped me. "So much for romantic."

Emma stared. I cleared my throat and swiped my hand down my face. "Jesus fuck, I'm sorry, I don't know why I just spilled all that."

Emma looked at me, her eyes narrowing. "Are you still in love with her?"

I couldn't tell you why the image of Annie's face immediately came to mind, but I quickly brushed it aside. "With Margo?" I shook my head. "No. I realized a long time ago that what we had and what I *thought* we had were two very different things. The girl I dated and the woman who wrote me letters were like two completely different people. Once I was back, I couldn't reconcile the two, and things just fell apart."

"So what's the problem then?"

Her soft voice encouraged me to keep going. I shrugged. "It's a small town with big opinions. I couldn't escape everyone constantly reminding me about her or reminiscing about our love story. And seeing her parents all the time? It was brutal. It makes me sound like an asshole, but I was so relieved when they moved away."

"A small town with big opinions." Emma scoffed. "They need to change the welcome sign to *that*. It's far more accurate."

I nodded and scoffed in agreement.

Emma sighed. "Sounds to me like holding on to her memory is a safety net. It makes sure you never let anyone get too close. Maybe it's a little too convenient to lean into the whole *Poor heartbroken Lee. Can you blame him for being unable to commit?*"

It was something I hadn't ever considered, but her words settled over me. We sat in silence as I considered her fresh insight.

Finally, Emma bumped her shoulder affectionately into mine. "Fuck 'em."

I raised my eyebrows at her.

Her smile spread wide. "I refuse to let the opinions of others rule my life. I suggest you do the same."

Wanting to talk about anything other than myself, I looked down at Emma. "So now that I've unloaded all my emotional baggage on you, let's hear it," I said. "What's *your* deal?"

Emma shrugged and smiled a sly smile. "I don't have a deal. I'm perfect in every way."

I smiled back with a playful roll of my eyes. "Clearly."

Emma lifted a shoulder. "In reality, I'm a romantic at heart. I'm waiting for my Prince Charming to come whisk me off my feet. Someone I can laugh with. Amazing sex, that's a must. Someone I can be my true self around, where I don't have to hide anything."

My mind immediately flew to Annie. She was the only person who ever got a glimpse of the real me, but I buried the thought. "You *are* a romantic. I hope you find him."

"Thanks," she said with a smile. "I will. One day. I'm sorry I can't go with you to the gala." She shrugged. "Prince Charming and all."

"No, it's okay. I totally understand. Besides, I wouldn't want to stand in the way of true love."

NINE
ANNIE

I STARED down at the text message on my phone. My heart sank into my belly like it did every year when I received the text.

MRS. WEAVER

Happy birthday, Annie! Margo is smiling down on you.

I swallowed past the scratchy lump that formed in my throat. Every year it was the same text on my birthday and an almost identical one at Christmastime. No phone call, no card, no visit—just the text.

The Weavers were good people. They had taken me in as a child after being bounced around the state of Michigan's foster care system. I knew how lucky I was to end up with them in Outtatowner.

Their daughter, Margo, was my age. She was enthusiastic and welcoming, and we instantly became unlikely best friends. Margo was fun and popular and basked in being the center of attention. At that time, all I wanted was to fade into the background, but she wouldn't let that happen. She and her family took me in and gave me hope for a future I had always thought was for girls who didn't come from broken homes.

Trouble was that the Weavers weren't looking for another daughter, and after Margo passed away, it was too painful for them to remain in the town that held so many memories of her.

Without a second thought, the only parents I had ever known up and moved. The only remaining contact I had was a single text on my birthday and one on Christmas Eve.

My phone rang, and a picture of Kate's smiling face lit up the screen. I immediately released the breath I'd been holding and infused my voice with false cheeriness.

"Hey!" I answered.

"Oh shit. Are you crying?"

Damn it.

Kate and I were close. Before she had moved to Montana—before Lee stepped into the role—I would have considered her my best friend.

"No, I'm good." I cleared my throat. "Sorry."

"Okay, well, everything is set for tonight. We're going to be at Tootie's—have a few drinks down in the speakeasy, then move on up to the back patio. Everyone's going to be there. We are all so excited!"

"Wait, wait, stop. What are you talking about?"

Kate groaned in exasperation. "Your birthday, silly. We're all ready to celebrate!"

Fresh tears prickled beneath my eyelids. "Oh, I didn't know if you—"

"You didn't think we weren't going to celebrate your birthday, did you?" Kate interrupted.

It was true. The Sullivans celebrated my birthday every year without missing a beat. It started with their mother,

June, who loved to throw parties. I think she saw my sad little existence as an excuse to be surrounded by children and the town she loved so much.

As a child, birthdays with the Weavers were quiet, understated affairs of a birthday cake, candles, and a single present. At the time, it felt like more than enough.

But as I got older, I realized that the way the Sullivans wrapped themselves around you was the greatest gift I could imagine. Things fell apart for a while after June died, and got even worse when Red got sick, but for the past year, with both Wyatt and Kate returning home, things had started to turn a corner.

Gatherings with the Sullivans weren't quite so strained these days, and everyone was finding their groove. That groove also included me, and I had never felt more loved. Whether they knew it or not, the Sullivans were the only family I had.

Which was why I certainly should not be thinking of Lee Sullivan in anything other than brotherly terms.

A renewed sense of love and belonging washed over me. With them, all was right in the world.

I smiled for real this time. "What time should I show up?"

ARRIVING at Tootie Sullivan's house when a gathering was in full swing was like stepping directly into swirling chaos. Chickens pecked at the grass, Duke Sullivan's dog—aptly named Three-Legged Ed—chased any car that turned down the driveway, and soft, upbeat music played from a speaker.

The Sullivan farmhouse had recently been transformed by Kate and Beckett. What had started as a renovation to rehab the crumbling structure had taken on a life of its own. Kate launched *Home Again*, an Instagram page documenting the historical renovation, and it went viral. The virality was one part home renovation and *fifty parts* watching Kate's ex-boyfriend's grumpy older brother fall head over heels in love with her, one post at a time.

Le sigh.

As I navigated down the driveway, I tried my best to not turn the dog into Two-Legged Ed. Beckett pulled Kate into a loving embrace and buried his nose in her brown hair. My chest pinched. I was so happy for my sweet friend.

I parked my car next to Kate's Jeep and hopped out.

"There she is!" Ms. Tootie's loving voice rose above the chatter and music as she made her way toward me.

"Hi, Ms. Tootie." My cheeks heated with the thought of all eyes being on me. I lifted a square box. "I brought Huck's strawberry rhubarb pie."

Tootie's strong arms pulled me into a motherly embrace with the box between us. Her soft floral scent wafted over me, and I sighed and relaxed into her hug.

"You did not have to bring anything to your own birthday celebration." She peeked down at the box and winked at me. "Though I do love that man's pie."

I grinned at her. Tootie had an uncanny way of saying the most innocent things and making them sound downright *sinful*. Her playful little wink at the end didn't help.

I looked around at the small family gathering. "No Red today?"

My chest pinched.

Tootie's arm wrapped around my shoulders. "He's on his way."

A smile bloomed across my face. Red Sullivan may have suffered from early-onset dementia, but he'd been having a string of good days lately. He was a fighter and the sweetest man. A Sullivan get-together wouldn't have been the same without him.

Kate made her way down the steps of the wide wrap-around porch with her arms flung open. "Get over here."

She wrapped me in a side-hug, and I leaned into her. Kate straightened to look at me, her green eyes dancing with delight. "I have it all planned out. Cocktails in the speakeasy, and by then Duke should be back with Dad. We'll move the party upstairs for dinner."

"And cake!" Penny shouted from the background.

"And cake." Kate laughed. "Definitely cake."

Lee walked up with a grin and a little hen tucked under his arm. He hip checked his sister out of the way. "Move it. She's my best friend."

My stomach somersaulted.

"Once upon a time, she was my best friend," Kate shot back and poked out her tongue.

"I'm not the one who moved to Montana. You snooze, you lose."

"What's with the chicken?" I asked.

Lee looked down at the little yellow hen and smiled. "It's Henrietta."

Kate laughed and rolled her eyes as Lee adjusted the chicken to make her more comfortable. "Henrietta's been following him around since he got here. She won't leave him alone."

He clucked at the hen, who looked more than cozy in the crook of his arm. "She's in love with me."

Kate looked at me with a mischievous grin. "She's *obsessed*. We've been calling her Horny Henrietta."

I laughed as Lee grimaced and set her on the ground. She continued to peck around him, oblivious to anyone but him. Lee wrapped me in a quick hug, then draped his arm across my shoulder. "Let's get you birthday drunk, Annette."

Heat prickled at my cheeks as I was led around the back of the house to the door that opened to the mudroom. It was in that room where, during the renovations, Kate and Beckett had uncovered a hidden trapdoor that led to a long-forgotten Prohibition-era speakeasy.

The door was open and I peered into the square hole in the floor. The narrow stairs had been refinished, but they were still tight and rickety. I walked down, carefully gliding my hand along a smooth banister. My foot slipped slightly on one of the small steps, and Lee's hands clamped around my waist.

"Easy there." His deep voice danced across the shell of my ear.

I sucked in a breath. His hands didn't leave my hips as we continued down the dark staircase. Before I hit the bottom stair, Kate flicked on a light switch, illuminating the small space with soft, warm light. It smelled like earth and lemon-scented wood polish.

It was a bit cramped, but the speakeasy was a wonky rectangle with a bar at the back. A table with chairs was off to the side, leaving space in the middle to stand and mingle.

As we all filed in, Wyatt moved to the corner of the room to turn on a record player. Soft jazzy music filled the space as Kate dipped below a wooden plank to stand behind the bar.

She popped back up with a tray of glasses and a wide grin. Next to her, Beckett rifled through the built-in liquor cabinet.

"We have everything to make a tart cherry gin fizz."

Kate started assembling the cocktail ingredients along the bar.

"Sign me up for that!" Lark called with a smile.

I was acutely aware of Lee's presence, his front nearly touching my back as he looked over my shoulder at the ingredients Kate began to lay out. "I'll have some of that white lightning."

Kate laughed and slid an ancient-looking bottle of liquor away from her older brother. "Not a chance. Don't you see this label?"

The amber bottle still had liquid in it, and the label was faded and worn from time. Despite its age, you could just barely make out the words *King Liquor* on the bottle.

"As far as we know, this could be poison. Even then they could have been out to get us." Kate's expression was serious.

"I don't know . . . ," Lark piped in. "I still can't get over that picture you found of all of them. They looked pretty happy together."

"We still haven't figured it out." Kate shook her head. "And Bug King isn't giving up any details."

Truth was, Kate didn't have as much time to devote to unearthing the reason behind the King–Sullivan feud since she and Beckett had become so consumed with their thriving *Home Again* business. It was an interesting mystery they had yet to unravel.

Kate made a show of shaking up her version of a gin fizz and poured each of us a serving in embossed antique crystal glasses.

She popped back underneath the bar top to join us on the other side and held her glass high. "To Annie Crane, the best sister a girl could ask for."

Wyatt held up his glass. "To Annie, the best sister a guy could ask for."

"Hey!" Kate cut in, slapping him on the arm as his deep chuckle filled the room.

"To Annie. The best sister life brought into our lives," Wyatt corrected.

I swallowed thickly.

"To Annie. The most amazing, creative, and talented friend. You're sunshine on a cloudy day." Lark beamed at me. If anyone was pure sunshine, it was her.

"To our Annie, who deserves all the love this world has to offer." Tootie gently saluted me with her crystal cup before taking a sip.

My eyes shifted to Lee, who had yet to move from my side. He looked down at me.

Did his eyes just move over my mouth?

My heart hammered. "To Annette. You were always meant to be a Sullivan."

"Hear, hear!" Katie shouted.

I used my glass to hide the emotion welling in my throat. When I was with the Sullivans, I wasn't Little Orphan Annie, but a part of a unit.

Their unit.

Beckett broke the simmering tension by twirling his fiancée gently and pulling Kate into the small open space next to the table. "Get over here, woman."

Kate and Beckett moved together toward the bluesy jazz music. Lost in each other, lost in love, they swayed.

The tart cherry gin fizz tickled my nose, and I let the bubbles soothe my tense stomach. I had always wanted a love like that—a love that left you so consumed with the other person that you couldn't imagine taking a single breath without them.

Too often images of Lee in that role flickered in my mind, despite my attempts to place him solidly in the *Friends Only* column.

Against my will, my best friend had become the measuring stick next to which all other men came up sorely lacking. But looking around, I couldn't imagine risking it—risking *them*—just to see if Lee felt the same way about me.

As a group we danced and laughed and let the mood and ambiance of the speakeasy carry us into another round of cocktails.

"Are we going to eat? Or are you all just going to get stupid drunk down there?" Duke's agitated voice rolled down the narrow stairwell.

"Oh look! The good-time assassin is back," Lee shouted up the stairs to goad his oldest brother.

"You let them have their fun," Red said from the top of the stairs.

At Red's voice, Penny unwound herself from a hidden compartment cabinet she had been exploring and ran up the stairs. "Granddad!" Her footsteps rattled the glasses on the bar top.

Kate grabbed the tray of cocktails and shot me a playful wink. "Follow Pickle. We can take the party upstairs."

Outside, the weather was warm, but the coastal air danced through the trees, so I was grateful when we all agreed to eat on the back patio. Tootie fussed over the meal she had prepared, swatting at the greedy fingers that tried to steal a sample before it was properly plated.

When Lee ripped off a hunk of freshly made bread and dunked it into the sauce she had been cooking all day, she slapped at his hand. "Annie, will you please control this boy?"

A barking laugh shot out of me. “Fat chance.” I laughed again, and it was natural and easy.

Lee shot me a wicked grin along with a wink that sent my belly flip-flopping.

On the patio, beneath a massive pergola, was a long farm-style dining table that could comfortably fit twelve people. The Sullivans gathered around it, all talking over each other, laughing and teasing. A hard lump formed in my throat. It wasn’t that long ago that any time I thought of this beautiful, found family my heart ached.

When June Sullivan had died, it seemed as though they would never be the same, especially after Red’s diagnosis. I looked at each member of the Sullivan family.

In time, Wyatt had found his way home, and Lark had found her way to him.

Duke was still grumpy as hell but seemed to be fulfilled by grueling farm work.

Kate had finally made her way home from Montana and discovered her love for home renovation. I couldn’t have found a more perfect match for her than Beckett.

And then there was Lee.

My best friend sat next to me, laughing and joking along with his siblings. The smile he wore was always freely given, but I also knew the pain that he was hiding. The deep pain of being the only witness to his high school girlfriend’s tragic death. She had died in his arms, and a part of Lee had died right along with her.

I risked another glance at him, and when he looked back, he smiled. I gently laid my head on his shoulder. Lee’s hand dropped to his side. My own hand twitched nervously.

I lifted my head and continued my conversation with Kate over dinner.

Tension rippled off Lee. When I shifted in my seat, he seemed to inch impossibly closer. Carefully, I moved my elbow, pressing my back into the wooden chair, all while keeping my face calm and smiling.

Inch by delicious inch, I could feel my body pull toward his. My breath quickened. My heart pounded.

I sucked in a breath, pulling his spicy, masculine scent along with it.

Gently I tilted my head in his direction, realizing our mouths were only inches away while his family sat around us.

Silence stretched between us.

I couldn't allow myself to imagine a life where this was yet another Sullivan family get-together and I wasn't Little Orphan Annie, adopted sister, but I was *with* Lee.

His woman.

But I knew it was impossible, because nothing about Lee was permanent or serious. He had let that part of himself die a long time ago on that dark stretch of country road with Margo.

My place in his life was as a devoted best friend. It was a place that, no matter what, I was unwilling to ever give up. It didn't matter that every part of my soul craved to be his.

Glasses clattered when Pickle plopped onto the seat next to me. I jumped and put space between Lee and me.

"Do you want to see my new chicks?" Penny pulled my arm in the direction of the chicken coop.

Placing my napkin beside the plate, I smiled at the littlest Sullivan. "I would love to."

I was keyed up and relieved to get a break from whatever the hell had been happening between Lee and me. I walked with her across the lush grass toward the cheery, yellow chicken coop.

"Stay away from Bartleby. He's been grumpy," Lark reminded Penny.

Beckett scoffed. "Yeah, he's a real di—"

Wyatt cleared his throat and pinned Beckett with a harsh *Dad* look.

"Mean guy," Beckett corrected. Kate laughed beside him. It was common knowledge that Tootie's Old English Game rooster had an ax to grind with Beckett. Despite the fact he was huge, with a pale-blond head, rust-colored wings, a black body, and gorgeous tail feathers that shone hunter green in the sun, he was known to be prickly. While renovating the farmhouse, he'd taken a particular dislike for Beckett Miller, though I saw Beckett sneak Bartleby little treats from his pocket a time or two.

Pickle grabbed my hand and led me toward the coop. Enclosed in a small area inside were baby chicks that appeared to be only a few weeks old. Their soft, downy feathers and tiny wings were precious, and little cheep-cheep noises carried on the breeze.

Penny pointed each of them out in the box. "That's Phyllis, Molly, and Benita. This brown one is Eggburt 2.0. But we won't eat this one." She shrugged. "Probably."

A laugh burst from me.

"There will be no eating Eggburt." Tootie's voice came from behind us, and she smiled at her great-niece.

I stretched my legs and moved toward Tootie, wrapping her in a hug. "Thank you for today."

Her strong hugs were an anchor in a swirling storm of emotion.

"Hey, you little rat," Lee called to his niece. "Let's see if we can't find some wildflowers with your grandpa."

Pickle zipped past us and joined her uncle and grandfather as they walked toward the row of wildflowers that separated the yard from the blueberry fields beyond.

I rested my arm around Tootie's middle and sighed. "Red seems so . . . good today."

She patted my hand. "He was approved for a national clinical trial, which means an intravenous infusion every two weeks. We're cautiously hopeful." Emotion was evident in her voice. She'd cared for her brother and his children when he became a widower, and more so since his diagnosis. It was a weight she seemed unburdened to carry, but I knew it was still heavy.

"I'll send all my prayers up." I squeezed her again.

We made a lap through the yard and circled back to where the rest of the Sullivan family was gathered.

"You're going?" Kate asked Wyatt.

"Of course I'm going. It's for charity." Wyatt planted his hands on his hips as Lark laughed.

"You're only going because you have me and won't be up for auction. Besides, if I *were* on the auction block, you wouldn't let anyone else bid on me." Lark wound her arms around Wyatt's waist and squeezed.

"Damn right. I dare anyone to try to outbid me."

Lark preened at him. "I would let the bids on you rack up and then swoop in at the last minute to disappoint them all."

"Better be careful," Duke added. "Ms. Tiny can be ruthless."

"What about you, Katie?" Lark asked.

Kate smiled. "Beckett and I will be busy next weekend. We've got a lead on a new house and want to be sure everything is ready if we land it."

"Duke . . . ?" Kate prodded her oldest brother.

Duke's face twisted. "Fuck no. The gala is a meat market disguised as charity."

"Aww c'mon," Lark teased.

"Always so serious," Kate teased Duke with a mock frown and a laugh.

"Well, Annie is going, so we'll be there to support her." Their eyes shifted to me in unison. I scrunched up my nose, trying to think of *any* excuse to get out of that ridiculous gala.

Maybe Emma was right—that I was looking at this all wrong. Instead of dreading the auction, I should have shifted my attitude. In high school, boys like Lee dated girls like Margo. Popular girls with perfect teeth, shiny blonde hair, and no freckles. They didn't date the weird, quirky artist friend who burned in the sun and whose hair could alternate between smooth ringlets and Krusty the Clown.

There was a time I thought maybe I could be someone else. But I wasn't that girl anymore, and the Sullivans had played a huge hand in helping me value myself, just as I am.

With a sigh, I looked out over the yard into the fading sun as Lee's long legs ate up the distance between us. "A call came in. Oakey is sick and they asked me to cover."

The tension in the group was immediate. Lee's eyes shifted to Duke's. "You can get Dad back?"

Duke's face remained stern. "Course."

"Sorry to bail on your birthday, Annette. Duty calls." Lee's cool green-slate eyes looked down on me, but his smile was tense. Unexpected calls always set him on edge, and that tension pulled on the invisible tie between us.

"We'll finish celebrating. The night's still young." Kate smiled at me in reassurance.

She was the only one who knew what I had done. How Margo had begged and pleaded. How I had thought I was helping her and being a good friend, before it morphed into something else entirely. But an emergency call, just like that one, had changed all our lives forever. Not only was Margo taken from us, but my opportunity to tell Lee the truth had died too.

I smiled tightly at him and waved a weak goodbye.

It was clear that if Lee wasn't willing to move on from her, then I had to. I would go to the gala with an open mind and an open heart.

But one horrifying thought burrowed its way into my mind and ran itself on a loop.

If Lee ever finds out, I'll lose them all.

TEN
ANNIE

Lee was nowhere to be found and, for once, I breathed a sigh of relief. It would be far easier to relax and try to make the best of the Matchmakers' Gala without his handsome face muddying the waters.

I'm here to have fun.

The words raced through me, over and over, like a mantra.

For a name as fancy as Matchmakers' Gala, there was not a ball gown in sight in Outtatowner's high school gymnasium. I did, however, put some effort into leaning into my feminine side with the mid-length chiffon party dress. It was a blend of green and gray—a color that always reminded me of Lee's eyes.

Shit. Scratch that.

A *smoky, sagey* greenish gray that had absolutely nothing in common with my best friend or his eyeballs.

The dress was sleeveless with a high neck, but a keyhole scoop hinted at cleavage. I'd even scrubbed my nails free of pottery clay and painted them a complementary blush pink.

My hair was unruly, so I'd pinned the sides behind my ears and let the rest flow down my back.

"Looks like you could use this." Lark appeared with two flutes of bubbly wine.

I immediately scooped one up and drained it before letting out an audible sigh. "Thank you."

Her eyes were wide. *So much for harnessing that feminine energy.*

"Sorry. I'm nervous."

"Don't be." She leaned in. "I've already got this under control." When her grin widened and her shoulder lifted, panic danced beneath my skin.

"What are you talking about? What did you do?"

Lark laughed. "Nothing, really. I just made sure Wyatt kept Stumpy Larson in check, and I may have dropped a few *very* subtle hints to charming Mr. Attwater regarding the date auction."

"You didn't."

She grinned. "I did."

My eyes searched the crowd, and my palms grew sweaty. Sure enough, in the corner, Wyatt was waiting to get a drink, but shooting daggers in Stumpy Larson's direction. The man shrank back when he caught Wyatt's glare.

A laugh bubbled out of me. "Oh, Lark." I squeezed her shoulder. "Thank you."

"Attention, everyone!" Aunt Sissy's voice crackled over the sound system, and a hush came over the crowd. "Thank you all for being at Outtatowner's annual Matchmakers' Gala! This Western Michigan tradition has been going strong for nearly a century! Records at the Remington County Historical Association have documents of a similar local auction dating back to the mid-1930s!" Polite oohs and aahs surrounded me.

"Now please make your way around the outer perimeter to see all the very generous and downright amazing items in our silent auction. Bidding will close by eight, and we'll move into everyone's favorite part of the evening . . . our *live* Matchmakers' Date Auction!"

A soft round of applause rippled through the crowd, and my stomach tightened. Across the gymnasium, I spotted Charles.

He was dressed in black suit pants, a crisp white shirt, and black tie. His hair was styled back, and his face was freshly shaven. I willed myself to feel . . . *anything* at the sight of him.

I held my breath.

One. Two. Three.

I paused.

What. The actual. Fuck.

I promised myself that the lack of physical reaction to the very handsome sight of Charles was due to nerves.

Lark looped her arm in mine. "Let's walk around and see what we can't spend our money on."

A waiter, sixteen-year-old Buddy Green, came by, and I placed my empty glass on his tray. Together, Lark and I made a circle around the gym to check out the items up for auction.

Farmer for a day with Duke Sullivan. *He definitely got guilted into that one . . .*

A collection of wines from Charles's personal wine cellar.

Six pottery classes, donated by yours truly.

Brewery tour for four from Abel King's brewery.

One pie a month for a year from Huck Benton at the Sugar Bowl.

A free tattoo from Royal King.

Outtatowner Fire Department sexy firefighter calendar. *Well, I'll be bidding on* that. I looked at the bid sheet. *Two hundred dollars?*

I laughed, and affection for my hometown washed over me. They were generous and quirky and downright hilarious.

I turned to Lark. "See anything you can't live without?"

She grinned. "I already told Wyatt I wanted your pottery classes."

"Lark! You know I would give you lessons for free. You don't need to do that."

She lifted a shoulder. "It's for charity. Besides, it's better than Stumpy Larson's *personal tour of Blue Star Highway.*"

I shuddered, then laughed. "Good call."

Together we wound through the crowd. I caught the eye of Mrs. Fritz, and she smiled at me before leaning in to whisper. "My money is on that handsome Mr. Attwater bidding on dates with you!"

"Thank you, Mrs. Fritz. That would be lovely."

Her hand squeezed mine. "We're all rooting for you two!"

Before I could answer, Bug King cleared her throat, and Lark and I turned toward her. "Excuse me." She held a clipboard, and her glasses were perched on the tip of her nose. "Just confirming that you will be participating in the Matchmakers' Date Auction, Annie?"

I cleared my throat. "Yes, ma'am."

"And Lee?" She looked at me over the rim of her glasses.

I shrugged. "Haven't seen him."

Her frown deepened. Word had gotten out around town that after a string of unsuccessful blind dates, Remington County's most sought-after bachelor may be, in fact, making an appearance on the auction block. This year, it meant big money for Remington County Child Protective Services. My chest pinched, thinking back on my time in the system.

She checked her list again and handed me a small cardboard circle with the number eight on it. "Please meet by the stage in ten minutes."

I swallowed hard. "You bet."

Lark rubbed her hand along my bare arm. "It'll be fun! You got this."

I sighed and laughed. "This town is so weird."

"Before we begin, please recall our very strict set of rules." Mabel, a sweet older woman in the Bluebirds, cleared her throat and spoke loudly into the microphone as she read from a piece of paper. "The Matchmakers' Date Auction is for entertainment and charity purposes only. No one shall be entered into dates against his or her will."

A snort shot out of my nose, and all eyes turned toward me.

Fuck.

I looked behind me, pretending it was someone else who'd made the noise as my face grew hot.

Mabel smiled and continued: "There are a set of six prearranged dates for each winning couple. For each date the couples attend, the board of directors for the Matchmakers' Gala will happily donate additional funds to the chosen charity. We have a list of eligible bachelors and bachelorettes, each assigned a number. We will pick a number at random. Once a bachelor or bachelorette is won, he or she is already committed and may not be eligible for dates with anyone else. So let's get started!"

The crowd cheered, and the band played a drumroll.

"First up . . ." She dug around the small basket, and my heart raced. "Chad McClintock."

He was known in Outtatowner as *Other Tall Chad.* Because, you know, the nickname *Tall Chad* was already given out, and at six foot five, he was *tall.*

Other Tall Chad strutted up the stairs and walked across the stage with a friendly wave and wide smile as the band played along. He even turned and did a little butt wiggle, which spurred the crowd to life with whoops and hollers. It was hard not to laugh. I released my clasped hands and tried to lean into the *fun* my town was trying to have.

Not everything had to be so serious.

"Let's hear it, ladies and gentlemen. What do I hear for this young man?"

"Five dollars!" Ms. Tiny shouted over the crowd, opening the bidding.

"Ten dollars!" Aunt Sissy smiled widely as her husband frowned down at her.

"Fifteen!" another called from the back.

"Twenty!" Ms. Tiny clutched her handbag closer to her chest.

"I have twenty dollars from Ms. Tiny. Going once. Twice. Sold!" The crowd cheered as Ms. Tiny made her way up to the stage and Other Tall Chad bowed to kiss the top of her hand.

Mabel swirled her hand into the bowl again. "Number four, Huck Benton!"

Loud claps erupted from the crowd as our burly resident baker made his way onto the stage. Unlike Other Tall Chad, there was no showboating. Instead, he stood with his feet planted wide and his thick arms crossed over his chest.

I leaned in to whisper to Lark. "I thought only *single* people were in the auction?"

Lark giggled. "Word is, Sylvie King penciled his name in as a joke, and it slipped past everyone."

"Twenty!" Before poor Mabel could even open the bidding, someone in the back shouted above the crowd.

"Thirty!"

"Forty!"

"Fifty dollars!"

The shouts of bidders began to roll into one another. "I think I heard fifty," Mabel called into the microphone.

From the left, Cass, Huck's fiancée, strode across the stage with her shoulders back and fire in her eyes. She leaned in close to Mabel's microphone. "Five hundred dollars!"

A gasping murmur rolled through the crowd as they cheered. Huck threw his head back in laughter.

"Sold!" Mabel called into the microphone with a hearty laugh.

Huck scooped up Cass and twirled her in a circle as the crowd roared to life.

"Well," Mabel said. "This is exciting! Next up we have . . ." She looked at the clipboard. "Annie Crane!"

My eyes went wide. *Shit.*

I lifted my hand and walked onto the stage. Lark slapped my butt in playful encouragement, and I narrowed my eyes at her. A few whistles and catcalls forced a nervous laugh from me, until I saw it was Lark whooping from the sidelines. She shot me a quick wink.

"Come over here, dear." Mabel gestured for me to stand beside her. "Ladies and gentlemen, here she is! Our resident redhead and talented artist. What do I hear for an opening bid?"

I laughed nervously as I searched the crowd. Part of me hoped I *wouldn't* see Charles and die of embarrassment.

"Fifty dollars." My eyes whipped right to find Charles smiling widely. Relief washed over me.

"Seventy-five." Not recognizing the voice, I looked around to see Royal King grinning at me.

What the hell?

A subtle gasp shook through the crowd at a King bidding on me. Everyone knew my ties to the Sullivans.

"One hundred." Charles gave me a reassuring smile.

Mabel jumped in. "Going once. Twice. S—"

"One fifty." Royal crossed his arms, the tattoos from his forearms peeking out of his suit jacket onto the tops of his hands. There was a dangerous glint in his eyes.

"Two hundred!" Lee's voice boomed over the crowd as he pushed past friends and neighbors to make his way toward the stage.

My eyes went wide, and my heart pounded against my ribs.

"Two fifty." The muscles in Royal's jaw twitched as though he were fighting back a smile.

"Five hundred dollars." Charles's elegant voice rose above the commotion of the crowd.

I sighed in relief.

"One thousand dollars." There was fire in Lee's eyes as he glared at Charles. From the background Royal laughed.

My brain clicked off-line.

What has he done?

"Sold!" Mabel shouted into the microphone. The crowd erupted into cheers and applause. "Okay, okay. That was exciting, but let's keep that charity money coming. Next up we have . . ." Mabel's voice faded into the background, and I numbly made my way off the stage.

Lark stood at the base of the stairs with wide eyes. I kept moving, past her and out of the gymnasium. Needing air, I ran down the hallway. Only the clack-clack of my heels on the hard floor followed me as I pushed open the exit door into the night air.

I planted my hands on my hips, still reeling from what had happened only moments before.

"Annette."

I whipped around at Lee's harsh voice.

"What did you do? Why?" I was breathless. Confused. *Angry.* I stepped closer to him. "I'd understand if it was to protect me from Royal, but Charles had the winning bid! Why would—"

In a heartbeat, Lee crowded my space. His large hand cupped the back of my neck as he pulled me into him. He hesitated only a fraction of a second before pulling my mouth to his.

In one searing kiss, Lee Sullivan completely changed the rules.

ELEVEN
LEE

I WAS KISSING my best friend.

Not kissing—*devouring*.

My mouth moved over her like I had done it a million times before. Like every single time I had imagined kissing Annie.

And she was kissing me back.

A soft, needy moan hummed in her throat. I deepened the kiss, swiping my tongue over her lips and demanding entrance. She opened for me, and I surged forward, pressing her back into the brick of the building. My hard body covered hers.

My dick twitched and hardened between us. A million sparks of electricity ignited under my skin.

My hand tangled in her soft curls as I tilted her head to deepen the angle. Her heartbeat thrummed under my hand.

I had kissed a lot of women, but none of them compared to her.

My Annette.

The soft curves of her body fit perfectly against the hard

lines of mine. Her hands gripped at my waist, balling the fabric of my shirt in her tight fists.

I wedged my thigh between her legs and groaned as her hips made the tiniest movement forward. My free arm wound around her waist, pulling her body against me. She lifted onto her toes.

My other hand moved from around the base of her skull, down the column of her neck, lower.

Lower.

My hand brushed across the lush peak of her breast. My rough palm grazed the hard tip of her nipple, and the awareness of that taut bud sent a lightning bolt straight to my cock.

I wanted to dip below her dress. To tear her underwear from her body and rail her long and deep and hard against the side of that building.

My fingers spread over her rib cage, teasing the bottom curve of her breast. Annie's arms wound around my neck. I let my thumb skim over the hard tip of her nipple.

More than anything, I wanted my mouth right there. My hips drove forward, pressing her harder against the brick wall.

She pushed my shoulders and I took a step back. Her hand flew to her swollen mouth. Her eyes were wide, her breaths ragged. "What are you doing?"

I searched her wide-eyed stare. *Didn't she feel it too? The shift?*

"I . . . I don't . . ."

"Jesus, Lee!" Annie shouldered past me and ran toward the parking lot.

"Fuck," I muttered. "Annette! Wait!"

She didn't look back before disappearing between a row of cars.

I sighed and braced myself against the wall of the building. I didn't have the balls to go back into the school to face my family and my community over the scene I had just made.

Undoubtedly there would be a thousand questions. For years people had speculated there was something more between Annie and me—something we had adamantly denied our entire lives. Over time, those speculations shifted to comments akin to *Of course Annie would never be with Lee. Look at him. He's a playboy and she's such a nice girl.* I stuffed down the anger that bubbled with the thought.

I hated the fact that they were right.

In one moment of recklessness, I had brought into question the very foundation of our friendship.

Typical fucking Lee.

Instead of facing them, I headed toward my truck. I scanned the parking lot, hoping to see Annie waiting. Maybe I could explain whatever it was I was feeling. With no trace of her, I dug the keys to my truck out of my pocket, climbed inside, and headed home.

Once inside my apartment, I tossed my keys on the table in the dish Annie had made. I pulled the dress shirt from my pants and worked open the buttons. As I walked to my bedroom, my dick was still hard from the kiss I had shared with Annie.

Resting my hands against the bathroom sink, I let my head hang. I was still worked up, not only from the kiss, but from the realization that Charles had almost won those dates with her.

My dates.

It hadn't bothered me that Royal had thrown out a bid for her. He was a shit-stirrer and everyone knew it. But the minute Charles stepped forward with his smug smile, I snapped.

Turning the water to the shower just above tepid, I stripped off the remainder of my clothing and stepped inside. The cool water moved over my tense muscles but did nothing to calm my raging hard-on.

Maybe it was because of my self-induced celibacy, or the way Annie looked, dolled up in her gorgeous party dress. Maybe it was because I had finally—*finally*—given in to the urge I had to kiss her and claim her as my own. Whatever it was, my cock surged with every thought of her.

I closed my eyes and clamped my hand around my aching cock. I thought of her like I had done a thousand times before. I imagined her smooth curves in front of me as my hands moved over her rounded hips.

I could still taste her kiss in my mouth and imagined my tongue gliding over the freckles on her shoulder. I would drag my teeth over the delicate skin of her collarbone and feel her shiver beneath me.

A soft moan would escape her lips, and her heartbeat would quicken under the thin skin beneath my mouth. Her arms would wrap around my neck, her legs around my waist, her nails biting into the skin on my back, spurring me forward as I worshipped her body.

I imagined she wasn't Little Orphan Annie, my best friend, or the foster sister of the woman I was supposed to never get over.

Instead, she was simply Annette.

Mine.

I would have her naked, panting and greedy, as I moved my hips between her legs and dragged the head of my cock against her glistening pussy.

Please . . . she would whisper against my ear.

I groaned as I stroked my cock. When I started talking dirty, telling her every sordid detail of the things I would do to her, her full pink lips would part in a sexy little *oh*. Her blue eyes would go wide and dazed with anticipation.

My fantasy flashed forward with my head buried between the soft pillow of her thighs, working her clit until her hips were grinding into my face. I'd grunt and demand more as I reached up to play with her nipple. She wouldn't be afraid of all the dirty, delicious things I wanted to do with her, because she knew me. Trusted me.

Annie knew I would do anything to take care of her, as if it were my dying oath.

In fact, she would ask me for it.

Beg.

I threw my head back and groaned in the shower. As the fantasy became too much, I tightened my fist and pumped harder and faster. Her name escaped as a desperate moan. I came in hard, hot pulses against the shower tile, one hand bracing myself to keep my knees from buckling.

When my heartbeat quieted, I turned the water even colder and let the icy shower roll across my face and neck. I couldn't help but wonder if she had made it home okay. I wondered if she really was pissed at me for what I had done. Was she still mad? Excited? I wondered if I'd made the wrong decision to bid on her dates.

But bidding on her was the only thing that felt *so right*. There was something between Annette and me, whether she wanted to admit it or not.

And I had six dates to prove it to her.

TWELVE
ANNIE

HIS BODY, his mouth, his hands.

Oh god, those hands.

Nope.

I turned the radio louder, but not even Van Halen could drown out the thought of Lee kissing me last night.

When an old woman in the shop fussing with my arrangement of ceramic dishes frowned at me and the volume level of the music, I turned it down and gave her a sheepish smile. "Sorry."

I returned my attention to the piece of pottery on my wheel, but nothing about it was right. The walls were an uneven thickness, wonky and sagging. The concept itself was just . . . *off*. I scraped the clay from the wheel and inelegantly plopped it in a lumpy ball in the center to try again.

And again.

And again.

The bell to the door of Sand Dune Studio chimed, and I lifted my head to offer whoever it was a welcoming smile. Emma wore a shit-eating grin as she blew through the door, and she twirled like a ballerina in the middle of the shop as soon as she entered.

She planted her elbows on the counter and rested her chin in her hands. "Tell me everything."

"It's Sunday. What are you doing here?" I began to wipe the clay from my hands, giving up on the piece entirely.

"Tell. Me. Everything."

I laughed and moved to the sink at the back of the shop. "What do you mean? There's nothing to tell."

"Bullshit!" she yelled.

"Emma," I chided.

She turned to the elderly woman. "Sorry." She then offered a smile to the patrons milling about the shop. "Excuse me."

"I'm so sorry," I offered to the mother with two small children. "She has a condition."

The woman with kind, tired eyes looked at Emma with sympathy. "I understand. I have a nephew who suffers from similar outbursts."

"Oh, no, she's just an idiot."

Emma laughed as I pulled her to the side of the shop and whispered, "Cut it out."

She raised her hands. "You're right. I'm sorry. But this is *Lee*."

"Exactly. It's not a big deal."

"I'm totally going to sponsor you. Pitch in some flowers or something." Her smile widened. "John Mercer bid on me, but I already know you two will be chosen as Top Couple."

I rolled my eyes to the ceiling and prayed for patience. To bring in even more funds for the chosen charity, townspeople could donate things like flowers, small gifts, and other extras to enhance the couples' date-night experiences and help their favorite become Top Couple.

It was ludicrous, and my face told her as much.

Emma furrowed her brows. "Annie, come on. It's for *charity*."

I moved around the shop in a flurry, trying to ignore my growing sense of panic. "What is this, *The Hunger Games*?"

"Please," Emma scoffed. "Six dates with Lee Sullivan?" Emma stood and raised three fingers in the air. "I volunteer as tribute!"

"Shh!" I looked around to see everyone staring at us. Ms. Tiny shook her head, and I offered a polite smile even though she always walked around my shop and never bought a single thing. "Stop that!" Laughing, I pulled Emma's arm down. "It's just weird because he's my best friend."

"And you've never thought of him in that way?"

Oh god . . . how many nights would I lie awake wishing Lee had looked at me the way he looked at Margo. At the many faceless women he left the Grudge with . . .

"Not really."

Emma dipped her chin and shot me her best *yeah freaking right* look.

I sighed. "Fine. A long, *long* time ago." I turned my back to her to clean my mess in hopes of changing the subject.

"Well, do you want to grab a bite to eat? We can talk all about it then."

I paused. "I can't. I'm meeting Charles for a late lunch."

"Charles? Why?"

I shrugged. "I bolted after the auction, before we could talk. I wanted to clear the air and let him know that these dates with Lee were just his idiotic way of protecting me from Royal King."

Emma pressed her lips together and stood. "That's not what it looked like from where I was standing."

"Well." I looked around, unsure of what else to say. "It was."

"Okay. If you say so . . ."

"What?"

She lifted her hands. "Nothing. I gotta run. I'll see you at work tomorrow."

After closing the shop by three p.m., most of the Outtatowner residents were back in their homes, prepping for dinner or a quiet Sunday night in, and tourists were making their own dinner plans.

By then the visitors were dragging their overly tired children off the beach, and purchasing custom pottery was low on their priority list. Slightly defeated after another day of meager sales, I locked up and climbed the stairs to my apartment so I could change to get ready for my date with Charles.

Not a date.

Somehow, after the events of last night, calling it a date felt misplaced.

Wrong even.

I checked my phone again, still no texts from Lee all day, which was fine by me. I was still mad at him, but a tiny part of me was irked he hadn't called. Lee had not reached out to explain himself—to explain that kiss and what the *hell* he had been thinking.

I did, however, have five missed texts from Katie and Lark, collectively. Mentally tired, I left them on *Read* and promised myself I would text them back once I had a better handle on the situation myself.

Stripping off my clay-splattered canvas pants, I slipped into a pair of straight-legged jeans, cuffed at the bottom. My silky white cami had delicate lace trim and a trail of flowers. The coordinating long mauve sweater would ward off any chill inside, but was still lightweight enough that I wouldn't die of heatstroke on the walk over to the Grudge.

Satisfied that I looked feminine and put together, I locked my apartment door and headed out.

As I looked down the road before crossing the street, I spotted Duke storming up the sidewalk. I paused to take him in—his suit jacket and pants were comically short. I waited for him to storm toward me, and a little laugh escaped me.

Relief washed over me. If the Kings and Sullivans were back to ridiculous pranks, maybe it was all fine. Back to normal. Maybe I'd had some sort of fever dream where my best friend pressed me against a wall in a darkened alley and kissed the *fuck* out of me.

Duke was irate and spread his arms wide when he heard my laughter. "Does this look like a fucking joke to you?"

My eyes went wide. "Duke, I . . ." Another small laugh escaped. "I have no words."

He pinched the bridge of his nose. "This is the only suit I own, and before taking it to the cleaners, it fit."

I looked over his large frame, having sympathy for that kindhearted beast of a man. "We can fix this."

I looked him up and down once again, considering how I was going to hide the fact that his suit was about three sizes too small for him.

It had to be a prank. It was the only explanation for how

a suit for a man who was well over six feet tall was somehow tailored to fit a scrawny high schooler.

I tapped my lip, then pointed at him. “Lose the jacket.”

He paused, the furrow between his brows deepening before he grumbled and struggled to get it off his large arms.

I held up one finger—“Hold, please”—and dropped to my knee to put a cuff in the already-too-short pants in the same way I had seen Charles do to his slacks.

I stood and beamed at him. “There.” I put my arms out in a *ta-da!* gesture, hoping he would buy it. “You look . . .”

“I look like a tool.”

I swallowed back another laugh threatening to bubble out of me. “You look like a hipster.”

Duke frowned his signature scowl before giving me a terse nod. “Thank you.” He glanced at me as though he was just noticing my appearance. “You look nice,” he commented, dragging a hand through his hair.

“Thanks.”

“Meeting up with Lee?”

My mouth dropped open. “Uh, no. Just grabbing a late lunch.” I hurried to change the subject. “Where are you going in a suit?”

“I need to get to city hall before five o’clock. They’re technically not even open today, but Joss Keller was in his office and doing me a favor. I needed to make a good impression.”

I frowned, recognizing the name. “Joss Keller, isn’t he an attorney? Is everything okay?”

“That’s what I need to find out. Ever since Katie unearthed that speakeasy, someone’s been asking too many questions. I got wind that there was an inquiry about the mineral rights on Sullivan properties. It has the Kings’ stink all over it.”

I slowly shook my head. "Surely that wouldn't be a prank. I can't imagine even the Kings would go that far."

He harrumphed. "I guess you don't know the Kings as well as you think you do."

"I guess not." I looked over the oldest Sullivan. His eyes were tired, and the grumpy line that creased between his eyes looked deeper lately. "I can help, if you need it." I tipped my chin toward my shop. "It's been really slow. I have time to look through some paperwork if you need me to."

Duke looked at me and softened. "Thanks, Annie. I'll think about it." He sighed, resigned. "I have to run. After city hall, I need to head up to Haven Pines and check in on Dad, but I look like a fucking idiot."

I smiled. "Give Red a hug for me. Oh, hey, when you make it over to Haven Pines, if MJ's working, can you please tell her that the Bluebirds are meeting Tuesday instead of Wednesday?"

He grumbled. Apparently, interacting with any of the Kings was low on his priority list—even if MJ was Red's primary nurse and the sweetest one of the bunch.

"Yeah, will do." Duke nodded and stomped away in the direction of city hall, his pants creeping higher on his legs with every step.

When I walked through the door to the Grudge Holder, soft music was playing on the jukebox. Sunday nights meant casual dinners for townies or a quick to-go order for parents who were dragging their children, tired and cranky, off the beach. I waved to the bartender, Cricket, and scanned the crowd for Charles.

My eyes landed on his pressed oxford shirt.

He was sitting on the east side, dangerously close to

King territory. I eyed several open high-tops on the Sullivan side of the bar.

Safety.

He caught my eye and lifted a hand with a friendly grin. Though uneasy, I painted on a bright smile and walked toward him.

"I thought this spot had great table service. Is it all right?"

I looked again at the proximity to the Kings. "Sure." I slid onto the high stool and my knee began to bounce. "Thanks for meeting with me."

"Of course. It's always nice to spend time with a beautiful woman."

I still was not used to the way Charles freely doled out compliments.

Pretty.

Cute.

Girl next door.

Quirky.

Those were all the typical ways I was used to being complimented. *Beautiful* was rarely among them.

I exhaled nervously. "What did you think of the Matchmakers' Gala?"

He smiled. "I think it's a unique way of raising charitable funds." Charles let out a small laugh. "Outtatowner sure is something else."

My eyes went wide and I laughed. If he could see the humor in the situation, maybe I could too. "I know, right? Especially the date auction. So silly." I let out a laugh in hopes of sounding relaxed, but the way it bubbled out of me made me sound on the wrong side of unhinged.

"I guess I didn't realize the auction would be so . . ." He cleared his throat. "Competitive."

I smoothed my hands down the denim on my thighs, remembering how Charles had tried to bid for me before Lee and Royal screwed it all up. "Oh yeah. I'm sorry about that. I think Lee was just feeling protective because of Royal trying to get under his skin. It was nothing."

Charles offered a soft smile. "Look, I believe you, but I also don't want to get in the middle of something."

"There's nothing!" My words were hurried, insistent, and completely hollow.

"Still," he continued, looking at me with soft eyes. "I think we should focus on enjoying the dates. For charity."

I blinked at him, not really understanding what he was getting at.

"Oh, I suppose you left before it ended." Charles gently sipped his water. "I put out another bid, and I'll be escorting Mia Bradley."

Oh.

I wanted to feel . . . *something*, but surprisingly, there was nothing. Mia was a townie and had always been kind and friendly. Before I could respond, my phone vibrated with a text.

My stomach tightened.

LEE

You get lost or something?

My head whipped up to scan the crowd, and I saw my best friend across the bar, leaned against the wall with his thick arms crossed and a mile-wide grin. It looked as though he was having a few beers and some food with several of his fellow firefighters.

My heart flopped over in my chest at his grin.

Why was it so hard to stay mad at him?

I looked at Charles, who was attempting to signal our server. "I'm sorry. I have to take this."

Charles smiled as he stood. "It's no problem. I'm going to walk over and see if we can't get our server. Sit tight."

As he walked away, I immediately started typing a reply to Lee.

I'm surprised you didn't run over here as soon as you saw me sit down and throw a temper tantrum.

LEE

A tantrum? You've got me all wrong. I have the patience of a saint.

A true, genuine laugh burst from me, and I willed the butterflies in my stomach to settle.

Are we really doing this over text? I can literally see you.

Lee shook his head and smiled down at his phone. Three bubbles popped up, then a text.

LEE

Just break up with him already.

You're mine for six dates and I don't share.

Tingles spread low in my belly. Lee didn't realize that his words, no matter how playful, affected me.

Charles and I aren't dating. He's got his own dates with Mia Bradley.

LEE

Just a heads-up . . . I picked up a few extra shifts at the station this week so that I can have the time off for our dates. I made some trades at work, so I won't be ignoring you, just not really around.

My heart beat wildly.

LEE

Date number one is Saturday.

I hope you're ready.

There was no way I could ever be ready for a date with Lee Sullivan.

THIRTEEN
LEE

ANNIE WASN'T TOO FAR off base assuming I'd throw a tantrum. When I saw her walk into the Grudge, looking sexy as hell and smiling at Charles, I wanted to ram my fist into his chiseled jawline.

I'd always felt protective of Annie, but never quite so *possessive*.

Relief washed over me when our texts contained the familiar banter we'd always shared. I may have caught Annie off guard with that kiss, but I wasn't completely in the doghouse. A few shift trades at work and I'd have plenty of time to figure out why the hell I'd snapped and why Annie was consuming so many of my thoughts.

In the break room, I walked up to Whip and tossed him a can of Coke. He looked down at it and set it aside.

"Relax. I didn't fuck with it." *I only shook it up a little.*

"What do you want, Lee?"

I cracked open my own can and took a sip. "I noticed you pussied out on going to the gala."

He made a face but ignored my dig.

"Well, I'm in. Can I count on you to trade some days?"

Never one to turn down a shift or the possibility of overtime, Whip considered for a moment. Probably because trading days would be a favor to me.

He looked me up and down again. "Fine. But leave me out of your pranking bullshit. I just got my truck and don't need you fucking with the paint job."

A slow grin spread. After the auction *someone* had spread peanut butter under all the door handles of Royal's truck.

Stupid and childish? Yes.

Effective at being completely asinine and endlessly infuriating? Also yes.

I crossed my arms. "Well, maybe tell your shit-stirring brother to back off."

Whip scoffed and opened the can of soda. It fizzed and bubbled at the top so quickly he had to suck down the bubbles. He shot me a knowing glare.

After the carbonation subsided, he shook his head. "Why don't you just piss on her and claim your territory already?"

I rolled my eyes and popped off the counter I was leaning against. "Shut the fuck up, *Bill*."

"Annie Crane is a beautiful woman. It's a shame she sided with the wrong family. Had I been at the gala, I may have made a bid on her myself."

"Tell me. Are you trying to be a dick or does it just come natural for a King?"

"That's enough." Chief Martin's booming voice caught me off guard, and I stood at attention. "I told you boys to leave that shit at the door. There's no place for it at the station."

In unison, Whip and I sounded like a couple of kids being scolded by their father. "Sorry, Chief."

"Sullivan." He turned to me.

"Yes, sir?"

"Someone put five empty jars of peanut butter in the trash cans outside without a bag, and raccoons got into it. Clean it up."

I tamped down the childlike giggle that threatened to rise. "Yes, sir." With a smile, I headed straight for the back door, popping Whip on the back of the head as I passed.

"Aren't tulips more like a *May* thing?" Beside me, Annie stood at the edge of the farmland leading to the Outtatowner Tulip Festival, which served as Matchmakers' Gala date number one. Nerves radiated off my best friend as we watched tourists and townies filter into the crowded Dutch-themed festival.

A few miles from town square, a local farm had been transformed into a colorful Dutch wonderland, with wooden windmills and vibrant tulips of every shade. Even the canoes on the river looked like a makeshift canal running along the edge of the property. It was like stepping into a postcard.

I fiddled with the small key chain in my pocket. It was a little pink pigeon with wonky eyes and a stupid fucking grin. I'd found it online, and it came in a set of eight other weirdly cute animals. He was hideous and he was perfect.

Sometime today I'd planned to slip it into Annie's bag without her knowing.

Beside me, Annie sighed, taking in the enchanting scene laid out in front of us. "Leave it to Outtatowner to make the impossible possible."

My thoughts immediately went to my best friend, and

the opportunity to change everything was standing right next to me.

Damn right we make the impossible possible.

"*Hoi!*" Aunt Tootie waved enthusiastically as she hurried toward us. She was dressed in a deep purple skirt, striped apron and jacket, a shawl, and a high, pointed bonnet.

"Tootie, you look amazing!" Annie wrapped my aunt in a hug.

Tootie held her at arm's length. "As do you, my dear. *Hoi* means hi in Dutch! Are you two lovebirds ready for this?"

Annie was about to correct my aunt when I slung my arm over her shoulders and pulled her into me. "Yep. All set."

"Wonderful!" Tootie was downright giddy. "Here are your stickers." She dug into the small basket on her arm, scribbled our names on two sticky name tags, and placed them on our shirts. "Have fun, you two!"

With a wink and a wave, tornado Tootie was gone, and Annie was staring at her back.

Annie took a tiny step in retreat. "I don't know about this, Lee."

With my arm still banded around her, I gave her a squeeze. "We're going to win you that money, raise a fuck ton for an important charity, and have a damn good time."

Also, you know, make you fall desperately in love with me. No big deal.

"But," I continued. "If they're going to buy it, we have to sell it."

"What are you talking about?" Annie wiped her hands along the sides of her pretty blue sundress and looked at me.

I shook my head. "There's no way in hell I'm going through the remix."

Her eyes went wide. "Shit."

Yep. As I'd suspected, she'd forgotten about that. If at any time dates were unhappy with their matches, the matchmakers would take it upon themselves to rematch people.

From across the field, Annie glanced at Stumpy Larson, who was attempting to close the distance between him and Sylvie King. Apparently that man had a death wish, because he was completely oblivious to the King brothers and their hawk eyes watching over their sister.

"Let's just get through this and have a little fun." I looked down and winked at Annie as she visibly gulped.

Together we wound through the growing crowd to the area where the gala dates were meeting. As we approached, Royal King and his date came into view, and I nearly choked.

Annie also stopped short. "Lee, why is Royal King dressed in lederhosen made for a child?"

A laugh tumbled out of me, and I resisted the urge to grab her hand and squeeze. Sure as shit, Royal was wearing lederhosen that were in a tug-of-war, challenging the limits of their snug dimensions. The trouser legs, barely extending beyond his balls, exposed his tree trunk thighs, covered in tattoos. Below were a pair of knee-high socks adorned with whimsical patterns.

He even wore the fucking hat.

I cleared my throat and leaned down to whisper in her ear. "He *may* have gotten a package, signed from the Bluebirds, saying couples received preference points for wearing the provided costume."

Her eyes went wide as she shook her head, sending

wafts of her shampoo swirling around me. To me, Annie always smelled like apples, sea salt, and sunshine. "Where do you even come up with this?"

I pressed a hand to my chest. "I swear, it wasn't even my idea!" Duke required payback for the stunt they'd pulled off with his suit, and my sister had bought the lederhosen on Amazon.

Annie gestured toward Royal with his booming laughter and smug smile. "I hate to break it to you, but I think he's enjoying this."

Sure enough, Royal's snug attire had drawn the attention of a gaggle of women, and he was reveling in it.

Damn it.

Undeterred, I could always find another way to get the Kings. Looking at the gathering of tourists and people from my hometown, I breathed in the fresh air mixed with the scent of soft-baked pretzels. Crowds gave me energy. Allowed me to be *on* and appear happy.

To hide.

But most importantly, it was the perfect excuse to *finally* touch her.

At my side, my hand found hers and gripped tightly. I tipped my face toward hers. My eyes flicked down to her lips, and the undeniable ache for her rattled through my bones.

My voice dropped, barely above a whisper, to give her fair warning. "Ready or not, Annette."

FOURTEEN
ANNIE

I WAS, in fact, very much *not* ready.

The Outtatowner Tulip Festival was a casual affair, an opportunity for matches to ease into their series of dates with each other. There was, however, a very large, and very ridiculous, dry-erase board. On it, each couple's names were printed, like some kind of scoreboard.

In big, blocky letters, *Lee and Annie* stared back at me from the top of the list. Little hearts beside the couples' names indicated additional donations or special gifts that were purchased by town sponsors.

Through the crowd, I saw Emma talking with Aunt Tootie beneath the ridiculous scoreboard, as Tootie drew a bright-red heart next to our names. Emma caught my eye and shot me a smile and thumbs-up. I rolled my eyes but smiled and waved back at my friend.

I scanned the crowd, my eyes picking out each of the other auction couples in various states of comfort, giddiness, and unease. Royal was still reveling in his comedic glory, doing lunges in his tight lederhosen while several of the old biddies in town swooned and clapped for him.

Sylvie and Stumpy walked with at least three feet between them. Sylvie took a step away for every step Stumpy moved toward her. They also had JP King as a very obvious shadow.

Huck had his fiancée, Cass, hiked up on his back, piggy-back style, as she laughed and proudly held a salted pretzel above her head like an Olympic torch.

She leaned forward and pressed a kiss against her man's lips as he rubbed a large palm up her thigh. Happiness for my friend spread through me. They were so obviously in love, and it was almost painful to witness.

Next to Lee, everything felt off kilter.

Our normally playful and relaxed banter was stilted and uncomfortable. Suddenly a man I had known for years felt like a stranger. Old Annie would have laughed and told him about how I was walking downtown when a pair of my underwear found their way out of the bottom of the pants. Apparently they'd been stuck to the inside of the pants, and I hadn't noticed. I had to quickly use my stealthiest maneuver to snatch them up before anyone noticed a hot-pink thong in the middle of the sidewalk. Lee's face would screw up in disgust at my story. His handsome features would twist up in horror before he would break out into a devastating grin and bend over with laughter.

Instead, we awkwardly stood next to each other and let the silence stretch like a cavern between us. I looked at him and took a deep breath. I still had no idea why he didn't just let Charles win the dates. For years I watched Lee dodge commitment and anything even remotely resembling a real relationship since Margo.

He was the kind of man who could make you believe in fairy tales and happily ever after, only he's never been there in the ever after.

Losing Lee would mean losing my entire family, and I could *never* risk that.

Watching Lee with another random woman after knowing what it felt like to be kissed by him would be hard enough. The thought of losing my relationship with the Sullivans as well felt like drowning.

I tried taking a deep breath and sweeping those thoughts aside. We were already here, and curious eyes were sliding over us, soft smiles playing at my friends' and neighbors' lips.

All I could think about was the fact I knew exactly what his kiss tasted like and how it felt to have his wide palms creep up my rib cage—an image that caused dangerously low flutters in my core.

When Lee's rough fingers brushed against mine as we walked through the crowd, my hand jerked up, and I crossed it to rub the opposite arm, trying to act casual and completely failing. A nervous chuckle was all I could manage.

While my feelings were very, very real—and rapidly spiraling out of control—the years of tamping down giddy giggles or batted lashes made it nearly impossible to contain myself when Lee openly flirted, or complimented me and leaned in close.

It was like the Lee I had come to know had been dialed up to eleven.

When I spotted Lark and Penny up ahead, I sighed in relief at the escape from the awkwardness.

"Hey, there's Lark!" I picked up my pace and left him behind as I walked up toward her and Penny.

"Hey, gals!" I called out with a wave.

Penny beamed up at me. "Ahoy!" she shouted with a wide, toothy grin.

Lark laughed, and her hand lovingly stroked down Penny's hair. "I think it's *Hoi*, Pickle."

Penny shrugged and took a generous bite of a caramel stroopwafel. Around the bite of the chewy waffle and caramel, she grinned. "*Ahoy* sounds way cooler." Her assessing eyes slanted toward Royal, who was still showing off in his lederhosen. "These people are weirdos."

Lee stepped up behind me, and he placed a hand over my shoulder, his fingertips grazing my collarbone. I immediately stiffened under his touch.

He sniffed visibly. *Sniff. Sniff.* "Does someone smell . . ." He looked around and continued to sniff at the air. "A rat?"

A smile broke across my face as Penny's eyes went wide. Her uncle Lee was constantly calling her his little rat. He grunted in her direction like a boar and a squeal peeled out before she took off running. Lee chased behind her as she dodged through the crowd. He quickly caught up, hoisting her into the air and onto his shoulders.

I breathed a sigh of relief that a little space finally broke the tension.

Lark returned her attention to me. "You haven't been answering my calls or texts."

I gave her a pleading smile. "I'm sorry, I know. This is just . . ." I gestured between Lee and me. "Weird."

"Really?" she asked in disbelief. "I feel like the entirety of this town let out a sigh of relief when Lee bid on you. It's like we were all just waiting for it with bated breath, and the unbelievable *finally* happened." Lark was practically swooning.

I laughed nervously and pushed a curl away from my face. "Yeah, I don't know what that was. I think Lee just got all worked up because Royal was showboating." I gestured toward Royal. "Again."

Together we looked at Royal, strutting like a peacock with Millie Reed as they moved toward the area to play a game labeled *Sjoelbak*. It kind of looked like some kind of Dutch shuffleboard.

Royal was one pair of wooden shoes away from being completely ridiculous.

Lark shrugged. It was common knowledge that Lark had some strange soft spot for Royal King, though no one really knew the true reason behind it. Seeking any excuse to get the attention off Lee and me, I decided to just go for it and ask, "Are you ever going to tell me what the deal is between you two?"

Lark looked at me, and a small smile hooked at the corner of her mouth as she looked around. "You really want to know?"

My eyes went wide. "Yes. Oh my god, I've been *dying* to know."

Lark took a step in close and lowered her voice. "Wyatt is the only other person who knows the full truth. I've been sworn to secrecy. Can you keep this quiet? Not even Katie knows the whole story."

I silently crossed an X over my heart. Little did Lark know, I was a pro at keeping secrets.

My true feelings for Lee, the truth behind the letters, years spent convincing myself and others of a reality that didn't exist.

"Royal has . . ." She paused and I felt like I was going to die on the spot if she didn't continue. "He has a secret. It's kind of an embarrassing one. Something I promised I would help him with. I'm still working on it, but I . . . I don't know. I kind of feel *bad* for the big lug."

"Well, what is it?" I asked, dying to get to the juiciest parts of her story.

Lark's nose scrunched. "I really can't tell you that part."

I loved Lark's loyalty, but at that moment I hated her for it. "Are you seriously going to leave me hanging? Lark . . . you're practically a Sullivan, and he's a King. Come *on*."

"I know." She sighed. "And Wyatt understands, which is why he even puts up with Royal's antics. But I'm sorry, Annie, I just . . ." Her eyes pleaded with me to understand the position she was in. "It's not my secret to tell."

Though frustrated, my heart softened for my kind-hearted friend. She was loyal and honest and sincere, even if that meant keeping a King's secret. "Does it have anything to do with the mineral rights or the farm?" I asked, still worried that maybe Lark was too new to Outtatowner to understand the gravity of the situation. Something had *definitely* put Duke Sullivan on edge, and I wouldn't put it past Royal to use Lark's kindness against them.

Lark raised a hand. "Oh no, no, nothing like that." She leaned in close. "Trust me, this is very personal."

My lips pressed together, and I fought my frustration of not knowing. "Okay, fine. I understand."

"Are we spilling secrets over here?" Lee came up with Penny on his shoulders, a fresh stroopwafel in her hand and the glint of mischief in her eye. My ovaries exploded at the sight of how comfortable he was with his niece.

Daddy . . . ?

Stifling a laugh at myself, I shook my head and focused on Lark, who paled at his question.

I subtly shot her a wink. "I offered to help Duke do some digging after those people were snooping around the farmhouse after Kate and Beckett found the speakeasy. I guess someone has also been looking into Sullivan Farms, but Kate's too busy with her renovations." I shrugged, feeling horribly guilty for being evasive with Lee.

It isn't technically *a lie.*

I *had* offered my sleuthing services to Duke, trying to figure out who's been cruising on their land and asking too many questions.

Lee shrugged. "Fuck it, I'm in."

From her perch on his shoulders, a laugh shot out of Penny's tiny little body. She thought swearing was hilarious.

Lark's eyes flew to Penny. "Do not repeat that in front of your father."

Lee pulled Penny from his shoulders and planted her feet on the ground. "Sorry, Lark. Where is Wyatt?"

Lark smiled proudly. "Defensive lineman workshop."

During the summers Wyatt organized camps, checked in on players, and often spent days recruiting and helping new players for Midwest Michigan University get settled in.

"Well, when he gets back, tell him to call me. I miss that grumpy bastard."

A shotgun burst of laughter erupted from Penny again. Lee offered a small grimace. He swung an arm around my shoulder and pulled me in close. "All right, you ladies have a good time. I've gotta go show off my girl."

The tulip festival passed in a blur. The rest of the day, Lee found ways to touch me. His arm subtly found my shoulder. His hand settled on the small of my back. From the outside, I had no doubt I looked like a prisoner, with wide, round eyes and a twitchy, panicked smile. Everything about being out in public, *with Lee Sullivan*, was totally surreal.

A few times I caught Charles looking over at Lee and me and frowning. More than once his attention wandered from his date, Mia. I attempted a small smile, but he didn't return it.

Finally, after a flight of German-style beers from Abel's Brewery and one too many soft pretzels, Lee offered to take me home.

At my apartment building, I fumbled with my keys as my brain struggled to find the correct one. Lee leaned in, bracing his arm on the building behind me. As he crowded my space, his masculine scent blanketed me, and my nipples stiffened beneath my shirt.

I turned to him, giving up on the key. "Lee, I think we should set some . . ." I swallowed hard, willing the words to unclog from my throat. "Boundaries."

His eyes bore into mine, a furrow deepening in his brow. "Boundaries."

"Yes."

"Okay," he said slowly, giving me space to continue, but not contributing.

"It's just that when we kissed, that made things . . ." I struggled for what it really was. *Amazing. Wonderful. Something I'd hoped for for years.* "Things kind of shifted, you know?"

His full lips were pressed into a firm line, his arm still planted above my head, caging me against the brick wall of my building.

"I'd be lying if I didn't admit you were right with what you said about Charles. I think maybe him seeing that I wasn't just waiting around for him got his attention."

I worried my lip. *Did I even really still care about that?*

I cleared my throat and found the courage to continue. "So if we're really going to do this for five more dates, I think we need to set some ground rules. Boundaries."

A smirk hooked the corner of Lee's mouth. "Like kissing."

A hot flush crept up my neck. "Definitely kissing."

"We're going to do that." The confidence in Lee's deep voice caused a pooling ache to throb between my legs.

I could barely breathe, let alone talk. "Then it should only be because it's a part of the act. So neither of us gets confused."

His voice was practically a growl. "I'm not confused, Annette."

My breath escaped as a huff. "You know what I mean."

His chuckle was low and deep. "So what you're saying is I can kiss you, but it just has to be in front of other people?"

The way he said those words made it sound like a dark and delicious fantasy. One that I had no idea would be so fucking hot.

I swallowed hard and hoped he couldn't hear my heart rattling around in my chest. "Yes, exactly."

He leaned in closer. "I can handle that."

Lee's large hand trailed down the bare skin on my arm, sending shivers racing through me. "What about this?"

I sucked in a breath, trying to gather my scrambling thoughts. "Um, touching, you mean?"

I could feel his warm breath on my skin. "Yes, touching. Being close to you. It's what two people who were dating would do."

I wanted to argue, to resist and tell him that public displays of affection weren't really my style, but the heat pooling between my legs, the way I went slick at the very idea of him touching me, made a liar out of me, and the argument died on my tongue.

Closing my eyes, I sought my last shreds of courage. "I also think that maybe we shouldn't spend too much time together outside of the dates."

Lee frowned. "That doesn't make any sense. We've always hung out together during our free time."

I straightened my back. "And you changed things when you decided to very publicly pretend like there was something between us after we spent years denying it to every single person who knows us. You changed the rules. I think a little time apart is the only way to make sure things don't get confused."

"No." Lee spat the word.

"Good." I breathed a sigh of relief. "What, what?" Lee's body was simmering with tension in a way I had never seen him before. He was disagreeing with me, and clearly not happy about my idea.

But if there were boundaries, some rules in place to keep Lee at arm's length, then my heart may have a sliver of a chance of surviving the next five dates.

A car drove past as Lee shifted his hips, and his shadow enveloped me as I pressed my palms against the cool, scratchy brick of my building. He reached up to cup my jaw as he moved his mouth forward.

"Lee, I . . ."

His soft mouth moved over mine as his fingers flexed on my jaw. His tongue swept through my lips, hot and demanding. His frustration was palpable and desperate. My body reacted in kind. My arms wound around his neck and pulled him closer. My leg hitched up, and his free hand gripped my thigh and squeezed. Through my sundress, I could feel the length of him, hard and hot against me, and a needy hum buzzed through my throat.

I moaned against his lips and wondered if anyone would notice if Lee fucked me against my front door in the middle of town. I wouldn't even care if it meant he would finally put me out of my aching misery.

Lee broke the kiss. My desperate breaths came out in pants. My thoughts were a jumbled, needy mess. "I thought we just agreed—"

His thumb stopped my words with a brush against my swollen lower lip. He leaned down close, and the deep rumble of his voice sent molten waves coursing through me.

"Bootsy just walked by. So technically that kiss was in public." Without another word, Lee turned, and I stared at the muscles of his back, rippling beneath his shirt as he walked away from me.

Then he turned. "Hey, Annette?"

I blinked and managed only a strangled sound.

Lee grinned. "This is the best day of my life."

I sank against the brick building. My head swam with questions, but there was one thing I knew for certain.

There was no way my heart was getting out of the next five dates unscathed.

FIFTEEN
LEE

It had been a week since I'd seen Annie, and I was practically crawling out of my skin. Before the gala, I'd never go more than a few days without hearing her laugh or watching her sink her teeth into her lower lip as she concentrated on her pottery wheel. A week was too long.

I sure as fuck didn't like it.

The sun glistened over the tranquil waves of Lake Michigan as I eagerly made my way to the arranged beach date. As I strolled across the sandy dunes, my heart danced with anticipation, mixing nervousness and excitement. Set apart from the public beach, I smiled at the sight of the other couples scattered across the shoreline.

I walked across the beach, my toes digging into the warm, powdery sand as I scanned the crowd, looking for my girl. Up ahead I saw my cousin Matty. He was a distant cousin, but still a Sullivan by blood. I tipped my chin to him and offered a wave. He returned it and walked on over.

We shook hands and I grinned at him.

"Hey, man, how's it going?" he asked.

"It's going. I saw your show the other night. You guys

are getting good." Matty had a band and often played at the Grudge during tourist season.

He gestured toward the area of the beach where the auction dates were getting settled in. "So the rumor is true?" he asked. "You finally woke up and took your shot with Annie?"

I readjusted the backpack on my shoulder. "Something like that."

Jesus, had everyone been thinking it behind our backs?

"Well, when you get ready for the next flavor of the week, you can send her my way." A pit opened in my stomach. I stared down at my little cousin and reminded myself that it wouldn't do anyone any good if I punched him in the face.

"It's not like that," I grumbled. My reputation as a player, though probably earned, was getting really fucking old, and I didn't like the implication of Annie getting caught up in the shitty decisions of my past.

I refused to be the reason she looked bad.

Frustrated and annoyed, I said goodbye to Matty and stormed up the rest of the beach toward the group. I still hadn't spotted Annie, and a moment of panic skittered through me.

Had she backed out? Changed her mind? Stood me up?

I scrubbed a hand against the back of my neck. Jesus, I felt like a teenager again, worrying about whether or not a girl liked me. I was about twelve seconds away from scribbling on a note, *Do you like me? Check YES or NO* and handing it to her like a schmuck.

Finally, I recognized her hot-pink-painted toes peeking out from underneath a huge striped beach umbrella. I could recognize those Flintstone feet anywhere, and an affectionate chuckle rolled through me. Annie hated her slightly large big toe. I didn't really think it looked weird at all, but I still liked to tease her about it.

As I got closer, I realized that apart from her bare feet, every other square inch of her was completely covered. From ankles to wrists to neck, she was covered in some kind of workout outfit.

I peeked around the umbrella. "Expecting a snowstorm? You do realize we're hanging out at the beach today, right?"

My voice caught her attention, and an immediate smile bloomed across her face. The pinch in my heart released, just a bit, at the easy way she smiled up at me.

"Just don't want to get too much sun." She pulled, tugging the sleeve of her shirt a little lower. "You know I fry on days like these."

I glanced up at the clear, cloudless sky. It was hard not to notice the shade of blue was a near match for the exact color of Annie's eyes. A tiny row of sweat droplets gathered at the base of the hair she had piled up on top of her head in a messy riot of curls.

I rolled my eyes and removed the backpack from my shoulder as I plopped down beside her. Digging through my bag, I pulled out the 70 SPF sunscreen I had packed for her and tossed it into her lap. "I got you."

Annie stared down at the bottle of sunscreen as though I had just gifted her a newborn kitten.

As she looked down at it, her voice was barely above a whisper. "Thank you, Lee."

My heart squeezed because Annie wasn't the kind of girl to swoon over grand gestures and flashy gifts—it was early-morning hot cups of coffee or remembering sunscreen that did it for her.

"So come on, get out of that sweatsuit before you pass out from heatstroke. I'm off duty." I shot her a wink and enjoyed the stain of pink that swept across the apples of her cheeks.

Cautiously, Annie lowered the zipper to the jacket and slid it off her shoulders. I swallowed hard and tried to not stare as I reached behind me and yanked off my T-shirt by the collar.

Her eyes moved over the tattoos I had inked on my arms and back. When I caught her staring, she lowered her gaze to the sunscreen and started rubbing the lotion into her arms as I pretended to search for something in my bag.

"Will you get my back?" she asked softly.

My heartbeat ticked higher. "Of course."

Sure, I could have packed a spray suntan lotion, but I'm no fool.

I moved behind her, letting the lake breeze waft her perfume in my direction. I quietly sucked in a lungful as I settled in behind her.

I took my time rubbing the lotion between my palms to warm it up before gliding over the rounded slopes of Annie's shoulders. Under the protection of the sun umbrella, I could hear the soft inhale and exhale of her breath.

Beneath my fingertips, her heartbeat hammered under her skin.

Though I hadn't gotten to see it all yet, her swimsuit was one I had never seen her wear before. It was a one-piece suit, but the way it was constructed almost looked like a high-waisted bikini. The top was white with small navy pinstripes. The fabric wrapped around her tits and tied in a tempting little bow in the back. Her creamy skin pushed the limits of the fabric with every inhale. The bottom of the suit was a dusty blue that disappeared into the waistband of the pants she still wore. A tiny sliver of skin hinted at a cutout just below her chest.

I can't wait to see the rest of it.

From behind her, my hands moved over the tops of her shoulders and across her collarbone. Her eyes widened softly. My palm inched upward to rub more lotion across her neck. The image of Annie beneath me with my hand gently across her throat as I drove into her flashed through my mind.

I quickly cleared my throat and moved to a safer area of her back. I reapplied lotion to my palms and moved my fingertips under the strap of her bathing suit. I had seen my brother do the same for Penny to ensure she didn't burn if the straps shifted.

"What are you doing?"

"I like to be thorough, Annette," I rasped.

She had sucked in a breath as though she was about to say something when Bug King popped her head around the edge of the umbrella. "It's about time for lunch, and then we're getting on the boats."

Annie planted her hands in the sand and popped up, dusting her palms and gathering her jacket and bag in front of her chest. "Okay, thank you, Bug," Annie croaked.

She looked back at me when I didn't move. "Are you coming?" she asked with a cute little furrow between her eyebrows.

I cleared my throat, willing the aching hard-on between my legs to go down. I swallowed. "I think I need a minute."

Her crisp blue eyes flicked down to my lap and then up to my face as the color in her cheeks deepened. Her lush mouth made a pert little O. "Oh, I . . ." A shotgun burst of laughter erupted from her.

She looked around for what to do. "Well, you can stand

behind me. I can . . ." She shrugged. "I don't know . . . block it?"

Goddamn, she was so fucking cute. If Annie was offering to let me stand close enough to her, knowing my rock-hard dick was between us, then I was going to take it. I stood, and she watched as I reached into my swim trunks to adjust myself.

Maybe I should have been embarrassed for how hard she made me from simply applying suntan lotion, but I didn't care. The way her tongue darted out to lick her lower lip told me she didn't mind it all that much either.

She turned around and placed her arms out like a petite bouncer at a nightclub. "All right, Sullivan, I got you covered."

I stood and stepped behind her before curling my fingers around her hip bone. I lowered to whisper in her ear. "Let's do this."

I kept my hand planted on the lush curve of Annie's hips as we walked across the beach. The sand made it tricky, and more than once her round ass bumped against my front, completely negating the fact she was trying to hide my erection.

I ignored her scent, her soft skin, the curve of her waist, and instead focused on the sun blaring in my eyes, the warmth of the sand beneath my toes, the old guy down the beach sporting a very tiny neon-green Speedo.

Anything beside how good it felt to be in Annie's space.

We met up with the rest of the group by a folding table near the edge of the water. Picnic baskets were lined up with labels indicating each couple.

As the group gathered, Bug waited for a hush to come over the crowd before she spoke. "You'll have one hour to enjoy your picnic lunch before the charter boats take us in groups of six for your adventurous fishing date."

A few light whoops and hollers sprinkled through the crowd. I pulled Annie closer to me. I knew she wasn't particularly sporty, but I had been fishing a thousand times with Dad.

"To add a little more fun and competition to the date, the couple with the biggest fish and the couple with the most fish will each win an extra prize!" Bug held up two large white envelopes.

I leaned in close to Annie. "It's in the bag."

She may not be very athletic, but Annie had a competitive streak a mile wide. She turned her head with a smirk and a glint in her eye. "Let's do it."

I glanced at the large whiteboard with each couple's name scrawled across it. Annie and I had a red heart next to ours. I knew Annie desperately needed that bonus prize money to make her dreams come true. When I saw Royal and Millie had three hearts next to their names, my competitive nature kicked into overdrive. No fucking way was he walking away with Annie's prize after his brother all but evicted her from her shop and her home.

Fucking Kings.

If Annie wanted to create the art experience of her dreams, she needed money. Besides, my plan was working. I hadn't had a single biddy from town corner me and try to set me up with their granddaughter. In fact, mostly they just hugged me and told me how happy they were for Annie and me or to warn me not to break Annie's heart.

Only a few still managed to bring up Margo.

All I had to do now was get Annie on board. This plan was fucking perfect.

I grabbed our picnic basket and was relieved when

underneath the striped umbrella, it was almost as if nothing had changed between Annie and me. She watched the waves while we ate the freshly made deli sandwiches. I used my backpack as a makeshift table to try to keep sand out of the potato chips. The beach was bustling with energy, and while she watched children splash in the sand and a group of teens play sand volleyball, I was watching her.

When a kid decided to showboat and took a header in the sand, she laughed, and as always, calm and reassurance settled over me. Part of me wondered why I hadn't seen it before—seen her in this new light, where she was no longer just my best friend but my entire universe.

Then it hit me that I had *always* seen her that way. Only now it felt like her seeing me in that same light was becoming more and more of a possibility. Every one-night stand, every girl whose number I took and never called back, every time I made a show of my dates to prove to everyone I was over Margo, was like an arrow to my heart.

I wasn't that person anymore.

I didn't want to be.

If I was being honest with myself, I wished I could say that he wasn't the real me, but the pathetic reality was that it had been. The future I had envisioned with Margo fell apart when I got home and she was like a totally different person. Then she was gone. Friends, neighbors, hell, even my own family took to constantly reminding me of what I lost.

I couldn't imagine a life without the woman I had come to love in those letters. Instead of dealing with the pain, I drowned it out with recklessness and the facade of a *don't-give-a-shit* attitude.

I may have enacted a self-imposed celibacy for the past

several months, but it didn't change who I was and what I had become. Even now I knew Annie deserved someone better, but there was an invisible tether between us, one that I would never be willing to cut.

A life without Annie felt like a life without oxygen. I had taken my first breath after being trapped underwater, and now I couldn't stand the thought of going under again.

If I wanted things to truly change between us, then I would have to change. It had already started.

By the time Bug rang the bell to alert everyone it was time to head to the boats, the sun had climbed even higher in the sky, and the sweltering heat pressed down on us. We were instructed to clump together into groups of six for the boat.

Emma had muscled her way next to Annie, threading her arm through Annie's and locking their elbows together. "We'll go together!" Emma shouted.

John Mercer tipped his chin to me, and I returned the greeting.

Sylvie King and Stumpy Larson got shoved in with us despite Royal trying to muscle his way into a grouping with his sister.

Everyone knew Stumpy was a creep, and I'm sure Royal was trying to keep an eye on his little sister. I couldn't fault him for it, because I would have done the exact same thing.

Royal pinned Stumpy with a menacing glare as he jabbed one long tattooed finger in the air. "You keep a *respectable* distance."

Stumpy visibly swallowed and managed only a nod. Royal's eyes slid to mine as if to communicate, *Keep an eye on her*.

I pressed my lips together in a silent agreement. The Sullivan–King feud may run back generations, but there were some lines we would never cross. Allowing Stumpy Larson to try anything with Sylvie was one of them.

The groups walked down the beach toward the marina. My back stiffened when we passed a fishing boat with *Noble King Fishing Tours* painted on the back.

I recognized the sleek lines of the fishing boat my father once owned. Back when he was himself and operations on the farm had run so smoothly he was branching out into other tourism opportunities. The boat, and Dad's dream of hosting guided fishing tours, had flown out the window when he'd gotten his diagnosis, and things went to hell so fast. It pissed me right the fuck off to see the King name on *Dad's boat.* I immediately regretted my kindness toward Royal.

Fuck that guy and his family. Especially his father, Russell King. He had never been an honorable businessman like his father, Amos. Russell was a scavenger. Even after all our families had been through, he was greedy enough to capitalize on our misfortune with Dad's illness, and I hated him for it.

Annie's hand pressed between my shoulder blades. She looked up at me with her big, round eyes and a soft, understanding smile. She knew how quickly everything had fallen apart for my family when Dad got sick. She knew how hard it was to see Dad's dreams fade away along with so many of his memories.

I want that fucking boat back.

Refocusing on our date, I stepped one foot onto the charter boat, holding on to it while offering a steady hand to Annie. Carefully, she slipped her hand into mine and got her balance before climbing onto the boat deck. I took the opportunity to lace our fingers together and hold on. When she looked up at me, I gave her a wink.

Captain Jimmy instructed us to sit at the perimeter of the boat while he and his first mate and daughter, Stevie, got us out onto the water. Music pumped out of a small speaker, and the wind whipped at us as we made our way onto the open water of Lake Michigan. While Captain Jimmy navigated, Stevie was busy checking poles and the bait we would use.

As the boat cruised over the waves, the passengers bumped and bounced. We gripped the sides of the boat to remain steady, and Sylvie's knuckles went white against the seat she was clinging to. On a larger wave, Annie yelped, then laughed at herself. Taking the opportunity, I pulled her onto my lap, wrapping my arms around her and keeping her secure. She looked back, then repositioned her hips.

"Don't be a tease, Annette," I whispered against her skin. "It will get you in trouble."

Her head turned to me, her breath fanning over my face as she said, "Maybe I need a little trouble in my life."

My fingers dug into the flesh of her thighs, my fingertips going white. I wanted to claim her, mark her. Leave behind pale purple signs of what she did to me and how she drove me wild.

With every bump of the waves my cock grew painfully harder. The thin fabric of her swimsuit and my trunks were the only barrier between us.

I imagined how easy it would be to slip between her lips and watch her eyes go wide as she took in my size. I planted a gentle kiss at the slope of her neck and used the opportunity to shift her closer, more fully seated on my lap. My heart thunked against her back as I held her close.

About fourteen miles offshore, Captain Jimmy slowed to an area he claimed was his "secret spot." The afternoon sun was beating down, but the lake breeze made it almost bearable. Annie stood, taking up space at the back of the boat as she, Emma, and Sylvie whispered and shot glances my way. I stretched my arms across the back of the seat and let the June sun warm my skin.

As the captain and first mate arranged our gear, the group made small talk. I laughed at jokes and contributed to the conversation but never let my eyes wander too far from my girl. She'd given up her battle of wills against the heat and had finally stripped down to only her swimsuit. The back cut high up on her ass, and I could see the perfectly round apples of her butt.

Despite the heat, tiny goose bumps formed on her smooth skin under my gaze. Fire danced in her eyes and I had to turn away to prevent giving in to the urge to walk up behind her and squeeze that delicious ass. Over her shoulder, Annie shot me a smirk and my chest squeezed.

Oh, that girl knows what she's doing.

Though she was still holding back, I could see her walls beginning to crumble. I held on to the hope that, however slowly, those walls were coming down.

Captain Jimmy and Stevie worked efficiently as they set each couple up with rods and bait. After a brief safety lesson and a demonstration on how to properly cast, we were left to try it out as they made their rounds to assist each couple.

The late-afternoon sun painted streaks of gold across the rippling waters of Lake Michigan. The waves were rougher than I'd anticipated, so to keep her safe, I locked Annie between my arms, abandoning my pole so she could keep her balance and concentrate on her cast. Each wave beat against the hull of the boat, rocking us together. I soaked in the hum of the engine and the call of the seagulls above us as I watched her purposeful movements cast the line into the water. It was a little awkward, with her having to maneuver around my body, but I held her centered.

Annie's line disappeared into the shimmering waters of Lake Michigan as she slowly reeled the line back in. She smelled like sunshine and coconuts as her warmth enveloped me in a comforting embrace. Annie's anticipation of a bite was palpable as she stared intently down into the water.

When her fishing rod jerked in her hands, she turned to me with wide, exhilarated eyes. "Fish on!" she yelled, as our captain had instructed us to do.

Captain Jimmy stepped up to guide her as she focused on the tug of the fish at the other end of the line. I reached into my shorts to pull out my phone and capture the moment. As she reeled it in, her laughter filled the air, blending with the sounds of splashing water and the joyous cries of seagulls.

Annie glanced over her shoulder and caught my eyes sparkling with pride, mirroring her own excitement. We shared the triumph and exhilaration of her catch, our unspoken connection deepening with every flicker of joy in her eyes. In that perfect instant, I snapped a picture, her wild red hair dancing in the wind and a wide, toothy grin smiling back at me.

"You're perfect," I said as I snapped several more pictures of Annie with her catch.

As the afternoon of fishing went on, I forgot all about the gala and auction. I allowed myself to enjoy a beautiful day with a gorgeous woman. The sun sagged in the evening sky behind a plume of thick clouds as Captain Jimmy informed us we were heading in to beat the evening storms.

On the ride back, a stiff breeze picked up, and I was glad Annie had her pants and jacket to keep her warm. The boat rocked and pitched, and we bounced off the waves. Stevie held on to the boat as Captain Jimmy attempted to get us off the water. The sky was darkening, and the earlier camaraderie faded into worried glances. John Mercer pressed a hand to his belly, the rocking of the boat seeming to upset his stomach. He groaned moments before leaning over the side of the boat and losing his lunch.

In a horrible wave of slow motion, I watched as everyone around me groaned. Annie paled before me as her eyes went wide.

I gripped her hand. "Are you okay?"

She only nodded and leaned into me. I wrapped my arm around her shoulders to try to protect her from bouncing around the boat. It was useless as we were all tossed around the angry waves. Under my arm, Annie's breath came out in pants. She pushed me away and slid across the bench.

"Oh my god, Lee." She held up one hand. "Don't look at me!"

Before the words were even out, she was throwing up off the side of the boat. Unfazed, I placed my hand at the center of her back and patted gently.

Captain Jimmy, Stevie, and I were the only ones who didn't succumb to seasickness. As we finally pulled into his spot in the marina, all the initial playfulness of our group had died and only soft groans could be heard over the slapping of water against the hull.

Annie groaned and gripped the side of the boat with quivering hands. My fingertips rubbed a small circle between her shoulder blades.

Without waiting for her to argue, I scooped her up. "Come on, champ. Let's get you home."

SIXTEEN
ANNIE

For the entire ride from the marina to Lee's apartment, I had to focus on breathing through my nose. Every bump on the road sent a fresh wave of nausea coursing through me. I tried to focus on something, *anything*—how hot Lee looked on the water, the way Emma looked at us with little hearts in her eyes, how *enormous* Lee's erection was and the fact I'd offered to help him hide it. Literally anything to keep myself from barfing in his truck.

Come on, champ. Let's take you home.

His home.

My head throbbed, and when he threw the truck in park, I fumbled for the handle.

"Don't even think about it," he warned. I watched as Lee rounded the hood of his truck and ripped open the passenger-side door. Once again Lee scooped me up in his arms. Too drained to resist, I closed my eyes and leaned into him. My stomach was at war with my heart.

In his apartment I was hit with the smell of fresh laundry along with the masculine smell of *him*. Scrambling to get my legs beneath me, I wiggled out of his arms.

Hurrying down the hallway, I burst into his bathroom and threw myself on the floor. The hard tile bit at my knees as I flipped the seat up and emptied my already hollow stomach.

Sweaty, embarrassed, and tired, I flushed and rested my head against the cool wall. I sensed him before I had the will to even open my eyes. I wished the floor could open up and swallow me whole.

"Sounded like an exorcism in here. Jesus." Lee's chuckle dragged out my own weak laugh.

I turned my head to find him leaned against the doorjamb, his muscled arms crossed. His biceps tested the strength of the cotton, as they always did.

My head still throbbing, I lowered it into my hands. "Can you please let me die in peace?"

His soft footsteps got closer, and he crouched next to me. Across my body, Lee reached for a small strip of toilet paper. He dabbed at my mouth as I stared up at him.

Lee and I shared everything—well, *almost* everything—but allowing him to see me with vomit on my face was too much. Heat flooded my cheeks.

"I feel like we're still moving." A fresh wave of nausea had me gripping the porcelain bowl.

Lee gathered my hair from the nape of my neck and lifted, softly blowing cool air across my clammy skin. "Just gotta get your sea legs, that's all."

A sad little groan was all I could manage.

Lee dropped a kiss on my shoulder and stood. "Be right back. Don't move," he warned.

A weak lift of my hand was all I could muster. I wasn't going anywhere.

When he came back, Lee was carrying a glass of water

and a cool, wet washcloth. A T-shirt was slung over his shoulder.

I reached for the water and took a tentative sip. "Thank you."

"You don't have to thank me for taking care of you."

I swallowed hard, my throat burning despite the cool water. Lee worked quietly as he dabbed the cold washcloth against my forehead and let it drape across the back of my neck.

He pulled the shirt from his shoulder, then gestured toward the jacket I was wearing. "Can you handle that?"

I looked down to see small splatters of vomit on my jacket and the edge of my swimsuit. I quickly unzipped it. With me hunched on his bathroom floor in workout pants and a swimsuit, embarrassment flooded my system. I snatched the shirt from his hands.

"I got it. Thanks."

His lips pressed together and he stood. "I'll be . . ." He gestured toward the door.

I nodded weakly and quickly closed the door behind him.

Oh. My. Freaking. God. I just puked all over myself in front of Lee.

Hot, embarrassed tears sprang beneath my lashes. My emotions were so out of control, I couldn't stand it. Carefully rising to my feet, I stripped off the jacket and pants. For a moment I debated pulling the T-shirt over my swimsuit, but the constricting material made my stomachache worse.

I removed my suit and pulled the large shirt over my head. Immediately I was enveloped by Lee's masculine scent. Fresh, clean laundry and his natural musk poured over me. In the privacy of his bathroom, I gathered the material at the collar and pressed it into my nose. The rolling in my stomach quelled.

Taking a steadying breath, I looked myself over in the mirror. My eyes were bloodshot, my pale face ashen, and my hair wildly out of control.

His soft knock at the door startled me, but I cracked it open. He offered a soft smile and held up a brand-new toothbrush and travel-size toothpaste. Sheepishly, I curled my fingers around them and tucked myself away in the bathroom.

When I gathered the courage, and the stomach, to exit my hiding place, Lee was sitting on the couch. Naked beneath his T-shirt, I nervously tugged at the hem. Lee's eyes flashed to mine before dropping low, pausing at the way my nipples peaked the front of the cotton. Lower still, his eyes moved over my bare legs.

Covering his mouth with a cough, Lee popped up from the couch. "Sit tight."

"Why are you doing this?" My eyes pleaded for him to understand what I was asking.

His sage-gray eyes pinned me in place. The deep rumble of his voice filled the apartment. "Because I want to."

"Why?" I pressed.

Lee only scoffed lightly before moving toward the kitchen. He turned to smirk over his shoulder. "You're my girl."

Blood drained from my face and I felt light-headed all over again.

Words I never dared to dream out loud played on a loop over and over in my head.

You're my girl.

You're my girl.

You're my girl.

It must have been the nausea. Maybe the dehydration. Or the overwhelming knowledge that I was wearing nothing but Lee's T-shirt in the middle of his living room, but it was all *too much.*

My legs wobbled and I sank into the couch, pulling my knees to my chest and covering as much of my body as possible.

Minutes later, Lee came back with a steaming mug. "Tea. For your stomach."

I nodded as he handed it to me and settled into the couch next to me, not allowing an inch between our bodies. Casually, as if he'd done it a thousand times before, Lee wrapped one arm around my shoulders and pulled me close. With his other arm, he found the remote and pulled up a movie.

Lee caught me staring at the side of his face, and he gave my shoulder a squeeze. "Just relax, Annette. I've got you."

I had no words to describe the jumble of emotions running through me, so I managed only a weak nod. In the background, the movie played, and all I could think about was him. Us.

You're my girl.

Awareness dawned on me slowly. Chirping birds. Sunlight filtered through curtains. Limbs tangled with an inferno.

Lee.

As soon as I realized it was Lee's long, heavy limbs wrapped around me, I stiffened. His masculine smell was everywhere. His steady breathing wafted in my hair as the rise and fall of his chest moved in time with my own breathing.

Somehow we'd ended up in Lee's bed with one of his legs slung around me, his other arm draped across my ribs and . . . cupping my tit.

I blinked away the sleep and looked down to see Lee's wide palm over his T-shirt, stretching across my boob.

My nipple immediately stiffened under his palm. My hips inched backward, quietly testing the limits of a cuddle session with Lee—*in his bed.*

His hips shifted forward, a low growl of awareness forming in his throat.

Lee's nose buried deeper into my hair as he pulled me impossibly closer, and I had to stifle a groan as my center clenched hopelessly around nothing. I wasn't a strong enough woman not to arch my back and grind into his morning wood like a cat in heat, so instead I slowly attempted to roll and face him.

His long dark lashes fanned out over his chiseled cheekbones.

Why is it that men get the good eyelashes? Totally unfair.

As I moved, his legs straightened to give me room, but his arm stayed banded around my rib cage. Facing him, I continued to study his sleeping face until a smirk tugged at the corners of his mouth.

"You're awake." I slapped at his shoulder, and he pulled me in closer with a hum. I buried my face into his neck, embarrassment washing over me.

I pressed my eyes shut. "I'm sorry I got seasick and puked all over your bathroom."

Lee rested his chin on top of my head, not letting me go. "I've seen you sick before."

I considered a moment that, yeah, I guess he had. But

something about how our relationship had shifted made me uneasy about him seeing that side of me.

Still embarrassed, I stayed silent.

His arms gave my body a squeeze. "I'll always take care of you."

Blinking up at him, he was looking down at me. He smiled a sleepy morning smile and all I could think was, *Oh shit.*

There was no way I was ever getting out of this unbroken.

A hard mass pressed against my leg. I looked down but couldn't see past where his bare chest pressed against my T-shirt. "Are you *naked*?"

His chuckle rumbled through me. "No, of course not. After you slept through the movie, my arm fell asleep, so I moved us in here. I'm not naked, but it is morning, and you're wearing nothing but *my* T-shirt."

His hand disappeared below the sheet to adjust himself, and molten heat flooded between my legs at the primal, masculine gesture.

With a little distance between us, I took in his bare chest in a way I rarely allowed myself to. One tattoo blended into the next as they swept across his chest and down his arms.

Tentatively I dragged one finger across his pecs. "You've added more."

An appreciative growl rumbled in his throat at my gentle touch. "A few."

Old tattoos, like the sun and moon Lee had gotten when he turned eighteen—and regretted—or his mother's name written in her handwriting, faded into fresher black ink. Many he got around his time in the Army, but others he'd added over the last few years. Across his ribs, my fingers paused. My eyes widened as I read the faded, looping script over and over.

There is no distance between your heart and mine.

My fingers traced over the words that stretched across the bumps of his rib cage.

My words.

Tears burned at the corners of my eyes. "Lee, I . . ." My stomach rolled. I fought against every blaring warning bell inside me. *Don't do it. Keep the secret. He will never forgive you for this.* "There's something you should . . ."

Lee's hand covered mine, pressing my fingers flat. His heartbeat thrummed against my hand. "That tattoo was a mistake." Lee shifted and sat on the edge of the bed with his back to me. "Those words saved my life, and she didn't even remember writing them."

Without another word, Lee stood and stalked toward the bathroom, leaving me to gather the sheets and hold them tightly to my chest.

A hard lump formed in my throat. I had kept Margo's secret, and mine, for so long that it almost felt like the truth.

Only it wasn't.

Lee deserved to know the truth, and I was terrified. He would be angry—hell, I would be *livid* if the roles were reversed, yet . . . my hope was that he would understand why I had done it for her and every other microdecision afterward that had kept the truth hidden for so long.

Sitting at the edge of the bed, I took a deep breath. *It's time.* "Hey, Lee?"

His head poked out of the bathroom, a toothbrush stuck in his cheek and a grin across his face. "How did I never know how good you looked in my T-shirt?"

My heart squeezed as love, affection, and *desire* for my best friend tugged at me.

Lee's handsome face made me dumb, and that was all there was to it.

So when, around a mouthful of toothpaste, he said, "*This* is the best day of my life," I could only smile and blink back tears.

SEVENTEEN
LEE

ANNIE

Our date tonight is at Abel's Brewery. Are you going to be able to control yourself?

I make no guarantees.

Do not mess with them tonight. As your date, I demand it.

Fun-ruiner.

Fine. I'll pack extra bail money.

That's my girl.

I SMILED DOWN at my phone before slipping it into my pocket and climbing out of my truck. I looked up at the friendly and welcoming sign of Haven Pines. My stomach still twisted at the fact my father had to live here, but I knew taking care of him full-time had been a hardship on Aunt Tootie. Duke buried himself in work, and my schedule wasn't consistent enough for me to do it myself.

I sighed as I walked across the parking lot. So many

times I wished things could be different for my father. For all of us.

A smaller sign near the front entrance boasted a special memory care neighborhood, and I followed the arrows that led the way, though I knew the directions by heart. For residents in the memory care ward, each door was painted and decorated to look like the front door of a home. Each had residential door numbers, and many hung decorative wreaths around the knocker. Lampposts even lined the hallway to mimic a stroll in downtown Outtatowner. It was common knowledge the sconces outside each door were a silent signal to other residents. Flipping the light on meant you were open to guests.

Dad's light was on, and it made me smile to think he was likely having a good day where he wanted to interact with others and enjoy their company. As I approached the door, I found my dad sitting on a rocker outside his room. When I came into view, Dad stood and a warm smile spread across his face.

"Lee." He clapped his hands together and laughed. "This is a surprise."

It wasn't.

I typically spent every Wednesday morning visiting him because it was a day Duke had to go to work early to deliver berries around town, fulfilling weekly orders.

I stepped into his space and pulled my dad into a hug, slapping him on the back. "Looking good, Dad." I held him out at arm's length.

He nodded. "Feeling good these days, Son."

A contented sigh washed over me. Dad had been accepted for a drug trial, and while we might never get the old Red Sullivan back, this medication had been our first glimmer of hope that it may slow the progression of his early-onset dementia.

The small cotton ball bandaged to the inside nook of his elbow let me know that today was an infusion day.

"I have a shift at the firehouse but thought you might enjoy breakfast and maybe a walk."

My dad smiled at me. "Hell, I'd like that."

As we walked down the hallway toward the exit to the courtyard path, I offered small nods and polite smiles to the residents as we passed. Dad often stopped to shake a hand or offer a kind word on our walk.

Stationed near the exit door in nurse's scrubs and behind a rolling laptop cart stood MJ King with a friendly wave and a bright smile. "Morning, Red." She nodded in my direction. "Lee." MJ typed in the code on the security pad to allow us outside access before holding open the door. "Enjoy the sunshine."

Typically I'd take this opportunity to toss back some flirty line. MJ was friendly and cute, and even though she was a King, my flirtatious nature didn't really care. But I was different now. This time I just took the door from her and smiled. "Thanks, MJ."

I let Dad walk in front of me as he wove his way down the crushed limestone path that meandered through the manicured flower beds and garden paths on the sprawling property.

"Off your game today." He smirked. "Normally you try to charm the pants off that girl."

I chuckled and ran a hand through my hair. "Not today."

We fell in step together, and I enjoyed the silent comfort of walking with my dad. "The truth is there's someone else. She's . . . special."

Dad looked at me with a sideways smirk. "No shit?"

I pulled my phone from my pocket and pulled up a picture of Annie and me. It was one of my favorites, taken years ago. It was of me making a goofy double-chin face with buck teeth and Annie crossing her eyes and puffing her cheeks out like a fish. I couldn't help but laugh as I tilted the screen toward Dad.

"Yeah"—he laughed—"she sure is something else."

I flipped the image to a more typical one, a solo picture of Annie that I had taken one day at the beach. She was looking out onto the rolling waves, and I had snapped the picture without her realizing. It was one of many of her I had saved under my favorites.

Dad looked at the picture of Annie. "So you finally did it, huh?"

I looked at Dad, my brows pinching together. "Did what?"

He scoffed and shook his head. "Woke up. Saw what was right there in front of you."

My mouth opened to speak, but Dad waved a hand to stop me. "I know Annie. Been watching you two give each other googly eyes for years when you think the other's not looking."

I lowered the phone and frowned. Of course he'd know Annie.

Dad kept his pace as we walked. "I know your brother likes to shelter me. Some days I'm not all right up here." He tapped his temple and my heart squeezed. "I've been having more good days than bad. Besides, Annie comes on Mondays."

"Mondays?"

"She visits from time to time, usually on Monday. Lately she's been asking a lot of questions about what I remember regarding our family history. Our people. It's been fun trying to reminisce, look at old pictures. I guess Duke's got her on some wild-goose chase."

Mondays.

The one day each week Annie has off and she spends it with my dad.

"I think she even knocked a few things loose." He chuckled. "I recalled a few long-forgotten memories. Felt good."

"That's great, Dad."

I fell into step with him as he continued talking about drama between residents and his unofficial job as handyman as we continued down the blooming walkways.

He lifted a finger to point out a construction site in the distance. "They're building assisted-living houses on this back part of the property. Semi-independent homes, they're calling them. Already got my name on a list for one."

Dad looked out over the construction site in the distance. He looked proud, hopeful. I had no idea if his condition would remain stable enough for him to live in a place like that, but if he could hope, then so could I.

I clamped a hand down on his shoulder and squeezed. "I think that sounds great, Dad."

A few moments later, Dad stopped abruptly and turned toward me. "Your mom is gone."

My mouth pressed together and I nodded, unsure of where this conversation was going and whether it would end with Dad being agitated and angry.

He looked out onto the property. "Now, I know that my Juney is gone, but sometimes it feels like she's still right here with me, clinging to my ribs. It's easy to forget all that's changed . . . though I guess that's a part of it."

I only nodded and held back the emotions that expanded in my throat.

"There's someone out there who's lucky enough to find her way in here." With two fingers Dad thumped against the center of my chest. "It'll hurt like hell, but you'll be a better man for it."

The only face that came to mind was Annie's.

I COULDN'T SCREW this up with her.

Once I had realized there wasn't a world in which I could exist without Annie, that was it. My mind was made up.

Waiting for me outside of her downtown apartment, Annie was radiant. She wore a simple white V-neck tank top with slim straps. It was tucked into a satiny gold skirt that fell past her knees, but had a sexy little slit that showed off her thigh.

Her long muscular legs were sun-kissed and freckled from her time spent on the beach, baking in the warm Michigan sun. I knew from our morning in my bed how soft and supple her thighs felt beneath my fingertips, and I itched to drag the hem of that skirt up higher to explore more of her still undiscovered parts.

When Annie stepped up to my truck, I shot her a look that stopped her in her tracks before climbing out of the driver's seat and pulling open the passenger door.

"A girl could get used to this," she teased.

I nodded and suppressed a smile. "That's the point."

Annie's apples-and-sunshine scent filled the cab of my truck as I adjusted the air conditioner. The evening coastal air was cool enough to have the windows down, but I didn't want any reason for that scent to escape.

Annie kept to her side of the cab, and I longed to invade her space—to reach over and plant my palm on her thigh as we drove the few miles out of town to Abel's Brewery.

I was determined to respect her boundaries, to make her turn those walls to dust herself, until I could show her that fighting this thing between us was utterly useless, and she was begging at my feet.

"What?" Annie asked.

I cocked an eyebrow. "*What* what?"

She spun a finger in the air between us and narrowed one eye. "You've got that look."

"What look?" I laughed.

"That *I'm up to no good* look. I know you, Lee Sullivan."

She did know me. All parts of me, and she hadn't gone running yet. I was determined to hold on to that until my fingers bled. "Just excited about date number three."

"You promised you would behave."

I pulled into a space and put the truck in park. "I promised I wouldn't pull a prank on the Kings." My smirk spread. "I never promised I would behave."

With Annie on my arm, we entered the brewery, and all eyes turned toward us. The brewery made the perfect spot for a town spectacle. The back portion of one of the tasting rooms had been converted into an area to mingle before heading to the back for a behind-the-scenes brewery tour and tasting. The main bar and seating area were still open to paying patrons. Those who were on auction dates made the perfect specimens, like being plopped in a fishbowl, while the rest of the town watched behind the glass.

In the back, the auction date scoreboard was prominently displayed, and after my failed stunt with the lederhosen, Royal and Millie were still in the lead for Top Couple. Annie and I were close behind, with Emma and John Mercer third behind us. There were also a whole host of names with no hearts next to them at all. Couples who were at risk for the remix.

My eyes slid to Sylvie and Stumpy Larson. I doubted she would be upset if she and Stumpy changed partners. In fact, I'm sure she was praying for it. After tonight, any truly unhappy couples would be granted a remix.

As we walked in, Annie and I were greeted with handshakes and friendly hugs. At the bar, Royal was posted next to Millie, chatting with Charles and his date, Mia. Another group of women next to them waved to Annie.

She leaned into my space. "I'm going to go say hi to some of the Bluebirds."

My hand found the small of her back. "Have fun."

I watched as Annie moved across the brewery with the elegance of a dancer. The satin fabric of her skirt did nothing to hide her curves, and because I was weak where she was concerned, I watched her ass the entire time.

A low whistle sounded next to me, and I turned to find Whip King appreciating her ass too.

"Fuck off, Bill."

Whip only laughed and took another drink of his beer. "I don't think it's me you have to worry about."

Confused, I looked to where Whip gestured with his glass. Near the bar, Annie turned from her conversation with her girlfriends toward Charles. He was dressed in a white button-down shirt, navy slacks that were about four inches too short, and a pair of brown shoes *without socks*. He may look fashionable to some, but to me he looked like a total tool.

I straightened when I caught sight of Annie laughing at something he said and gently resting her hand on his forearm. Charles clearly saw the friendly gesture as an invite, because his body shifted and he leaned in for a hug.

That's it.

Leaving Whip behind, I strode across the brewery in seconds. My hand found his shoulder, and with a slightly harder than necessary squeeze, I'd grabbed his attention.

"Lee." He turned toward me with a hand outstretched. "Good to see you."

My eyes trailed to his hands, but I only grunted like a caveman. When I looked at Annie, she was clearly confused. "You almost ready? The tour is about to start."

Her eyes moved from my angry glare to Charles. "Um, sure. Charles and I were just catching up."

I glared at him like the jealous asshole I was. "I'm sure."

"I'm not typically a beer man myself, as I'm sure you could guess, but I love to see the process of how all this is made." Charles was attempting to redirect the conversation —away from the irrational anger that was making everyone uncomfortable.

"I'm just shocked Abel agreed to hosting the date here. He's usually so sullen and quiet." Annie sidestepped into me, and when my arm wrapped around her waist, I saw the jealous flare mirror in Charles's eyes.

"It was to get out of the auction," I ground out. Abel King kept to himself, and if opening up his brewery in exchange for opting out of the auction was on the table, I had no doubts he'd take it.

Aunt Tootie's date bell tinkled above the crowd. We turned to see her smiling and holding a clipboard. "This way, lovebirds! The tour is about to begin."

Slowly we filed in behind her and moved to the semiprivate room. From the back, Abel King entered from a long, dark hallway that I assumed led to offices or storage spaces. Of all the Kings, Abel was the most intense. He was quiet, reclusive, and built like a fucking tank. He'd even done a stint in prison, if the rumors were true. Looking at the cold, hard stare he shot over the crowd, I'd believe it.

Annie, along with a few of her friends, laughed and whispered as he stood before the group. His arms crossed, and a glare that could have been directed at any one of us settled on his face.

Tootie cleared her throat. "Mr. King so graciously opened his business for us. He'll be walking you through the beer-making process, and at the end, each couple will receive two tickets to redeem for a flight of the brewery's six signature beers. Before we begin, we have a special sponsorship to announce . . ." Her eyes moved nervously over the crowd. "Miss Sylvie King and Stumpy Larson have been gifted a private tasting."

Abel's nostrils flared, and he stepped forward. There was little doubt the "anonymous sponsor" was likely Stumpy himself.

Tootie's smile wobbled. Sylvie's shoulders slumped. "A tasting for four!"

Stumpy's head whipped up. "What?"

Unfazed, Tootie blinked and looked down innocently at her clipboard. "That's what it says right here." Despite the rivalry, my aunt had a kind heart.

"Royal and Millie can join us!" Sylvie practically shouted and sidestepped toward her overprotective older brother.

"Poor Sylvie." Charles leaned down to whisper to Annie. I didn't like his fucking tone and the way he lowered his voice for her. When Annie giggled under her hand, a fresh, irrational wave of frustration washed over me.

Abel barely spoke as he walked us through the brewery. He might make exceptional beer, but his people skills could use serious work. As we walked, Annie engaged in conversations around us and asked questions. I couldn't help but notice how her eyes would drift to Charles and Mia.

Was she jealous? Did I read this situation between us completely wrong?

Charles's fingers slid delicately over his date's shoulder. There was familiarity in that touch, and we both saw it. Annie may be mine, but I was smart enough to realize she'd had feelings for Charles at one point in time. Hell, getting him to commit to Annie was a selling point for this whole ruse in the first place.

As the tour wrapped and we waited for the flights to be delivered, I leaned into her space. "Kiss me. In front of him—in front of everyone."

Her eyes shot to mine, searching. "And what would be the point of that?"

To prove to you that what we have is real.

"Revenge, obviously. Served ice fucking cold like his cold, dead heart."

Annie gulped hard, but her voice was strong. "No."

Heat flared in my eyes. I liked Annie's backbone. Her resilience. Grabbing her hand, I led her through the door at the back of the brewery and down the dark hallway.

"Where are we going?"

Without looking back, I let my growing frustration bubble. "I need to talk to you."

I stepped closer to her, knowing the long dark hallway would keep us from view. Annie's back pressed into the wall, and I moved forward, leaving only a few inches between us.

Her head tipped back to look me in the eyes.

"Do you still want him?"

Her blue eyes narrowed. "Who?"

"You fucking know who."

"Charles?"

I placed one hand against the wall on each side of her, caging her in. "Yes."

Her eyes searched mine. My heart beat wildly, waiting for her answer. "Are you *jealous*?" she seethed.

A growl rumbled through me. "You're damn right I'm jealous. I also don't like the way he looks at you—like whatever's going on between you is some kind of game. You're not a game. You're the fucking prize."

Annie breathed out. "I thought this was supposed to be fake."

I leaned down to whisper. "Nothing about the way I feel about you is fake. It never has been."

Her breaths quickened, causing the tops of her breasts to tease the edge of her tank top. Using my fingertips, I traced the long line of her neck and across her collarbone, slipping a finger under the thin spaghetti strap.

"I can wait. Until you open your eyes to what this really is. I'm more patient than you realize."

"We talked about this. I thought we set boundaries."

I nodded toward the door where damn near our entire town was laughing and drinking beer. "Technically, this is in public." I leaned back to appreciate how gorgeous she looked, full lips parted in surprise and a sexy little flush staining her cheeks. "Fuck, baby, I'm getting hard just looking at you."

Annie's fingers dug into the fabric of my shirt as her fists twisted. My hips flexed forward as she wrapped one hand around my neck, pulling my mouth to hers. Her kiss was frantic, and I planted my hands on her hips, easing her into me. My tongue ran over the seam of her lips, and she moaned before allowing me access. I deepened our kiss, pressing my body into hers.

Clinking glasses, low music, and laughter filtered down the dark hallway, but I couldn't care less. Together, we were lost in our own world, where nothing and no one mattered.

No one but *her*.

My hands breezed over the silky material of her skirt, testing the high slit that exposed her thigh. I slid my palm over her leg, inching higher. I broke the kiss, opting to watch her eyes lose focus as I teased the edge of her underwear. I dragged one finger in a single, teasing stroke up her pussy.

"What do you say, Annette? Will you let me have a little taste?"

EIGHTEEN
ANNIE

My brain struggled to catch up, since my sole focus was the heat pooling between my legs.

I focused on my ragged breathing and how it drowned out the din of the crowd just beyond the hallway door. Lee's intensity was jarring. He was looking at me like he had a thousand times, only it was *different*.

Hungry.

For the first time in my life it dawned on me that Lee may have been serious when he made comments about me being his girl or that he wanted to take care of me.

I'd never allowed myself to believe that it might have actually been real. The affectionate way he looked at me. The possessive way he touched me. The way he had always defended me.

Every interaction between us jumbled in my mind as I attempted to sift through reality versus wishful thinking or outright denial.

The heat of Lee's breath moved against my neck as his fingertips continued to tease the lacy fabric of my underwear. Goose bumps erupted across my chest and arms, and my thighs squeezed around his hand.

"Annette, I need an answer." The deep growl in his voice sent tingles racing up my spine. Desire and need swept over me.

"What was the question?" I was breathy, nearly panting, but I couldn't find the will to care.

His mouth moved lower, brushing across my sternum as one hand dusted across the hard nipple poking through the fabric of my tank top. My mouth was dry, and I swallowed hard, desperately wanting to melt into him—to let him take charge so I didn't have to admit how badly I wanted this.

How I had *always* wanted it.

"Can I make you come? Then we'll straighten that skirt out and go back in there with your friends."

The image of me, sated and sex-rumpled, strutting back into the brewery with no one the wiser, was downright erotic.

"Yes." The word was out in a desperate whoosh of breath before I could rein it in. If Lee could live his life recklessly, then maybe, for once, so could I.

On a groan, Lee's teeth tugged at my nipple as his rough fingers slid farther between my thighs. A moan built in my throat as he lifted his head. His strong hand circled my throat as he looked down on me.

"Quiet. We can't get caught."

My eyes flashed to the doorway. I managed a weak nod and bit down on my lip as Lee's attention lowered. A squeak escaped my throat when he crouched, pressing a kiss to my stomach and gathering the material of my satin skirt.

Lee pushed the material into my hands, and I held it for him as he feathered a kiss over my underwear. The sight of my best friend, dropping to his knees before me, sent an aching throb directly to my clit.

I wanted him. All of him. His hands. His mouth. That cock. I didn't care where or when or how. I was desperate for it. Needy.

Lee's hands moved over my thighs, caressing the skin and muscle. I glanced at the doorway. No one seemed to be coming in or out all night, and we were somewhat secluded. The risk of being caught only spurred my desire. I lifted my skirt higher, granting him complete access.

Appreciation and heat flared in his eyes at the sight of me. Shifting his weight, he lifted my left thigh over his shoulder. My hand found his hair, and I raked my fingernails through it. His teeth dragged against my skin as he inhaled my scent and groaned in appreciation. With one finger, Lee hooked the edge of my underwear, tugging them to the side. I was already soaked for him.

His mouth clamped down on my pussy, and my head fell back against the wall with a thump. I struggled to stifle a moan as his tongue spread me open. Gripping the thigh draped over him, Lee shouldered it higher, opening me to him. Lee worked my pussy with wide, flat strokes of his tongue.

Every nerve ending was on fire, and I clamped one hand over my mouth to keep quiet. His tongue slid across my pussy, pausing to suck and tease my clit. The familiar, deep clench of muscles told me I was spiraling closer to the edge.

And fast.

"So fucking good, Annette."

"Oh my god." My hips bucked, and I was riding his face as he greedily ate my pussy. Tongue, teeth, lips. Lee's mouth was rough and demanding, and when he slipped a finger inside, then two, while he teased my clit, I was done for.

My fists clenched the gold fabric of my skirt as I held it out of the way. Looking down, I had the perfect view of Lee worshipping my body. My inner muscles pulsed around his fingers as he stroked in and out. He stared up at me, watching every whimper and squirm as he devoured me.

Heat clawed its way across my chest and through my belly, gathering in a hot ball at the base of my spine.

"Watch me," Lee demanded, teasing and licking while he pumped his fingers into me and hooked them to hit a place deep inside that made me melt. "Watch and know it's me who's making you come so hard that your legs are shaking."

With my fingers tangled in his hair and my eyes staring down at my best friend, I came apart. My pussy clenched around his fingers as he lapped up every drop of my cum with appreciative, encouraging hums.

A tingle from my scalp to my toes warmed me.

When I finished, Lee sat back on his heels, his eyes never leaving mine. "Goddamn, Annette. I always thought you were pretty, but you are fucking gorgeous when you fall apart."

Still panting and with his help, I lifted my leg off his shoulder. As he'd predicted, my legs were unsteady beneath me. With a smirk, Lee sucked the last of me off his thumb before placing a gentle kiss on my thigh.

"Let's get you fixed up, sweetheart."

When he stood, my eyes lifted with him. I was still trying to wrap my brain around the fact that *Lee* had just single-handedly ruined me for all other men. My best friend. The man I promised myself I would *never* fall for.

He toyed with my silky thong before pulling it down my legs. "These are soaked." Before I could argue, Lee slipped them into his pocket, and a fresh wave of desire rolled through me.

"Are you going to give those back?"

He smirked. A smile I'm sure would have incinerated those panties anyway. "Absolutely fucking not."

I laughed as Lee tenderly smoothed my skirt around my hips. I attempted to straighten my tank top. My nipples were still painfully hard, and my pussy ached for more. I planted my hand flat against my belly. Lee stood and towered over me, protecting me from view as I gathered myself.

He leaned in and finally kissed me. Gentle. Reassuring. I melted into him. The slight taste of myself on his lips stirred something primal within me, and I wanted Lee in a way I had never allowed myself to explore for fear of losing him. Losing *everything*.

"What do you say, Annette?"

My emotions stirred as my mind raced. "I think I need a minute."

Lee nodded and dropped a kiss at my temple. "How about this? I'll go out there and order us a drink. Mingle. Maybe try to earn us an extra heart or two on that damn scoreboard." He gently guided me down the hallway, back toward the doorway to the crowd. "Once I'm gone, you slip into the bathroom. Take all the time you need."

I looked up at my best friend. He always seemed to know exactly what I needed. Right now, I needed to stop freaking out and come to terms with the fact that Lee just ate me out *in public*—and I liked it.

No. Loved it.

I wanted *more*.

The earth was shifting beneath my feet, and he understood that I needed a few moments by myself to come to terms with it. I nodded. Lee shot me a soft smile and disappeared beyond the door.

After counting to thirty, I peeked my head around the door. No one seemed to notice me exiting the hallway.

No one except for Emma.

My cheeks heated as her eyes went wide, and she mouthed a silent *Oh my god!*

Emma immediately left her conversation to cross the brewery and grab my hand. I saw Lee, standing casually at the bar like he hadn't just been on his knees with his face between my legs only minutes before.

"Holy shit!" Emma's excited whisper had me shushing her. "Please tell me you just got railed in the back room."

"Emma!" I looked around but no one seemed to be paying us much attention. "Help me. Do I look okay?"

She stepped back to look me over. "Except for the JBF hair? Yeah, you look great."

My hand flew to my head. "JBF?"

She grinned and lifted an eyebrow. "Just been fucked."

"Crap." I attempted to fluff and untangle my wild curls.

Emma laughed again. "I'm kidding, but thank you for confirming." She leaned in close. "That's so fucking hot."

I shushed her again but couldn't stifle the giddy giggle that escaped on the tail end of it. "Emma, oh my god . . ." I gave her a look that communicated everything—my disbelief, my *happiness*. Everything I couldn't dare say out loud. "I need a drink."

NINETEEN
ANNIE

YOU HAVE GOT *to be freaking kidding me.*

I flipped two pages back, then forward again, using my finger to trace over the words as they settled in. I pulled out the small lockbox Kate and Beckett had found when they discovered the speakeasy.

Three people, two men and one woman, smiled back at the camera. The two men wore pressed pants and dress shoes. One had on a dark tie, loosened at the neck, while the other wore a light collared knit shirt with the top two buttons undone. The woman, in a dainty floral print dress and heels, had her hands on her hips and was captured mid-laugh. They looked *happy*.

On the back, faded cursive handwriting revealed three names—*James, Helen, and Philo.*

As the week unfolded, to distract myself from the mess of emotions I was feeling after the brewery date with Lee, I had gone to the public library to do some digging for Duke.

There wasn't a lot to sift through, but one name continued to snag my attention.

Helen Sinclair.

In one document, she was listed as Helen Sinclair, but there were other documents that listed Philo and Helen Sullivan. A few hours of research and I discovered that our assumptions were correct. Helen Sinclair married Philo Sullivan in 1931. Tootie was certain, even without a marriage certificate, because in the photo of Helen and the two men, it was clear she was the source of the devilishly charming Sullivan smile.

And there, on the printout in front of me, were deeds for land from the Homestead Act of 1862 for families King, Sullivan, and Sinclair.

Sand Dune Studio was quiet as usual, and my heart beat faster.

Each of the three families claimed land through the Homestead Act of 1862, which gave them each 160 acres of public land.

I looked over to Mel, the high school girl I had hired for the summer to help with the influx of tourists. "Hey, Mel? I have to run to the library for a little bit. Can you hold down the fort?"

Mel looked around the empty shop and smiled. "I think I can handle it."

After piling the papers haphazardly, I rushed toward the door. "Thanks so much. I owe you one."

I hurried down the sidewalk. I was definitely on to something, and I didn't want to lose momentum.

The Outtatowner Public Library was busy with kids out of school for the summer, and tourists popping in for a quick reprieve from the summer heat. The public library held special events for young kids all the way to teenagers, and those programs were bustling with activity.

I hurried through the stacks to the bank of computers in the far corner. My fingers raced over the keyboard to log in to the library's system and pull up the catalog of newspaper articles stored digitally.

Using the information listed on each certificate, I pulled up a map of Remington County and began digging. It took only a few pages of searching until I found exactly what I was looking for. Documentation for King, Sullivan, and Sinclair land, all 480 acres, and each property was side by side.

My heart beat faster.

At one point in time, they were friends and neighbors.

I freaking knew it.

"Can I help you find something, Annie?"

Bug King's voice startled me, and I quickly minimized the page. I turned with a nervous laugh. "Oh! Hey, Ms. Bug. No, I'm all good here."

She raised a skeptical eyebrow. "Doing some research?"

Nerves rattled through me. I knew Bug. She was stern, but generally kind. She was also a King. I wasn't entirely sure what this information meant and how it played into the strange goings-on at Sullivan Farms. Regardless, I needed to talk with Duke and the rest of the family before I uttered a word to anyone else.

"Oh, you know, just killin' time." I feigned fanning my face. "It's a hot one out there today."

"Mm-hmm." It was all Bug replied. After a beat, she looked me up and down. "You know the auction remix is coming up. Several of the couples are displeased. Will you be adding your name to the list?"

My stomach plummeted. Things had gotten so muddied with Lee that I didn't even know if we were really fake dating anymore or if it had morphed into something else entirely. I did know that there was no way in hell I was letting another woman get her hands on him. Especially not until I figured out what was going on between the two of us.

"No, ma'am," I replied. "Lee and I are having a good time with each other."

She pressed her lips together, and I didn't miss the subtle disapproving shake of her head. "Be careful with that one, Annie. As the Trisha Yearwood song warned, that boy's a Walkaway Joe."

My back straightened, and a lightning bolt of defensiveness, maybe even protectiveness, shot through me. I didn't know what the hell song she was talking about, but I understood what she was implying. Bug may be a matriarch in town, and I had been taught to respect my elders, but I sure as shit wasn't going to let her talk negatively about Lee.

"I mean no disrespect, but I believe between the two of us, I have a better handle on Lee's character. Don't you think?" I raised an eyebrow in challenge, hoping the nerves that simmered under my skin weren't written all over my face.

"Very well," Bug said before turning her back and walking away with a shake of her head.

I exhaled a sigh of relief and wiped my palms on the tops of my jean shorts. It didn't matter that Lee was a playboy and we had agreed to these dates for all the wrong reasons. He was still my best friend.

I quickly printed out the pages I wanted to take back to the Sullivans and hurried out of the library.

On the walk home, temptation got the best of me, and I pulled up the song that Bug had referred to.

My heart sank when I realized she just might be right.

~

LEE

Everyone from the station is doing the firefighter run. Meet you after the race.

I GRINNED down at my phone. Every year the Outtatowner Fire Department participated in the Fourth of July 5K run. Only they ran in turnout gear—pants, suspenders, and *no shirts*.

Brooklyn and Emery, the other female firefighters, also participated, and it always made me smile when they led the pack with the men huffing and puffing behind them.

I sure as hell wouldn't be missing an opportunity to openly ogle Lee as he ran past me shirtless and sweaty. A tingle settled between my legs, and I wondered how soon it might be before I could see him shirtless and sweaty in another, more private setting.

I had been keyed up since our brewery date, but with Lee's adjusted work schedule, we hadn't had any alone time since Wednesday night.

Fourth of July fell on a Tuesday, and even six days of not seeing him felt like a lifetime.

In a single dark hallway, Lee had somehow tipped my world upside down while making it feel as though it had been righted for the first time in my entire life.

I didn't know what to do with all the emotions I seemed to have on a daily basis.

Was this still fake?

Had Lee always felt this way?

What changed?

Why now?

Could I get over my own insecurities and anxieties in order to give myself over fully to Lee?

What would I do if things didn't work out between us?

How would I ever tell him the truth?

When Tuesday morning came, you bet your ass I had found a prime spot along the race route and set up a blanket and chairs for the Sullivan group. Those participating in the 5K would run ahead of the parade and then join their group before the parade began. The firefighters would lead the pack and then circle back to their trucks in order to honk their horns and toss out candy to the children.

I wasn't a runner, so I nestled into my lawn chair and waited for the rest of the Sullivans to arrive.

Winding through the crowd, I spotted Penny and raised my hand to call her over. Behind her, Lark was carrying a small beach bag, and next to her was Kate. I waved my arms to catch their eye.

"Oh my god, how did you get such a good spot?" Kate asked.

"Benefits of living downtown." I shrugged. "I put out the blanket and lawn chair at five a.m."

Lark leaned down and hugged me. "You are incredible."

"Where are the guys?" I asked, looking past them, expecting to see Beckett, Duke, or Wyatt coming up behind them.

"They're running. Can you believe it?" Kate laughed.

Lark shrugged. "Wyatt convinced them it would be a fun thing to do together. He even got a couple of his players to join in."

"Neither of you wanted to join them?" I asked.

Kate lowered to sit. "No." She laughed.

"*Hell* no," Lark added.

Penny reached for the plastic bag Lark had tucked away in the beach tote. "I'm just here for the candy." She grinned widely.

Soon the announcer began getting the crowd settled

and ready to cheer on the runners of the 5K as they made their way through town.

I smiled, content to be surrounded by my community and the Sullivan women who had become so much more than friends—they had become sisters. My chest squeezed, and my heart ached for the possibility that maybe, *just maybe*, this could somehow become a reality and not just a summer where Lee and I got tangled up and everything fell apart. Losing them would tear my heart out.

Lark bumped into my shoulder. "Here comes your man."

My eyes whipped to hers, and she winked. The familiar rush of heat flooded my cheeks. Fighting the morning sun, I shielded my eyes and looked down Main Street. Sure enough, cresting the hill and coming toward us was a group of firefighters dressed in nothing but suspenders and firefighter pants.

Leading the charge and brandishing the American flag over his head was Lee. My heart stuttered. Panting and already sweaty in the sweltering July heat, Lee's muscles strained with the weight of the flag waving above his head.

The crowd took to their feet, cheering for the brave men and women of the Outtatowner Fire Department. Appreciative whoops and hollers rose from the crowd.

Penny stood to watch them run down Main Street. "Why are they shirtless?"

"Because it's hot outside," Lark answered, giving Kate and me a sly smile.

Kate laughed. "It's *really* hot outside." Her eyes found Beckett and locked onto him.

My eyes never left Lee's face as I watched him scan the crowd. When his piercing eyes found me, they stopped, and my heartbeat stopped along with them. A wide grin split his face as he pumped a fist in the air, his muscles straining against the flag.

As he passed, Lee thumped his chest twice and pointed at me. A thousand eyeballs shifted in our direction, but I didn't care. I bounced on my toes and screamed even louder for him and the rest of the men and women in his unit.

Despite his reputation, Lee was brave and loyal.

Proud.

And I was proud to be associated with him, no matter the terms.

"Holy shit," Kate whispered next to me.

"You're lucky my dad's not around," Penny teased. She loved when adults cursed, and it irritated Wyatt to no end.

Ignoring her, Kate turned to me with wide eyes. "Lee is in love with you."

I leaned into her. "Stop. You know it's not . . ." The words died on my tongue because I didn't know what it was anymore, and I didn't want to lie to one of my best friends. "I don't know what it is," I finished.

"Well, I do." Kate scoffed. "That is the look of a man who is totally gone for you."

Lark clapped her hands together and sighed. "Oh, I'm so excited for you two!"

Lee and the rest of the firefighters led the 5K, and I watched him disappear around the corner. My face was hot and my insides were mush.

Needing to focus on *anything* other than how Lee Sullivan made me feel, I focused my attention on Penny.

"Okay, kiddo, in a few minutes the parade will actually start. Let's get you some candy. Remember . . . elbows out!"

Penny's rolling laughter soothed my soul as she grinned and shot her arms akimbo and growled like a tiny linebacker.

TWENTY
LEE

After the 5K race, I was on cloud nine. My unit and I threw on some shirts and climbed on the fire truck.

"Looking slow out there, Sullivan." Brooklyn smirked at me as she pulled her shirt over her sports bra. It struck me that the whole *shirtless firefighter* stunt was pretty sexist. Sure, Brooklyn and Emery always jumped at the chance to beat us in the race, but maybe next year we could think of something else to rile up the crowd.

I patted my abs. "It was the birria tacos. This is your fault."

She laughed as Whip scoffed. "Taco Tuesday is *tonight*. Find another excuse."

I laughed, enjoying the easy camaraderie of my unit. It was the sense of belonging I had missed from my Army days. Stressful jobs had a way of bonding people, and despite our relatively quiet town, we had each other's backs.

"Let's load up!" Whip bellowed out to the group, and we all climbed aboard the three fire trucks that would toss candy to the crowd. I found my spot on the right, beside a twenty-five-gallon bucket filled to the brim with candy.

Circling back through town, the trucks meandered to the beginning of the route. Whip blasted the siren and horns as we lined up to lead the parade.

As the truck rolled toward Sand Dune Studio, my heart ached. Standing and waving was Beckett with his arms wrapped around Katie. Lark leaned into Wyatt, who had Penny perched on top of his shoulders. In the middle of the two couples, next to my frowning oldest brother, Duke, was Annie, beaming at me and waving wildly.

She had never looked more beautiful.

I couldn't hear a damn thing over the sirens, but I could see Penny's excited giggles. I called back to Whip. "Be right back!"

Whip flipped me a middle finger as I hopped off the truck and jogged toward my family with a laugh.

Without even giving it a second thought, I ran straight for Annie, grabbed her by the back of the neck, and planted my mouth on hers. I swallowed her shocked little gasp and wound my arm tighter around her back when she melted into me. I pressed my forehead to hers and whispered, "Fair's fair. This is *very* public."

I grinned down at her before looking up at Penny perched on my brother's shoulders.

I held my hands out to Penny, who launched herself into my arms. I hoisted her up onto my own shoulders. "You want to go for a ride?"

She smiled down at me. I looked over at my brother Wyatt. "I'll meet you back at the fire station."

Wyatt smiled and nodded as he pulled Lark into his side.

I held on to Penny's legs. "All right, you little rat. Let's do this."

"Woo-hoo!" Her fists shot into the air.

I jogged back toward the fire truck. Grabbing the handle, I hoisted her inside before pulling myself into the truck. Her eyes went wide when she saw the large bucket of candy on the floor.

"Now, listen. We still have to give some of this away." I laughed.

Penny dug two hands into the bucket, scooping out candy. She looked at me with hopeful eyes.

I grabbed my own handful. "Okay, let's do it." I tossed the candy out of the truck to scatter on the roadway.

A delighted giggle tore through her. Penny tossed her two handfuls as children scattered like ants to collect it.

"This is epic!" Penny shouted. Her laughter was infectious and lifted the moods of everyone in the truck.

I couldn't help but wonder if Annie had ever wanted kids. She had a natural and easy way with my niece that made it all too easy to imagine her surrounded by children. It wasn't anything we ever talked about, and for the briefest moment I let myself fantasize about a funny little girl with Annie's freckles and wild hair and my grin.

I swallowed hard at how vivid and real that fantasy was. How *easy* it was to conjure up.

Another lifetime where none of this was fake. Where I woke up so much sooner and saw what was right in front of me. Maybe Annie could have been mine from the beginning.

Maybe she already had been.

By the time the parade was over, the buckets of candy were completely gone, though the bulging pockets of

Penny's stars-and-stripes shorts were a good indication that her sweet tooth would be satisfied.

In true overprotective fashion, Wyatt was waiting for us at the station when we arrived. Once the fire truck was parked, Penny hopped out and jumped into her dad's arms. "Have fun?"

"The best time!" She looked back at me. "Thanks, Uncle Lee."

"You bet, Rat-face."

Wyatt and I shook hands, and I watched him and his little family load up into his car and leave.

Outtatowner never did anything small, so after the 5K and parade, families would go home to barbecue before meeting down by the county fairgrounds for an epic fireworks display.

I was eager to get back to Annie when a call came in. Dispatch relayed the call for a residential house fire a few miles outside of town. The firefighters on duty, including myself, hurried to gear up and get our trucks on the road.

As with any call, adrenaline zipped through my veins. We gathered as much information as we could from dispatch as we hauled ass out of town to the rural farmhouse. Before we even got there, thick black smoke was billowing above the tree line.

I hadn't immediately recognized the address, but when we drew closer, I realized we were heading straight for the Robinsons' property.

Sloane was a single mother with twins, and she had recently moved back to her family's property. If the rumors were true, her ex was a bit of a psycho. A pit formed in my stomach. If this was her place, kids could also be involved. I exhaled three sharp breaths to calm my racing heart.

Whip's fist bumped my biceps. "Get your shit together, man."

Focus.

I swallowed hard and pressed my lips together before nodding once.

I reached back into my memory, trying to pull out details of the old farmhouse, but I came up blank.

"Hey, what did we know about the Robinsons?" I called into my headset over the blaring sirens.

Whip shook his head, indicating he knew about as much as I did.

Brooklyn called out, "Sloane is living there. She's got twins, a boy and a girl. If I remember right, the house is two stories. She might even have a dog or a cat."

A young, scared mother.

Two small children.

Pets.

Fuck.

Best-case scenario, the fire started when the house was empty. I prayed they had been at the parade and no one was home. Worst-case scenario—I couldn't allow myself to think about that.

As we approached the scene, the flashing lights of fire trucks and the piercing sound of sirens added to the chaos that engulfed the typically quiet, rural neighborhood. The adrenaline surged through my veins. Lives were at stake, and I focused on the task ahead, a knot of tension forming in my stomach.

The orange glow flickered through the downstairs windows, a sign of the relentless fire raging within.

The desperate cries of a mother and the urgent voices of my fellow firefighters reverberated in my ears as I jumped out of the truck. The heat of the inferno hit me like a wave. I scanned the surroundings, trying to gather as much information as possible.

Sloane was standing outside, clutching one small child and screaming while a police officer held her back. The mother and her daughter were safe, but the young boy was still trapped inside. I couldn't bear the thought of him, alone and scared, being consumed by the flames.

I charged forward to hear what she was saying.

"Ben is in there!"

My eyes whipped to my lieutenant, and with his curt nod granting me permission, I took off without another word. I raced to the truck to secure my oxygen tank before heading straight for the farmhouse.

As I approached the entrance, the acrid smell of smoke filled my nostrils, making it difficult to breathe despite my tank. My heart pounded, the weight of responsibility bearing down on me. With each step, the crackling fire grew louder, its ominous presence mocking my every move. The smoke billowed, obscuring my vision and making it hard to navigate the treacherous terrain.

Focus. Stay calm. Find the boy. You can do this.

I pressed forward, my training guiding me through the suffocating haze. The heat intensified, causing my skin to prickle and sweat to pour off my brow. The flames danced with a ferocity that seemed to mock my attempts to control them.

I shouted Ben's name, hoping he would hear my voice above the chaos. Along with my unit, I searched each room, battling the growing desperation that threatened to consume me. Time was slipping away, and the fire showed no signs of relenting. The thought of failure clawed at my mind, but I pushed it aside, knowing that I had to keep going.

Testing my weight on the wood floor upstairs, I pressed on. In the primary bedroom, a muffled cry reached my ears. My heart leaped with renewed hope as I traced the sound to a closed door. With swift hands, I turned the handle, revealing a walk-in closet rapidly filling with smoke. The boy was huddled in the corner, his eyes wide with fear and his cheeks stained with sooty tears. Relief washed over me.

"I got you!" I yelled, knowing he likely couldn't hear me over the roar of the fire.

After slinging him over my shoulder, I fought my way back through the fiery labyrinth, the flames licking at my heels. The smoke thickened, making it difficult to see, but I relied on muscle memory and instinct to guide me. When I reached the top of the stairs, I quickly realized my exit was gone, and my heartbeat ticked higher.

I turned back to the bedroom farthest from the flames. My legs burned, but with a final burst of energy, I reached a window. I looked down to find a sloping hill and a grassy area. I smashed the glass, the shards cascading around us. Cradling the boy, I jumped.

My body collided with the hard ground, sending a sharp pain radiating through my rib cage. As I lay on the grass, gasping for breath, a sense of relief washed over me. My arms held the crying boy tightly as EMTs rushed in to help.

My breaths came hard and fast. The boy was safe and would be reunited with his mother and sister. They would all be headed to the hospital to ensure there were no complications from smoke inhalation, but for now they were safe. I stared up at the crystal-blue sky as the chaos surrounded me. The tension and angst that had gripped me moments ago transformed into an overwhelming sense of gratitude.

Brooklyn's face came into view, silhouetted by the

bright sky. "Nice work, hotshot." She knelt beside me and pressed two fingers into my carotid artery to check my pulse.

I shook her off, removing my mask and gasping for air. "I'm fine."

She laughed. "You just took a header out of a window and used your body as a landing pad. You'll be lucky if you didn't break something."

I rolled to my side and stinging pain lanced through my ribs. "I'll live."

I groaned as I got to my knees. Before me, I watched as the rest of my team worked to contain the fire. The house would be a total loss. In a matter of minutes, the flames were contained, and the smoke and ash mixed with the indescribable, stomach-rolling smell of a home fire.

"You know the drill. Gotta get checked out." Brooklyn held her hand out for me, and I gripped it, using her strength to help me stand.

I can't really do a crowd right now.

ANNIE

Want to meet me at our place?

I GRABBED my keys and carefully loaded myself into my truck to make the few-minute drive to the water tower, where my girl was waiting.

As soon as I was out of the cab, her body slammed into me. "I'm so glad you're safe."

I braced myself and flinched against the impact. "News travels fast."

Annie pulled away. "Small town." She immediately

noticed the way I favored my right side. "What happened? Oh my god, are you hurt?"

I shook my head and headed toward the ladder. "Not too bad, but I had to take an emergency exit. Just a couple of bruised ribs."

Her delicate fingers danced over my T-shirt, testing where she guessed I might be hurt. My body warmed against her gentle touch, my stomach muscles clenching when she skated over the tender ribs.

"Lee . . ." The concerned way she exhaled my name sent warmth buzzing through me. She shook her head. "Sometimes you don't think."

"Don't worry about me." I stepped back, opening my arm to let her pass and ignoring the worry that crossed her delicate features. "Ladies first."

Annie's lips pressed into a small smile as she planted two hands on the ladder. Before hoisting herself up, she looked at me over her shoulder. She moved up two rungs, and I appreciated the faded band T-shirt she had knotted at her waist and the way her flowery skirt billowed in the soft breeze. In a few more steps, I'd have a hell of a view.

Annie tucked her hand beneath her bottom to keep from shoving her butt in my face, and I bit back a smile. She looked back at me. "Hey, no peeking."

I averted my eyes. "You're the one who wore a skirt."

"I thought this was supposed to be a *date*."

"I am not mad about it, trust me."

"Just . . . look somewhere else."

After some very unladylike sounds, Annie finally hauled herself up the worn metal ladder as I followed behind her.

It took hours for the adrenaline to leave my system, but when it did, I was completely drained. I sat next to Annie and sighed. Twilight was just settling over our small town. For long moments, we sat in contented silence.

Her soft voice finally broke the silence. "Are you okay?"

I shrugged to say *not really*, then sighed. "I will be."

"Was it bad?" She quickly shook her head. "You don't have to talk about it, but I'm here if you ever need to."

I pulled her hand into mine and placed them both on my lap, staring down at how her long fingers laced in mine. "I was scared."

I could feel her staring at the side of my face, but I continued to avert my eyes and instead looked out onto our town.

"I was worried we wouldn't make it or that I wouldn't find him. When kids are freaked out, they hide in the tiniest, most random places. All I kept thinking was that I was going to be too late."

"But you weren't."

"Not this time." Like it often did, my mind flipped back to Margo and how even though I was the first on the scene, I was too late to save her. Somewhere along the line, anyone in trouble became a glaring reminder of how I had failed her.

Hot tears burned behind my eyelids. With a thumb and forefinger I swiped them away and cleared my throat with a grunt. With the adrenaline crash came a rush of emotion, for me, often in the form of tears. I was used to being alone when that happened, but there was something comforting about having Annie with me when I finally fell apart.

I knew in my bones she would never turn away from me.

"When I was in Afghanistan, I'd get scared and repeat over and over, *My heart is always with you*." Annie stayed silent next to me. "It was something she wrote. Said it reminded her of a poem she'd read once. Another thing she didn't seem to remember when I got home, but at the time, it was something that had made an impact for me. It wasn't just those words, but the fact I could think about everyone I loved back home. Even in the worst times, I could find a way to feel connected."

"Lee." Emotion was thick in Annie's voice. "Do you remember, um, in the letters . . ." Annie was holding back tears.

Shit.

I hadn't meant to upset her. "Hey." I turned my torso toward her, shifting to spare my tender ribs, and brushed her curls behind an ear before holding her face in place. "I don't wanna think about that or talk about it right now. Can we just sit here for a few minutes?"

She swallowed. "Okay." Her voice was barely above a whisper.

In the quiet evening, as the sun set over the waters of Lake Michigan, I had an overwhelming need to be surrounded by her. To bury myself deep inside and get lost in the comfort of Annie.

I didn't want to think about scared little boys, horrific house fires, or the tangled-up feelings I was having for the one person who should be totally off limits.

Annie was my best friend, but I wanted nothing more than to be consumed by *her*.

The first boom of a firework startled us both. Annie sucked in a gasp as a riot of yellow and purple burst in front of us. Being on top of the water tower gave us a perfect view of our town's impeccable fireworks show in the distance.

With every blast, Annie's face was illuminated briefly in a soft glow before being shadowed once again by darkness. I watched her worry shift to joy as she watched the fireworks, and light danced in her eyes.

I breathed her in, and the anxiety and stress of the day melted away.

Annie was so much more than my best friend. She was a balm for my tattered soul.

I leaned in, nuzzling my nose against her neck, and breathed her in. Despite my tender ribs, I shifted my body to lean into her. My lips teased the delicate skin of her neck as I gave into my aching need and sucked her pulse point.

"Lee," she breathed, arching into my mouth. "What are we doing?"

"We're forgetting anyone else exists."

TWENTY-ONE
ANNIE

Lee's mouth made it nearly impossible to think of anything else. Only moments before I was about to spill it all. Tell him about the letters and the feelings I had buried for so long out of fear of losing him and his family.

Only, under the attention of his mouth, I couldn't think.

We're forgetting anyone else exists.

Lee traced his thumb down my throat, and a soft moan escaped my lips.

His name caught in my throat and my entire body reacted to his touch. Brushing my hair off my shoulder, Lee continued to tease and kiss my neck. His hand in my hair pulled gently, exposing more of my neck to him.

He tasted. *Savored.*

When he finally moved to my parted, waiting lips, we groaned in unison. He wrapped his tongue around mine, and my hips squirmed. The hard surface of the catwalk bit into the backs of my thighs, and our height only added to the intensity of the moment.

"Come here." Lee's demanding tone sent a bolt of electricity straight to my clit as it throbbed in anticipation.

Lee guided one leg over his lap and onto the platform beside him so I was straddling his hips. He was rock hard beneath me, and my hips moved slowly against him. My back pressed against the slim metal bar that would keep us from falling and the danger only ratcheted up my desire.

Lee's cock nestled dangerously close as my skirt fluttered around us. Only his pants and my underwear separated us.

Lee continued kissing my neck and collarbone, using his firm hands to rock my hips against his lap. Our mouths moved in a desperate, frantic rhythm as the tension thickened between us. Our tongues tangled in deep, long strokes.

His hands moved across my hips and up the valley of my sides, igniting a path of desire across my skin. I was wet and pliant for him. Begging for more as my hips rocked forward.

"Tell me you want this. That you want me." The low growl in his voice was feral, and I ground myself against him even harder.

"I want this. I want you. Right now."

The hot breath of his teasing chuckle danced across my skin. "Right here? Where anyone could see us?"

I glanced over my shoulder. We were high in the air and somewhat hidden from view, so the likelihood of anyone actually seeing us was slim, but the possibility was still there. The thought of getting fucked by Lee Sullivan, *out in the open*, in our spot was overwhelming.

"Yes. Here. Please."

My breasts dragged up and down his chest as my hips swiveled against his erection. Our kisses were frantic as our hands fought to memorize every inch of each other.

"I love this fucking mouth."

On a whimper, I raked my hands through his hair.

Gathering the material of my skirt, Lee's fingers traced up my bare thighs until they reached the seam of my underwear. His thick fingers traced the edge, teasing me.

"Take these off. *Now.*"

Swallowing hard, I shifted my weight to hastily remove my thong. As I did, Lee unbuttoned his shorts, reached in, and pulled out his long, hard cock. My eyes widened at how thick it was. I licked my lips, wanting to drag my tongue across the vein that ran along the side.

"Can I?" I blinked up at him, hoping he understood exactly what I wanted.

His jaw went slack, and he fisted his cock and squeezed. His forearm flexed, and I lowered my mouth to the tip of his cock.

"Just a taste," he warned. "I have plans for that pussy."

I lowered, and my lips parted around the head of his cock. Swirling my tongue, I tasted the salty drop that had already formed at the tip. I hummed in approval and was rewarded with a groan. Licking my lips, I dragged my tongue over that delicious vein from root to tip before gripping the base with my hand and sucking him deep.

He was big. Far too big to take all of him, but I tried my damnedest. Swirling my tongue and pumping the base while I sucked, he moaned, his head tipped back into the darkness. Fireworks were still exploding around us, and I sneaked a glance at him as I licked and sucked. His gorgeous face was tipped to the inky sky, and illuminations of gold and red danced over his face as the fireworks continued in the distance.

Desperate for him, I gave him one last suck before straddling him and pulling his mouth to mine for a kiss.

"I need you. I need more." We were both panting and desperate as he gripped my hovering hips.

Lee pulled a condom from his pocket and ripped it open before rolling it down his length. I watched in eager anticipation of how generously thick and long he was. I inched forward, letting my skirt hide my ass while watching intently as Lee lined the head of his cock up with my entrance.

Achingly slow, Lee's cock stretched me open. "Jesus, you're hot and so fucking tight."

My jaw clenched at how full I was, and it just kept coming—stretching me wider. Filling me up.

"More."

Lee shuddered as I sank lower onto his lap. My nails dug into his shoulders. My pussy clenched around him, and he hissed out a breath.

"Move those hips, baby."

Eagerly, I obliged, rocking my hips as his cock pumped in and out of me. I sank all the way to the base of his dick, my clit was teased with every stroke.

I chanted his name as his hands dove beneath my skirt to grip the flesh of my hips. His fingers slid over my ass, kneading and guiding me as we rocked together. His fingertips smoothed over my butt, diving even deeper to feel where his cock entered me.

"You feel that?" He teased my already sensitive opening as his cock pumped into me. "Feel how much I stretch that cunt open?"

Lee had never dared speak to me in such a way, and it only spurred my desire. My tits bounced in his face, nipples aching to be tasted and teased. "More. I need more."

With a playful grin, Lee's fingertips dragged higher, skating over my ass. I clenched, never having been touched there before and loving the feel of his hands across every inch of me.

"Pull your knees up."

Adjusting my footing, I pulled my knees higher as he sank even deeper, eliciting a cry from me. As he thrust, I gave up my last shreds of control and clung to him. Pressure built low in my spine as his cock continued to pull me closer and closer to release.

Lee grunted as he fucked me, and I rode his cock. His hands smoothed up my back, pulling my chest closer to him as we both panted.

"I can feel how close you are. I want to feel your cum drip down the sides of my cock."

His filthy words, whispered harshly against my ear, were exactly what I needed to crest that hill of my orgasm. Rippling waves of release washed over me as I came.

"Give it to me. More." He pumped into me as I ground down on him in one clenching stroke. He broke, moaning into my neck as he pulsed inside me.

His hard body stilled. "Annette."

I collapsed on him, allowing his body to hold my weight as I relished the feeling of sex with Lee.

The fireworks had quieted, but my heart maintained a steady thumping. "Looks like we missed the show."

Lee looked up at me, smiling. "I didn't miss a damn thing."

He studied my face, and I bit back the litany of things I wanted to say to him. Everything had changed. I could hardly breathe.

Slowly, I lifted myself off his lap and sat on the catwalk beside him. The streets of Outtatowner were eerily quiet, only a few cars circling the town square. I looked around and found my underwear, still soaked through. I balled them into my fist. "Well, these are ruined," I teased.

Lee removed the condom before tucking himself back

into his shorts. "One of many. Maybe next time don't even bother with underwear."

I swatted at his shoulder, relieved that our playful banter was still intact despite the monumental shift our friendship had just taken.

"You're awfully cocky."

A slow smirk spread across his handsome face. "You didn't seem to mind."

My laugh burst out into the night sky. "Definitely not. I'll be lucky if I can walk."

When I looked at Lee, he grinned and winked. "Don't worry. I can carry you."

I sighed and leaned into him, letting my head rest against his muscular shoulder. For once, I let myself enjoy the quiet solitude of our water tower. Finally, when I couldn't take the questions swirling in my mind, I sighed. "So it's you and me, huh?"

His lips pressed into my hair. "Glad you're finally catching up."

I tilted my head to grin at him. My stomach swooped at the soft way Lee looked at me.

He dropped a kiss on my forehead. "It's always been you, baby."

TWENTY-TWO
LEE

I SMELLED HER BRIGHT, sunshine scent before even opening my eyes. Tightening my arms, I held Annie's body against mine. Draped across my chest was a riot of auburn curls. I buried my nose in her hair and stilled.

I wanted to live in that moment forever.

Memorize every detail. The way her nose tipped up at the end. The freckles that danced across the bridge of her nose. The soft arm that draped across my abs and how her thighs caged my leg as if she were afraid I'd disappear somewhere in the middle of the night.

As if I could ever leave.

Annie's breathing was steady and even. We'd stayed up well past midnight, exploring this new aspect of our friendship. Before we'd even made it through the door of my apartment, I was hoisting Annie over my shoulder and grabbing another handful of her ass. I headed straight for my bedroom, and we never came up for air.

I was all too happy to drown in her.

Annie shifted and let out an adorable little morning moan.

"Good morning, sunshine."

She groaned and stretched before looking up at me. "You're still here."

I chuckled and looked down at her sleepy face. "It's my apartment. Where was I gonna go?"

Annie smiled and buried herself deeper into the nook of my arm. My bruised ribs protested against her embrace, but I bundled her closer.

For years I'd done impressive work of avoiding this very scenario. Waking up with my latest hookup in tangled sheets was a strict *no fucking way*. Usually after my dates got their fill, they were eager to pack up their shit and leave to tell their friends all about it.

But this was different. *She* was radically different.

Nothing about Annie could be compared to any other woman I'd ever been with. With them, I was careful not to reveal too much of myself or ever be vulnerable. I was good for a fun time—always the happiest guy in the room.

But Annie knew damn near everything about me. Over the years I'd given pieces of my true self to her, and she'd never turned away. Not once.

A sharp sting dug into my side.

It was inevitable that I was going to fuck this up, and it was going to hurt like hell to lose her.

Not. Fucking. Happening.

I had no clue how I was going to ever be enough for her, but I refused to go down without a fight.

"What's with this?" Annie peered up at me and pressed her index finger between my eyebrows, massaging out the furrow that had settled there.

Tension eased when I looked into her sleepy blue eyes. I should have known one look from her would make everything feel less daunting. I trailed my fingertips up her bare spine, then wrapped my fingers around her hip bone and pulled her even closer.

"How are the ribs?"

I shifted my torso, testing out the screaming pang that accompanied every movement. "Sore."

Concern flooded her eyes. "I'm sorry if we were too . . . athletic."

A laugh tumbled out of me, followed by a wince. "It was worth it, I promise. Come here." I shifted my weight, rolling to ease the pressure on my side while holding Annie beneath me. I took her in. Warm and naked and looking up at me with trusting eyes.

Light marks decorated her pale skin as I looked over her neck, chest, and tits. Possessiveness washed over me, and a single thought came to mind.

Mine.

"You are so fucking beautiful, Annette."

Blushing, Annie buried her face into my shoulder. I shrugged her off. "I'm serious. I've always thought so but never had the balls to tell you. You're stunning."

On a laugh, she squirmed beneath me. "Well, Lee Sullivan . . ." Her fingers dusted across my chest, down my back, and grabbed my ass. "You are hot as fuck."

My cock thickened at her touch, her playfulness. "Annie Crane? Do you have a secret crush on me?"

Her giggle was effervescent. Warmth and love spread through me.

Her eyes widened with humor. "Big crush. Huge."

I moved my hips against her, savoring how her legs opened for me and how my cock nestled between them. "Scandalous. What would the Bluebirds say? Everyone knows when it comes to women, I'm only good for one thing."

Annie's hand found the side of my face. Her eyes searched mine with a sudden seriousness. "Hey." I looked at her, hoping my humor would hide my shame, but she managed to stare past my defenses. "I have never thought that and never will. I know you, Lee. I'm not here *despite* who you think you are . . . I'm here with you *because* of the man I know you are."

If I wasn't already so far gone for that woman, it would have been the exact moment I fell in love with her. Only with Annie, it was a lifetime of falling for her.

Annie had never disregarded me as a player, like everyone else had. Instead, she'd fought to look beyond my shields to see *me*.

It was disorienting.

Overwhelming.

Intoxicating.

Everything I'd told myself was an impossibility was staring up at me like I'd hung the moon, and the only emotion I could muster was sheer panic.

I needed time. I needed to figure out how the hell I was going to show up and be the kind of man that Annie deserved, and I needed to do it before she figured out that she'd given herself to a man who had no fucking clue what he was doing.

"I'll make it worth your while." With a sly smile, I trailed a hand down her torso and between her legs.

On a soft moan, she arched into me, but shifted. "I have to go. I'm packing up today."

My brows pinched forward. "Packing?"

Annie stretched and slid away before sitting at the edge of my bed. With her arms overhead, she reached toward the ceiling before dropping her hands and looking at me over her shoulder. "Time's up on the apartment. I convinced JP

King to give me more time on the storefront, but I can't afford both the apartment and storefront since the rent increased."

I shook my head. *Fucking Kings.*

"Oh, but don't worry." She looked over her shoulder with a sly smile. "I already texted him and let him know I'd be moving all my—and I quote—*thongs* this week. I wanted to die of embarrassment." A short burst of quiet laughter made her shoulders shake. "Freaking autocorrect."

My palm moved across her back and over her curves. "He can think about your thongs all he wants. You're mine."

The subtle bite on her lower lip let me know my words landed exactly as I'd intended. Still, unease clung to my ribs. "Where are you going to go?"

Annie gathered the clothing scattered around my room. "Emma is letting me stay on her couch for a while. Just until I find something to rent that's not too expensive. I'll have better luck once the tourist season is over."

I sat up, gathering the sheets at my waist and frowning at her. No way in hell Annie was couch surfing, but what other option was there?

Move in. Let's go all in on this thing and see what happens.

The mere thought of living with Annie brought warring emotions of elation and total dread. Opening myself up completely was a mistake I'd made with Margo and not something I was in a hurry to repeat. It was safer to make sure I wasn't royally fucking things up with Annie by moving too fast.

But I could take care of her.

Finding her shirt tangled in the sheets, I playfully tossed it in her direction. "Get dressed. I have an idea."

~

STANDING at the threshold of the apartment above the barn at Highfield House, I swung the door open. "Home sweet home."

Annie looked at me before stepping inside. "Lee, what did you do?"

I shrugged. "I called and asked Aunt Tootie for a favor. With Lark and Wyatt building their place, you've got them nearby, but no one's using the apartment."

In high school, the small apartment had been the location of many, many Sullivan parties. Friends would dare each other to explore the giant, creepy-ass barn downstairs, and the apartment became a teenage gathering place of sorts. When Lark came to Outtatowner, Tootie had cleaned it up and offered the unused space for her to live while she nannied for Wyatt. It wasn't long before those two were hooking up and she moved in.

The apartment was perfect until I could figure out how to convince her I wasn't going anywhere.

How was I ever going to manage to keep her?

Annie twirled in the kitchen and sighed. "I've always loved this place."

I smiled. "I know."

Annie moved to the window, then separated the curtains and looked out across the driveway to Highfield House. "It's the dreamiest farmhouse. There's so much potential, you know?"

I swallowed thickly. Annie always saw potential in everything—mean old dogs, ancient farmhouses, playboys who peaked in high school.

"Will you live here for now? Please?"

She turned with a wide grin and a nod. "I think I can make it work."

I exhaled in relief. "Thank god. I thought you were going to be a pain in the ass and make me take you over my knee to get you to agree."

Playful desire flashed in her eyes. "Well . . . if that's on the table, then . . ." Annie crossed her arms with defiance glittering in her eyes. "I refuse."

She twirled, taunting me with a wiggle of that full, round ass.

I swatted her butt, and her playful yelp and giggle calmed my nerves. I followed as Annie walked through the space, letting her hand drag against the well-worn laminate countertops.

"Man." She sighed. "I haven't been up here in years."

I tucked my hands into my pockets and rocked back on my heels. "Lark dressed it up a bit when she was staying here, but since she moved in with Wyatt, it's been empty. I talked with Tootie, and she said that you could stay here as long as you need to. Rent free."

The apartment kitchen was small but had everything she might need to be comfortable—microwave, fridge, oven and stove, and a small dining table in the center with four chairs tucked beneath it.

The space opened to a living room that was only slightly larger. The sofa was sturdy, but I knew from a few nights laid out on it that it was worn and lumpy in spots. It would have to do for now.

In the corner, next to a side table that had a vase and some fake flowers in it, was the infamous green chair. A lifetime ago I had dubbed it my lucky chair because, well, I'd gotten lucky on it plenty of times. Suddenly the humor of broadcasting my conquests faded, and I hated seeing that chair in what was now Annie's space.

Her eyes tracked mine to where I scowled down at the recliner. "Well, look at that. The lucky chair has survived all this time."

Annie ran a fingertip across one of the armrests.

I shook my head. "Lark swears she has cleaned that thing within an inch of its life, but . . ." I shrugged. "I'll haul it out of here for you."

More than just haul it out, I wanted to burn that fucking thing.

"But, Lee . . ." Annie sat in the chair and seductively crossed one leg over the other. "This is your *lucky* chair."

She then spread her knees wide, and my eyes burned a path up her leg to where her shorts were cut dangerously high. I wanted to be strong, to be a good man, knowing full well she deserved more than getting fucked in my lucky chair, but *goddamn*.

Annie's fingertips started at her knees and trailed a path up her voluptuous thighs. "Don't you want to make me come?"

She teased the edge of her denim shorts, pulling them to the side and revealing nothing but a thin swatch of baby blue covering her pussy.

The truth was I *did* want to fuck her on that chair. I wanted to fill her so hard and so damn deep. Knowing she would be the last woman to ever touch it before I set the whole thing ablaze in a bonfire. And Annie *would* be the last woman I'd ever touch on that goddamn chair.

I walked to her, taking my time as I crossed the living room. My eyes were locked on her body as I licked my lower lip.

I palmed my cock through my pants. "Slip off those

shorts, baby. Show me that pretty little cunt before I bury my face between your legs."

Her breath whooshed out as she undid the button and lowered the zipper before shimmying out of her denim shorts.

"That's good, baby. I like when you do what I say."

"I like when you tell me what to do," she answered with a tip of her eyebrow.

"Then pull your tits out of that fucking tank top."

With a swallow and a sly smile, Annie lowered the straps of her tank top and undid her bra. Her tits bounced with their weight, and my cock throbbed in anticipation.

I sank to my knees in front of her and used my hands to roughly grab her hips and pull her to the edge of the seat. My fingers hooked into the waistband of her underwear as I peeled them down her thighs and tossed them aside.

"There's no one here watching. No one to catch us. It's just you and me."

"I know." Her breath came out in little pants. "But I want this."

"That's good. I just want you to know that when I eat this pussy, I'm not doing it for anyone else. I'm doing it for me."

I used my teeth to nibble up her thigh. Her hands found her breasts, tweaking her nipples as I took my time licking and teasing her soft skin. Her hips rocked against me as I denied her the pressure she desperately wanted, opting instead to lick and tease in gentle strokes of my tongue.

One hand threaded through my hair, and the rake of her nails against my scalp sent shivers down my spine. I dove in, devouring her, pouring every ounce of myself into making her feel good. Gripping her hips, I pulled her into my face.

My tongue slid over her ass as I worked my way to her

pussy, claiming every inch of her as mine. When she clenched against my tongue, I teased her opening with a stroke of my finger.

Fingering her tight little pussy, I licked her clit as she moaned. "More."

"I've got you."

"Oh my god, Lee, I'm so close. Don't stop."

"Baby, I'm not stopping until you're screaming my name." I worked her until she was bucking against my face, her back arching off the faded green fabric of the chair.

Crying out my name, she came. Every muscle of her body tensed around me and I pressed my palm on her stomach to hold her down as I continued teasing and stroking until the last ripples of her orgasm quelled. She sank into the plush fabric of the chair as I feathered kisses down her thigh and across her knee.

She stroked my hair as I tenderly loved on her. "Hey, Annie?" I looked up at her, willing her to see the emotions that swelled inside my chest.

She hummed, still unable to speak.

"This is the best day of my life. Hands down."

TWENTY-THREE
ANNIE

The Bluebird Book Club was a club that dreams were made of—sweet friends, the occasional smutty book, and lots and lots of booze. Feeling lighter than air, with my arms loaded down with a few bottles of Prosecco, I followed the voices coming from the back of Bluebird Books. Nestled in the reading nook, the Bluebirds sat in chairs and on cozy couches and cushy poufs. The familiar scent of old pages and fresh coffee filled my senses.

"Hey, gals!" I smiled and greeted everyone from Sylvie and MJ King to my high school chemistry teacher.

Women from all ages and walks of life in town—King, Sullivan, and everyone in between—came together as a part of the Bluebird Book Club. Outtatowner, Michigan, may be a small coastal town, but the gossip flowed like waves crashing on the shore. The Bluebird Book Club was a source of friendship and connection.

It was my happy place.

I deposited the bottles at the makeshift bar before popping the cork on one and pouring myself a healthy portion.

Raising the glass, I called out, "Cheers, ladies!"

I took a sip, and the fizzing bubbles tickled my nose. Conversations flowed around me as I settled into a worn-in high-back chair. I loved that chair. It cupped my butt perfectly.

As I settled into my usual spot, surrounded by friends and familiar faces, a sense of belonging washed over me. The Bluebird Book Club had become my sanctuary, a place where I could escape the uncertainties of life and indulge in laughter and friendship.

Tonight that sanctuary was exactly what I needed.

Kate and Lark were on either side of me with Kate leaned in and gushing over her latest *Home Again* project. A mixture of determination and dreamy happiness washed over her face. I was so happy for my friend. After a rocky path of wasted years dating a total asshole, she'd found her happily-ever-after—with her ex-boyfriend's hotter older brother, of all people.

Soon the discussion shifted to the upcoming date remix. Excitement and anticipation simmered throughout the group. Nothing was more exciting than stirring up a little drama in Outtatowner. The remix was a chance for those paired up in the auction to get a second chance with someone they were more suited to. I immediately glanced at Sylvie, who was practically salivating at the idea of *anyone* other than Stumpy Larson.

My heart skipped a beat as I listened, knowing I was still matched with Lee.

Suddenly a hushed whisper reached my ears. "Annie, have you heard? Charles wants to be paired with you for the date remix." MJ King leaned in, her eyes sparkling with mischief.

I blinked, caught off guard by the unexpected revelation. In the time Charles had been in Outtatowner, the suave sommelier had made quite an impression on the women of the town.

But the crush I had once harbored on him no longer held its appeal. Rather, it fell flat and out of place.

I mustered a smile. "Oh, really? That's . . . flattering."

"Charles can get bent." Kate shot a disgusted sound out of her nose, and Lark nearly choked on her vodka soda.

MJ's knowing gaze didn't escape me. She had always been perceptive, able to read between the lines. She leaned closer, her voice filled with concern. "Are you going to take him up on it? I mean . . . this could finally mean the next step for you two."

My heart skipped another beat as I thought of Lee.

The next step.

At one time, I'd hoped that Charles would be interested in something more than casual dates at random intervals. He was polished and charming and sophisticated. The only problem was, he wasn't Lee. And now that things between Lee and me had shifted, I couldn't imagine going back to feeling the same way about Charles.

"I'll take him." Sylvie King leaned in, inserting herself into the conversation. Her eyes were steady and serious, as they often were.

"You're interested in being matched with Charles?" MJ reared back and looked at her sister in dismay.

Sylvie shrugged. "I'd literally take *anyone* at this point," she whispered.

A titter of giggles erupted between our fivesome, and we all agreed that Stumpy was the *worst*.

I raised my glass. "He's all yours."

With determined eyes, Sylvie stood and marched up to where Tootie, Bug, and several other women were arranging, then rearranging, names on a board to come up with fresh combinations.

I genuinely hoped Sylvie and Charles had a fun time together. Despite the fact she was a King and a touch more reserved than her sweet-natured, outgoing little sister, Sylvie had a quiet kindness about her. Maybe she and Charles would hit it off.

"How did the move-in go?" Lark asked me, pulling my attention away from the remix.

"Totally fine. I'm all settled in. It's a cute place. Thanks again."

Lark laughed. "Don't thank me. I'm thrilled to have you close by! Besides, you're family." Her hand found my knee and squeezed. My heart thumped.

I'm family now, but what if things don't work out with Lee? Would you still feel the same?

Tamping down the intrusive thoughts, I forced a smile.

Kate leaned over. "Please tell me you burned that god-awful chair."

I blinked, schooling my face and willing the heat forming in my chest not to move north to my cheeks and totally give us away.

"I tried to throw it away," Lark cut in, "but Wyatt said it was Lee's ceremonial chair or some shit." She put both palms up. "I have no idea."

Kate made a gagging sound, and we laughed.

Was it wrong that I was more than happy to be counted among the women to be thoroughly fucked by Lee Sullivan on that green chair? Probably.

Did I still smile every time the chair caught my eye? You're damn right.

~

THE SUN KISSED my skin as I stood on the beach, taking in the sight of the sandcastle competition and sand volleyball games. It was the much-anticipated Beach Games date.

My heart raced with a mix of excitement and nervous anticipation.

As I watched Lee approach, he pulled a wagon with an arsenal of professional sandcastle-building tools—shovels, trowels, buckets in different sizes with the bottoms cut out, even a bristle brush.

I tipped my face to the sun and laughed.

"Seriously?" I eyed the tools. "Are we building a sand kingdom?"

He grinned, mischief dancing in his eyes. "You bet. We're not just here to participate. We're here to dominate."

His playful banter and intense stare sent shivers down my spine. He sauntered up to me, wrapping one arm around my middle and kissing me, right in front of everyone and without a care in the world. The sexual tension between us was palpable, growing stronger with each touch.

I pulled away. Internally, I was still navigating this uncharted territory of a romantic relationship with Lee, totally unsure of how to proceed. But every touch, every stolen kiss, ignited a fire within me that refused to be ignored.

Bug and Tootie stood before the crowd, pointing out the roped-off area for the sandcastles, introducing the newly matched couples, and giving the rules for the judges.

When Lee looked at me with determined eyes, I wiggled my eyebrows. As we began constructing our sand-castle, Lee's competitive streak took over. He meticulously molded the sand, his focused gaze fixed on our creation. The sand flew as he expertly sculpted turrets and intricate details. My background in pottery made it easy to get the sand-to-water ratio right, and while others struggled with crumbling structures, ours were built and stacked with ease.

"Let's get the basic structures done, and then you can add the magic."

"Magic?" I swiped a hand across my sweaty forehead.

Lee waved a hand over the rough sandcastle. "Yeah . . . all the cool designs and shit."

I barked out a laugh and shook my head.

"Then," he added, "we'll add the best part."

My head whipped in his direction. I knew that tone.

"Lee."

He wouldn't look at me.

"Lee. What do you have planned?"

He grinned and my insides turned to mush. "How do you feel about being buried?"

I shook my head and refocused on constructing a castle turret and etching out the windows. Sneaking glances, I watched him, admiration mingled with a touch of unease. I couldn't help but wonder if I was different from the many women who had captured Lee's attention in the past. Was I just another conquest? Would he eventually lose interest and move on, leaving me with a heart shattered into a million pieces?

My rambling thoughts were interrupted by the boisterous presence of Royal King. He was a few spaces down, pulling his usual showboating antics, drawing attention and laughter from the crowd. Next to him, his sister Sylvie was patting sand as Charles mounded more nearby. Neither spoke to each other, but Sylvie no longer looked like she was about to run away.

I chuckled to myself, shaking my head.

Lee leaned over and nudged me with his shoulder. "Hey, fuck that guy."

I pinched my eyebrows.

Lee gestured with his shovel toward Charles. "He snoozed, he lose'd."

"I don't think that's how the expression goes," I teased.

Lee gave me a smile that made my insides go liquid. "Hey, come here. I want to tell you something."

I leaned forward. As I did, he peered down my bathing suit top and popped a quick kiss on my cheek.

Blushing, I sat back on my heels. "You're a pig."

He winked and I fell a little more in love.

Lee continued to shape our sandcastle. His commitment to impressing me, to making us stand out from the crowd, meant more than he could ever know. It was in that moment that my doubts about his seriousness and intentions gently started to fade away, replaced by a glimmer of hope.

Next to the intricate castle, Lee had dug a wide, oblong hole. "Okay, Annie." He gestured to the opening.

"What?"

He gestured again. "Get in."

"Get in the hole? No way."

"Come on. You're the mermaid. I was going to make the sand piled on top look like a fin."

I leveled him with my stare. "You have the artistic talent of a three-year-old. You get in."

He knew I was right, and with a determined nod, Lee whipped off his shirt and centered himself in the hole as I quickly piled wet sand over his legs. Reaching around, he pulled the wide fabric belt from my bathing suit cover-up and wrapped it around his chest in a faux mermaid bra.

I burst out laughing and used a trowel to etch a scale design into the tail fin. Lee giggled like a schoolgirl, wiggling the sand with his toes.

"Don't move," I warned, stifling a fresh round of giggles. I stood, wiping sand off my butt. "I'll grab the judges!"

Racing across the sand, I found the three judges. As we approached, Lee leaned into his mermaid routine, batting his lashes and wiggling his fingers in a wave to the judges. My fingers pressed into my lips to keep from laughing. Though they were trying to appear impartial, I could tell by the humor in their eyes that we had a strong chance to win. When they walked away, I tackled Lee to the ground and peppered his face with kisses.

He quickly took over, rolling me and pressing my back into the warm sand. I laughed freely as Lee peppered kisses down my neck and collarbone.

"Hey, hey." Tootie looked down at us and smiled. "There are kids around." She winked as Lee rolled off me and helped to pull me up.

"Sorry, Aunt Tootie. Just got carried away." Lee had the sense to look guilty as his aunt reprimanded us.

"Well, I am happy to present to you the prize for Best Sandcastle. Congratulations!"

Tootie handed us a certificate and a basket full of wine, cheeses, and desserts. Lee set the basket down and hoisted me into the air.

My squeal of laughter floated across the water as he charged toward the lake and dunked us in the cool water, drowning me in love for him.

TWENTY-FOUR
LEE

It was a bit of a shame that the sand volleyball portion of the date ended early after Sullivans and Kings got into a shoving match over an out-of-bounds call, but it was worth it.

Fuck those guys.

After a dressing down by both Tootie and Bug, the teams decided to call it a draw and end the night early. Not that I minded—it only meant that I'd have more time alone with Annie. I couldn't seem to get enough of her.

Even before our relationship took a U-turn into *more than friendship* territory, she was always someone I never seemed to get sick of. Annie was generous, kind, and always knew how to have fun. Now that the fun included mind-blowing sex, it was damn near perfect.

Kissed by the sun, Annie's pinked skin had a glow to it as she circled my kitchen. After the beach date, she'd insisted on stopping at her place to shower. I let her know to pack an overnight bag and didn't miss the sweet smile that earned me.

Back at my place, she popped her head into the fridge,

as she'd done a thousand times before, but instead of looking away like I'd trained myself to do, I watched and appreciated the curve of her ass as she bent over.

A powerful feeling built inside me.

Possessiveness.

There was something bone-achingly right about having Annie there—comfortable and taking up *my* space.

Humming some tune in her head, her body moved as she scavenged for a snack.

"You better watch what you're doing with that thing."

Annie smiled at me over her shoulder and added an extra little wiggle. Desire unfurled in my gut.

"*Fuck.*"

Her head whipped around to watch me as I reached down to palm my thickening cock through my shorts.

"Don't look surprised. That little body of yours has been getting me hard for years." I strode toward her, still holding my dick through my shorts, aching to be buried inside her. Annie turned and leaned her back against the fridge. Her lower lip tucked between her teeth as one knee came up and she scissored her legs in a squirm.

I towered over her, reveling in the way her eyes darkened as they dilated. The pulse in her neck hammered at the base.

Tension and heat crackled between us, and our eyes locked. My hand moved up her side until my palm found her collarbone and then encircled her throat in a possessive grip.

"Tell me again," she whispered.

My hand flexed. "I denied myself this—told myself you were off limits, but now? Now that I've had you, there's no going back. You're mine."

Her hands gripped my hips as I shifted forward,

pinning her against the fridge and letting her feel just how badly I wanted her.

"Lee," she breathed. "This feels impossible."

"The only thing that's impossible is denying this thing between us. Looking back, it's so fucking obvious. It was inevitable."

My mouth crashed to her as I pinned her against the refrigerator. Her hands spread across my back, and her hips bucked forward. I smoothed my hands down her arms, tightening my grip at her wrists and holding her in place while my mouth moved down her neck.

I dug deep to move slowly, taking my time memorizing every inch of her skin. My body, and my heart, demanding more of her.

All of her.

I wanted to fuck her long and hard until she was as helpless as I was. Her hands flexed against my restraint, and she whimpered. I secured both wrists in one hand, as I dipped my fingers down the front of her shorts to slip into her pussy.

Wet and warm. My fingers came back soaked.

"Needy fucking girl." I admired how slick my finger was before sucking it with a moan. "I figured you'd be hot and tight, but I never imagined you'd be so sweet."

Annie gasped after I kissed her again, sharing her taste and swallowing the sexy moan that rattled from her to me. Desire tightened in my spine, settling low between my legs. Grabbing the backs of her thighs, I spread her open and lifted her. The bedroom was too far. Setting her on the couch, I crawled over her, never letting our bodies separate. Her hands tore at my shirt. When I helped her remove it, her fingers danced across my muscles, and I flexed for her, appreciating the desire that flashed in her eyes.

I cupped her breasts, hating the thin T-shirt that covered her incredible body. The V in the collar hid her freckled skin, and I wanted more.

"Is this shirt special?" I asked, already gripping the fabric at the collar.

She shook her head and tilted her hips. It was all the go-ahead I needed before ripping the shirt down the middle. Her tits bounced with the force of the ripping fabric. Back at her place, Annie had changed out of her swimsuit and into a light-pink lace bra that highlighted her tanned skin. Through the flimsy material, I could make out the perfect circles of her nipples. Her fingers fumbled for my waistband. When she slipped the button free and pulled the zipper down, her eyes went wide. I hadn't bothered with underwear after my own shower.

Repositioning Annie to the edge of the couch, I knelt on the floor, pulling her hips toward me. I ran a hand down her torso, worshipping her body splayed out in front of me.

"Don't. Move."

Annie bit her lip, wiggling in her jean shorts. "Or what?"

I pointed at her as I rose. "Fuck around and find out."

Her hand brushed across her abdomen, then disappeared down the front of her shorts. She moaned and tipped her hips up, then fingered her pussy with a soft moan.

"Such a brat." I shook my head and hurried to the bedroom, where I grabbed a condom and some lube.

When I returned to the living room, Annie had slipped off her shorts but left her matching pale-pink thong. Her hand was still tucked inside, playing with herself.

I dropped my shorts and knelt between her knees. My hard cock throbbed, knowing only the lacy fabric separated me and her tight, wet cunt. "You don't like to listen, do you?"

Her body rolled as she teased herself.

I quickly closed her knees and gripped her hips. In a single continuous movement, I flipped her, bending her over the couch and shifting her ass into the air.

I ran kisses up her backside to her lower back before hooking my fingers into the top of her underwear and slowly pulling them down. "I like you like this. Bent over, ass up. Offering it all to me."

I ran a fingertip down her ass and through her pussy. Her hips pushed against me, begging for more. I leaned over her to whisper in her ear. "I'm dying to be buried inside you, but once I am, I don't want to be gentle or go slow. I'm telling you right now, I'm fucking you hard tonight."

Thrusting two fingers deep inside her, she sucked in a gasp, her pussy tightening around my fingers. She was dripping, a trail of wetness slipping down her inner thigh. I worked my fingers, reveling in the way her hands clutched at the sofa while I teased her.

"God, I love watching how perfectly that cunt stretches for me."

"Please. Now," she begged.

Biting back a smile, I gripped my cock with my free hand to tease more parts of her. I stroked her clit with the head as my fingers stretched her open.

"Fuck, you have no idea how badly I want to sink this cock into you."

She looked at me over her shoulder, mouth parted and panting. "Do it. Please."

My teeth ground together. I was inches away from her hot, wet pussy, and I wanted nothing more than to feel her grip me with nothing between us. Fucking without a condom was an unbreakable rule. I'd always been careful.

But goddamn is she tempting.

"If that's what you want, tell me. Tell me you want me to fuck you bare."

"Oh my god."

I loved how my filthy words left her rattled and breathless.

"Tell me."

"I want you bare." She arched her back. "I'm on the pill. We're good."

I teased her entrance with the head of my cock and stroked my fingertips down her spine. "You are more than good, baby. You're fucking perfect."

With a tiny thrust, I fed her an inch.

Then another.

Slowly sinking into her, I pushed past her tightening walls until I was balls deep inside her. "Annette," I groaned, unable to handle how perfect she felt.

Her ass pushed against me, and I responded by pumping in and out of her. "That's my girl. You look so good, ass up, taking all of me."

A guttural moan streamed out of her as I set a rhythm. One hand slid forward, working her clit as I filled her.

"So fucking wet." If I wasn't careful, her body's response would put me over the edge before I made sure she could come, and that wouldn't do. In long, deep strokes, I filled her. I grabbed a handful of her plump ass and splayed my other hand across her back, holding her down against the couch as I fucked her.

Her moans grew more frantic, and she clenched tighter around me. My dick throbbed in anticipation. She was so close. Over the years I had craved Annie in a thousand different ways. Only in tortured solitude had I ever allowed myself to fantasize about my best friend, but there she was. Seconds from coming and eagerly taking every inch of me.

"You're going to come, and then I'm going to fill your tight little cunt, but I won't be done with you. Do you understand?"

Annie only moaned and clenched against me.

I cupped her chin, forcing her eyes to mine as I pounded into her. White-hot tension built at the base of my spine as I gritted my teeth. "I said, 'Do you understand?'"

"Yes, sir."

Her willful compliance broke us both. Waves of her orgasm squeezed me as I pumped in and out. Seconds later, my fist found her curly hair and I held her in place, filling her with long pulses of my own orgasm.

Annie sighed against the couch as I lazily slid in and out of her, enjoying the view of my pleasure mixed with hers, coating my dick. I pulled out of her, watching my cum seep down her thighs.

The urge to possess her completely was so fucking strong.

I trailed my fingers past her dripping cunt, using her own cum as lube to press a finger against her ass in a test.

To see if she would take me.

She moaned. *Fuck, she is too tempting.*

With one finger I continued to tease that forbidden little spot, while another gently stroked the soft skin of her back, tracing goose bumps as they erupted across her delicate skin. Reaching forward, I found her breast and gently pinched her hard nipple, then pushed another finger inside her ass.

"Holy fuck, Lee."

I had never been so hard so quickly. Only moments

after finishing and my dick was already perking up for round two. I was a desperate man. I fisted my cock and began to stroke.

Lifting her, I turned her body so her ass hung off the edge of the couch—so I could see her beautiful face.

To watch her take my cock again.

Grabbing the bottle of lube I'd dropped beside me, I covered my cock in the slippery liquid and stroked. With my free hand, I ran a finger down her pussy and teased her ass again. One finger, then two.

"Don't stop." Her blue eyes were hazy and wild with desire.

I let her watch as I stroked my cock and toyed with her ass.

"Come on, baby. Spread yourself wide for me."

Annie did as I'd instructed, lifting her knees and putting herself on display. I growled, seeing both of her holes glistening with our sex.

The need for her was overwhelming. I moved forward, running my cock through her pussy and lower, teasing her ass with the head of my dick. I took my time, massaging her with my fingers, gently teasing her with my cock.

A tiny smile spread on her face as she bit her bottom lip. "It's okay." Her voice was shy but thick with desire. "I want it."

I braced her feet, letting her lower back rest comfortably on the edge as her ass taunted me. I aligned the tip of my cock at her ass and let the head slip in, just until her tight little opening cinched over the crown.

My eyes rolled back as the heat and pressure of her tight hole overwhelmed me. The hiss of her breath had me opening my eyes. "You okay, baby?"

"Fuck, Lee. Oh my god, yes."

I gave her another inch, sliding easily into her. "Still okay?"

She nodded. "Play with my pussy."

A wolfish grin spread across my face as my hand found her clit. Annie's back relaxed, and she opened for me.

"Yes. God, yes. Play with me and fuck my ass."

I grunted, gently stroking in and out of her. I found a gentle rhythm, sliding in and out of her ass as I stroked and teased her clit.

It was incredible to watch her pussy clench as I teased and fucked her. I slipped my thumb in, giving her cunt something to squeeze, and her silky muscles rippled as I stroked out another orgasm. My cock ached with how tight she gripped me. I pulled out with a tortured moan before one final tug and letting my cum paint her chest and neck.

We were both breathless.

One arm flung over her forehead. "What the hell did you do to me?"

I chuckled, sitting back on my heels and taking her in.

"I feel so used, but like . . . in the best way."

My hand ran up her thigh. I had tried to be gentle but still needed to check in with her. "You sure you're okay?"

"I'm fantastic."

"Okay." I shifted to stand. "Don't move, and this time I mean it."

TWENTY-FIVE
ANNIE

It was official.

Lee Sullivan had ruined me for all future men.

Shit. Even past men paled in comparison.

I was still recovering, splayed out on his couch, when he came back with a determined look in his eye. Without a word, he scooped me up like I weighed nothing and held me in his arms. His nose buried in my hair as I sighed into his embrace.

Holding me, he made his way to the bathroom, where the tub was steaming and filling with bubbles.

"What's all this?"

Lee set me on my feet and tenderly stroked my hair. Instead of answering, he smiled down at me. Warmth and adoration shone in his eyes, and a swell of overwhelming emotion filled my chest.

"You relax. Get cleaned up. I've got a surprise for you."

I fucking *lived* for surprises, and Lee knew it. My toes danced, and I lifted to pop a kiss on his mouth.

With a smile and wink, Lee left me alone in the bathroom. It was as meticulous as the rest of his apartment but, feeling brave, I snooped. His tidy drawers were the opposite of my overflowing ones, with only a few basic toiletries. Studying the neat row with deodorant, toothpaste, and a toothbrush, I reached in and twisted the toothbrush, making it cockeyed, and slid the drawer shut.

Much better.

Feeling deliciously used up, I stepped into the hot bathwater and sank below the surface. He'd clearly used his bodywash to create the sad layer of bubbles, but I was all too happy to be enveloped in his clean, masculine scent. My ass was a bit tender, but mostly my pussy was swollen in the best way, and the warm water helped ease the tension in my aching muscles.

My eyes flew open when Lee's tender touch stroked down my jawline. I sat up, sloshing water around the tub. Blinking, I looked around. "I must have fallen asleep." Embarrassment stained my cheeks.

"You looked peaceful, but I didn't want you to drown. I don't have time to hide a body today."

I giggled and playfully rolled my eyes before gently tugging his arm. "Get in here."

Lee stood and stepped over the edge to join me in the bathtub. Before he lowered, I put a hand up. "Stop."

Staring, with his hips in front of me, I spotted a tattoo on his upper thigh I had never noticed before.

I pointed. "What is that?"

Standing in front of me with his thick dick at eye level, he stroked down his abs, along his cock, and brushed his fingertips across the faded ink. "It's my favorite tattoo."

"A flower?" I studied the intricate line work of the tattoo. It wasn't masculine and dark like most of his other tattoos. Instead, it was dainty and feminine. Since it rode high on his upper thigh, it was no wonder I'd never seen it, but in that there was a sense of wonder. I loved that after all these years, there was still so much to learn about my best friend.

"Not just any flower. It's a flower called dianthus 'Annette.'" I blinked as his hand covered the frilly flower design. "It keeps me grounded."

Reaching up, I gently slid his hand away to look at it again. The delicate lines were a faded slate gray and not the harsh black of a fresh tattoo. My heart lodged in my throat. "This tattoo . . . it isn't new." Realization flooded through me.

Lee sank into the tub, leveling his eyes with mine. His fingertips brushed down my cheekbones. "Nope."

"But, Lee . . ." My eyes ping-ponged between his.

I watched the muscles in his neck work as he swallowed. "I've had this a long time, Annette." Despite the earth-tilting news he'd just delivered, Lee smiled and turned my body so he could nestle in behind me.

He rested his head on my shoulder, pulling me in close. "Hey," he whispered.

I only hummed, my mind spiraling in a thousand new directions.

"This is the best day of my life."

I pinched my eyes closed, completely lost as to how I could possibly express the jumble of emotions I was feeling. Only one thing I knew for certain. I was going to tell Lee about the letters, and it was going to change everything.

After soaking in the tub until we were pruny, Lee surprised me again when we walked back to his living room. Instead of his typically neat and tidy space, Lee had transformed it into a pillow-and-blanket-fort oasis. Chairs had been pushed together, the couch had disappeared under a bedsheet, and throw pillows peeked out from beneath the covering.

"What is this?"

Lee walked to the entrance and held open the fabric. "Your castle, my lady."

Dressed in only Lee's oversize T-shirt, I sank to my knees and crawled through the pillow-fort opening.

On all fours, I shot him a look and tugged at the hemline that barely covered my ass. "No peeking."

"Ha. Not a chance."

With a squeal I scurried inside the cozy fort as he playfully pinched my butt. Blankets and pillows covered the entire area, while the television was queued up to a movie.

"You were busy," I teased.

"You were asleep," he shot back playfully.

A hard lump settled into my throat. Lee was thoughtful, kind, and sexy as hell. Everything I had never allowed myself to dream of was right in front of me, and I was about to ruin it all.

But I had to. I owed him that much.

As I settled into my plush surroundings, I gathered the shreds of my courage.

Lee nestled beside me, fluffing the pillows behind his back and wiggling until he was comfortable. His muscular arm stretched across the back of the sofa, and he gestured for me to cuddle up to him.

I obliged and sank into the cozy setup. Lee smirked at me and pulled me closer. He popped a kiss on my cheek. "I love your curls. They're as wild as you are." He pinched one between his fingers and let it spring upward.

Charmed, I tucked the rogue curl behind my ear. "I know you don't like redheads."

His brows pinched. "Who said I don't like redheads?"

A laugh shot out of me. "You did. When I was finding you dates, remember?" I bunched my shoulders and deepened my voice to a gruff man voice, *"No redheads."*

He laughed, pulling my hair to his nose. "This exact shade of copper and auburn is my favorite color in the world. I only said that because by then I already couldn't stop thinking about you."

I swallowed hard. "Oh."

He squeezed my shoulder. "Yeah. *Oh.*" Lee focused on the television. "Come on. I have the perfect movie for us."

As the opening credits rolled, realization dawned on me. I looked between him and the screen. "Stop it. No freaking way."

He laughed as the blaring techno music poured from the speakers. My face dropped to my hands. "We are *not* watching this."

"You bet your ass we're watching it. This is a classic."

I shot him an unimpressed glare. "*BMX Bandits* is hardly a classic."

BMX Brothers was, in fact, an obscure movie about a kid who dreamed of becoming a BMX bike legend. It was filmed locally, and in one of Margo's schemes, she had sneaked us on set. I had *one line* in the movie and had spent my lifetime hoping that film would die a silent death.

"Should we fast-forward to your amazing screen debut?" he teased.

I narrowed my eyes at him. "Don't you dare. Oh my god, this is so embarrassing."

"Do Lark and her friends know they've got some Hollywood starlet competition?"

This earned him a laugh. "Oh, right. My one line and incredibly awkward close-up is going to change my life."

"Will you do it for me?"

"Do what?"

He smirked. "The line. I want to hear it."

"Please tell me you're joking." I shook my head.

He moved his arm to nudge me forward. "Come on. For old times' sake. Let's hear it."

I rolled my eyes but crawled forward until I was kneeling in front of him. Heat flooded my cheeks. Everyone in Outtatowner had seen the movie a hundred times, but in front of Lee I felt foolish.

He grinned and cupped his mouth before whisper-shouting, "Action!"

I stifled a giggle and took a deep breath. My eyes widened as if I were watching something approaching from a distance. My arm shot out and I pointed. "Billy, look out!"

Lee's deep laughter filled the cozy confines of the blanket fort.

I plopped back down next to him. "I hate you."

He laughed. "You love me."

The air was thick between us. Normally I'd follow up his cocky statement with a playful eye roll or a *yeah, right* for good measure.

Only I couldn't.

I cleared my throat and laughed. "God, I remember how pissed Margo was that they had asked me to do the line. She'd spent all that time convincing me to go with her and sneaking us on set. She was convinced if the director would see her, he'd demand she have a starring role. She was always doing wild shit, remember?"

Lee was silent as I rambled. A soft huff of breath was his only response until his voice came out low. "Yeah. I remember. She never liked being second fiddle."

At that, I laughed. Margo was never second *anything*.

Ever.

Emotion welled in my eyes. I blinked at the screen and struggled to find the words. "Lee, you remember how things were before you left?"

His eyes searched mine, confusion written all over his handsome face.

I shifted so I could look directly at him, and *god* that was difficult. I placed my hand on top of his. "We were all friends, and you and I would cut up and laugh all the time. Margo was always so . . ."

"Jealous."

A nervous laugh trickled through me. "I don't know that *jealous* is the right way to explain it. But when you went overseas, Margo had asked—"

"Stop." Lee's hand gripped mine, and pain was evident on his face. "I don't want to talk about Margo right now."

"Lee, this is important." I cleared my throat and took a deep, shaky breath.

"Annette." My eyes searched his. "Tonight I want to enjoy *you*. No one else. Just you. I want to sit in a blanket fort and watch a shitty movie and laugh with my best friend. Can we do that? Please?"

I pulled my lips in and willed away the tears. It was the *please* that broke me.

This is too good. I can't ruin it yet.

I managed only a nod and cuddled into the nook of his arm.

He sighed and brushed his lips across my hair. "See

this? Right here with you? This is perfect. Best day of my life."

Shame and guilt consumed me, but selfishly, I shoved the past back into a box in the back of my mind and focused on Billy "Barspin" Crammel making his BMX dreams come true.

TWENTY-SIX
ANNIE

Nerves rippled through me, and the aroma of meat loaf with mashed potatoes and gravy filled the air as I set the table at Tootie's farmhouse for an impromptu Sullivan family dinner. Though I was more than content in the barn apartment, I'd asked Tootie to borrow her kitchen and have all the Sullivans in one place to tell them what I had discovered. The farmhouse was abuzz with excitement, and I couldn't help but feel a flutter of anxiety deep in my stomach. They were completely unaware of the important revelation I needed to share with the family, something that could change everything they knew about their family history.

As I smoothed the tablecloth and arranged the silverware, Lark was in the living room finishing up a delicate french braid in Penny's hair. Kate was chatting animatedly with her boyfriend, Beckett, their laughter filling the room. Kate's green eyes sparkled with happiness, and I couldn't help but smile. Seeing her so content made me realize how much I cherished the bond we shared and how grateful I was she had moved back home.

My attention was diverted when Lee entered through the front door. With his broad shoulders and easy smile, he exuded an undeniable charm that never failed to make my heart skip a beat. Only this time I didn't have to turn away and pretend not to notice. He caught my gaze and winked, causing a blush to creep up my cheeks.

"I thought you had work?" I asked.

"I do, but I can spare a few minutes to kiss my girl before my shift starts." Lee wrapped a possessive arm around me and pulled me in for a deep kiss.

My girl.

Heat flooded my cheeks as a fresh awareness of the Sullivan family eyeballs set squarely on us. If there was any doubt about the status of our relationship, Lee had cleared that up with one highly inappropriate kiss.

A low cluck drew my attention to the front door. Just beyond the screen, Henrietta was staring me down.

"Looks like someone's jealous." I laughed when he released me and quickly averted my eyes.

Kate rounded the table and leaned in so Penny couldn't hear. "That's because Horny Henrietta can't get enough of Lee's attention."

He smirked and swiped a few pieces of lettuce out of the salad bowl. I watched his back as he opened the door and tossed Henrietta her treat before offering a few neck scratches.

"You're only making her fall more in love with you," Kate teased.

I knew she was talking about the chicken, but heat flooded my cheeks. *I feel your pain, Horny Henrietta.*

Duke cleared his throat, drawing my attention away from Lee. "Annie, you've outdone yourself. Smells great," the grumpy but lovable farmer remarked, his voice gruff yet appreciative.

"Thanks." I grinned, grateful for the compliment and the change in subject. "I wanted tonight to be a little bit special."

Aunt Tootie walked into the room, her wispy gray hair piled high atop her head. Her eyes twinkled with mischief as she surveyed the scene. "What's all this fuss about, honey?" she asked, her voice tinged with joyful curiosity.

"I kind of have something to share with everyone," I replied, feeling a mix of anticipation and anxiety coursing through my veins. "I've been digging into the town's history, and I think I might have found something."

The room fell silent, and everyone turned their attention toward me. Even Lee, who stood by my side, squeezed my hand reassuringly.

"Okay, so," I began, my voice barely above a whisper, "it's clear the Sullivan family and the Kings were not always rivals. In fact, back in the late eighteen hundreds, I have proof that they were friends and neighbors."

Stunned silence filled the room, and I continued, the words tumbling out of me like a cascade. "I found out that they intentionally purchased adjacent parcels of land through the Homestead Act, and it seems like their families shared a close friendship. But something happened, something that tore them apart, and the feud began."

Kate's eyes widened, mirroring the surprise that rippled through the room. "How is this possible? Our families have been at odds for generations. What happened?"

"I'm not entirely sure," I admitted, my mind racing with possibilities. "But I think it's connected to the strange goings-on at the farm. The tire tracks, the evidence of someone on the property, someone looking into mineral rights—it all might be tied to the secrets buried in your family's past."

Beckett leaned forward, his curiosity piqued. "Secrets are never good. Some are downright dangerous."

I tamped down the ripple of unease at the truth in his words. I had to remind myself that he was talking about the farmhouse and not the major secret I was keeping.

I cleared my throat and pressed on, a surge of determination coursing through me. "It won't be easy, but if we keep digging, we might finally be able to put an end to the feud and discover what really happened all those years ago."

"End the feud?" Lee's voice was incredulous. "Why the hell would we do that?"

Duke sighed. "I'd really like it if the Kings would stop fucking with my truck, for one. Last week someone painted *Honk if you're horny* on my tailgate. It took me half a day to figure out why everyone in town kept honking and waving at me, grinning like a bunch of fools."

I stifled a burst of laughter, and Lee covered his own chuckle with a fake cough.

As we gathered ourselves, silence hung in the air, the weight of my words settling upon us. The Sullivan family were waiting for my next move, for my guidance. I looked at Lee, his eyes filled with unwavering support and affection, and something inside me shifted.

Beckett's words rattled around in my head. *Secrets are never good. Some are downright dangerous.*

"Is THAT RAT SHIT?" My stomach curled as I backed away from the corner of the barn.

Lee shrugged. "Probably."

I dropped the shovel with a clatter and raised both hands in the air. "Okay. I'm out."

I stomped toward the barn door, but Lee stopped me. His gloved hand squeezed my elbow. "Hang on." His hand reached into my hair. "You've got a cobweb crown happening."

I squealed and danced on my toes as Lee plucked the web from my messy bun.

Dusting the front of my jeans, I pleaded with him. "Remind me what we are doing here, again?"

"Tootie said there were stacks of boxes with old family records buried in here somewhere. One might have more information on our land."

I looked around the old barn. For as long as I could remember, all the kids in town swore it was haunted. Years ago, when Sullivan Farms expanded, the property around Highfield House was no longer the main property, so this barn was relegated to storage and housing mean old barn cats. Based on the evidence of mice, those cats weren't doing a very good job.

I stared up at Lee as he finished fishing cobwebs out of my curls. Studying his face, affection and desire pooled in my belly. For so long I'd trained myself to not stare too long, but now that our relationship had evolved, I could stare all I wanted. His jaw was stubbly and strong. It cut at sharp angles, and I loved the way it moved when he was thinking or annoyed.

When I looked up, his eyes were staring down at me. "Why are you staring?"

His full lips pulled up on one corner. "You started it."

I blushed and tried to look away, but his gloved hand caught my chin, forcing my eyes to meet his again. "Truth is, I've always been staring."

"Oh, whatever." I gave him a shy smile. "Always?"

His hand dropped to shake off the leather glove before his hand tangled in my hair at the base of my skull. His green-gray eyes drilled into me. "Always." His voice was molten and thick. "Far longer than I had any right to."

"How long?" My question was barely a whisper.

Lee took another step, crowding my space and pressing his hips to mine. "I feel you before you even step into a room. I know your perfume from two klicks away. You're the voice in my head when I'm not sure what to do." His other hand gripped mine and pressed it into his chest. His heartbeat pounded through his shirt and into my palm. "There's never *not* been a time where you haven't taken up space. Right here." His hand tapped mine.

I love you. Oh my god, how much I love you.

Emotion lodged in my throat, and I pressed my eyes closed. "I never thought . . ." I tried to find the words—to tell him that for me, it had *always* been him. I took a breath and lifted my chin. "Lee, you need to know that when Margo and I—"

"Don't do that." His features darkened. He took a step back, opening a cavern between us and filling my stomach with dread. His hand raked through his hair, sending its ends in a thousand different directions. "Don't do what everyone in this goddamn town does and make this about her."

"There is no distance between your heart and mine." I looked into his eyes and willed him to know. To understand.

The muscles in his jaw worked, and he took another step back. "It's getting late. I should get you home."

Without looking back, Lee turned and left me staring after him, alone with my mounting regrets in the dusty old barn.

TWENTY-SEVEN
LEE

The sixth and final date for the Matchmakers' Gala auction dates was finally here. On the outside, it would seem like the farmers' market was the least exciting date, but I was simmering with anxious nerves. I had been busy all week with work and my dad and helping Tootie, so by the time Saturday morning rolled around, I was aching for Annie.

The intensity of our interaction in the barn was still clinging with me. I'd nearly gotten on my knees for her and told her how punched-in-the-gut in love with her I was. Instead, I'd shut her out as soon as Margo's name passed her lips. More and more, it was like my memory was playing tricks on me. I'd never had any issues keeping the two women separate in my mind, but the closer I got to Annie, the more she and Margo got so tangled in my head that I felt like I was losing my goddamned mind.

Why would she ruin the moment by bringing up my dead ex-girlfriend?

Trying to ignore the strange, uncomfortable feelings I

was having, a few times the past week I had sneaked away to pop into Sand Dune Studio. Each time I'd used my spare minutes to give Annie flowers or drop a kiss on that lush mouth of hers. I had never been so head over heels, but I didn't give a fuck. For once the happiness I radiated on the outside wasn't all show. It was an accurate reflection of how I was finally feeling on the inside.

She did that.

I had also sent Annie on a wild-goose chase just as I went to pick her up for the market. I claimed there was something in Highfield House that Lark needed and bought myself a good fifteen minutes while she searched in vain. It was the perfect opportunity for me to hide all one hundred tiny resin ducklings in the apartment. They were numbered, so it was sure to throw her into a tizzy trying to find all of them.

The sheer genius—*the stupidity*—of it had me giggling to myself.

"What's so funny?" Annie asked, bursting through the door as I slid the silverware drawer closed.

"What? Nothing."

She raised an eyebrow, and her glance sliced to the drawer for the briefest second, but she let it go. "I couldn't find the purse you said she wanted, and when I texted Lark about it, she didn't know what I was talking about, so . . ." Her hands dropped to slap her thighs. "I give up."

I shrugged and looked at my watch. "We need to go. I've got a date to take you on." I gave her a playful wink and enjoyed the way her cheeks pinked.

A vibrant charm seemed to radiate from every nook and cranny of the Outtatowner farmers' market. I gripped Annie's hand as we ventured beyond the quaint downtown area and onto a side street alive with the pulsating rhythm of the market.

The air crackled with an energy that mingled the fresh tang of the nearby lake breeze, along with the earthy scent of freshly harvested vegetables. Sunlight, filtered through the swaying leaves of ancient maples, painted dappling patterns on the worn cobblestones beneath our feet. The vibrant stalls burst with an explosion of colors—ripe red tomatoes, golden ears of corn, and plump purple eggplants vying for attention, while baskets overflowed with vibrant blooms of every hue, infusing the air with their heady fragrance.

"No stand for you today?" I asked as we headed toward the table where the Bluebirds were checking auction couples in.

Annie smiled but was still lost in thought. "Mel is running it today, but we can check in on her."

I frowned. Even though something was still off, I was determined to get us back on track with this date.

"My favorite couple!" Tootie smiled as she pulled Annie into a hug, rocking her back and forth. "Not that I am allowed to show favoritism." She winked at me over Annie's shoulder. Annie squeezed her back, and Aunt Tootie moved to search through an expandable file folder. She removed a white envelope. "For you two."

Annie examined the envelope before slipping her finger under the seal to open it and pulling out a slip of paper. "An *anonymous sponsor*"—her eyes flicked to Tootie, who wore a shit-eating grin—"has bought us pastries and coffee from the Sugar Bowl, along with a bouquet of flowers." Annie flipped the card for me to see.

"Go on now." Tootie scooted us away. "Enjoy the

market." She gestured toward the whiteboard with all the couples' names on it. "It's neck and neck for the town's favorite couple, but I've got my money on you two!"

Annie's soft laugh rolled over me. It was a sound I had heard a million times before but still wished I could bottle up. It immediately made me feel at ease.

My hand found the small of her back, and I guided her toward the bustling market.

The rich aroma of freshly brewed coffee beckoned, intermingling with the intoxicating scent of warm cinnamon pastries emerging from where the Sugar Bowl had a table and stall set up.

Behind the table, Sylvie King was handing change to a customer.

"Huh," Annie commented.

I turned my attention to her.

"It's weird she's not on a date with Charles." Annie shrugged. "I'm going to snag us those coffees and pastries and see what's up."

I nodded. "Duke is across the way. Meet me over there?"

With a nod, Annie slipped away. Across the street and a few stalls over, Duke was standing behind the long tables, discussing produce with a customer and looking thoroughly pissed off.

As he ended the interaction, I stepped up, laughing. My hand shot out, and my brother gripped it. His eyes were focused over my shoulder. When I glanced back, he was watching Annie and Sylvie talking over two steaming cups of coffee.

Duke was watching her. Anyone with half a brain could see his attention was focused on a particularly pretty blonde. I was loyal as a Sullivan, but not oblivious. Sylvie King may be a little cold and dismissive, but she was attractive, and Annie swore she wasn't quite the ice queen she had been made out to be. Regardless, it was my duty to give my oldest brother shit.

I leaned in close. "You should probably stop eye-fucking Sylvie King in public, dude."

His eyes whipped to mine, anger simmering in his stare. Duke was always a crabby motherfucker, but clearly I'd hit a nerve.

"Shut it." His warning was unmistakable, the anger he held on to so tightly just below the surface.

It was the perfect time to poke the bear. "Sorry, man. I just thought you had the hots for MJ, not Sylvie. That's all."

My oldest brother's face turned an angry shade of red. "You keep your mouth shut about them. *Both* of them."

I raised my palms and laughed. "Holy hell, I'm joking. Relax."

He nearly growled. "I am relaxed."

I laughed again and shook my head. Years ago I had stopped trying to figure out what the hell Duke had to be so pissy about. When our family went to hell, I chose to mask my pain with humor, sex, and laughter. Duke wore his pain like a badge of honor.

Changing the subject, I looked over his table, which was arranged with baskets upon baskets of fresh Sullivan blueberries along with jams and compotes Duke had made himself. "Do you have any of the blueberry lime? It's Annie's favorite."

Duke snatched a small jar off the table and placed it in front of me with a clunk. I dug for my wallet, but he shook his head. "On the house."

I patted his shoulder. "Thanks. You're a great brother."

A disgruntled noise rumbled from his throat, and I laughed, saluting him with the jar in my hand. "See you later, man."

I made my way back to Annie. She used one hand to sip her coffee while somehow balancing a white paper bag and my coffee in the other hand. I relieved her of the items and leaned in close. "You get the scoop?"

"Apparently Sylvie and Huck are taking turns behind the stand. She and Charles are meeting up later for their date."

I glanced at the scoreboard again. "That's good news for us. They were catching up." I winked.

Annie didn't laugh as I'd intended, but only offered a light smile.

A mixture of anticipation and unease swirled within me. Today Annie was still acting differently—her energy a bit subdued, her laughter restrained. It sent a shiver of worry down my spine, tapping into some unresolved fears I didn't like to think about.

As we meandered through the bustling market, I noticed that other couples from our close-knit town were in the idyllic setting for their own arranged dates. Laughter blended with the hum of commerce and the rustling of paper bags. The farmers' market was a patchwork of bustling stalls, smiling faces, and the occasional bark of a contented dog.

I looked down at my best friend walking beside me, her hair lifting with the gentle breeze.

I want this life with her.

Annie was oddly quiet beside me. I squeezed her hand. "Everything okay?"

She swallowed hard and nodded, but didn't answer.

I could be patient, to give Annie the space she needed to share her burdens when the time was right. Until then, I would enjoy the stolen glances, the gentle brushes of our hands, and the unspoken promises of affection that wove between us.

By the time we'd made our way through the market, Annie had made up some bullshit excuse and barely looked me in the eye when she disappeared into her apartment. She had thanked me for the flowers and the date and promised to be in touch later in the day.

Restless and uneasy, I found myself walking through the wrought iron gate of the Outtatowner cemetery. The sun filtered through the old trees as I walked down the path toward Mom. After dropping Annie at home, I'd gone back to the market and purchased a second bouquet. I stood for long, heavy moments and stared at the weathered gray headstone.

June Sullivan—beloved wife and mother.

My throat was hot and thick. I rarely made it to the cemetery. For whatever reason it wasn't a place I felt connected to my mother, and it dredged up too many unwanted emotions.

I sucked in a deep breath. "I remember the blue dress you wore. It had flour dusted on the front when you leaned down to scold me." I chuckled at the forgotten memory. Mom had caught me playing a trick on Dad, but I'd been caught in the act. I was certain I would be in a load of trouble.

"'Next time, walk on the right side of the hallway so the boards don't squeak.'" I recalled, so vividly, her mischievous smile and how she winked. I cleared my throat and whispered, "I remember you every day."

With an aggravated sigh, I ran my hands through my

hair. Over the years I'd worked so hard at keeping my emotions in check. Shoving them down so I didn't have to feel so lost. So fucking helpless.

"Remember that time you told me I was going to marry Annie Crane?" My hand found the ache in my chest and rubbed. "I think you might have been right, Mom."

I squatted and pulled some of the long grass around her headstone. "Things have changed between us. I don't know if you can see us from where you are, but we've gotten close. I told myself it would never be anything more than a friendship, but then an opportunity presented itself, and I couldn't help myself. I want to give her more of myself, but I don't know how. And I can feel it. I already feel her pulling back, and I don't think I can survive that." I choked back the tears that clawed at my throat. "Things are different. It's Annie, and I need her like I need the air in my lungs, but—" Self-doubt and uncertainty raced through me.

Soft footsteps sounded behind me. I swiped at my eyes and turned to find my sister, Kate, walking up next to me.

"Hey." She stood and looked down at Mom's headstone.

"Hey."

Kate leaned her head on my shoulder. We stood in silence, staring down at the headstone. Finally, Kate whispered, "She's a pretty good listener."

I cleared my throat and sniffled. "She's the best."

"Are you okay?"

I exhaled and stuffed my hands in my pockets, looking up at the crisp, blue July sky. "I don't know what the hell I am."

Kate leaned into me, nudging her shoulder against mine. "Don't fight it, okay?"

I looked down at my little sister.

She raised her eyebrows. "I'm serious. This feeling

here?" She patted the center of my chest. "Don't fight it just because it feels strange right now."

I pressed my lips together in a small smile. "I'm trying not to, but I feel like I've been fighting it for so long." I raked a hand through my hair and looked down at my mother's gravestone.

"Do you remember when Mom died, you and I hid together under the stairs?"

I nodded, hating the painful memories from that time that flooded back.

"I remember you told me that you'd always take care of me. Love me, just like Mom would have. You said that if I ever needed *anything* that you would be there. And you were. You always included me. Always stood up for me." She let out a small laugh. "You were the one who drove to Chicago and egged Declan's car, then plastered his telephone number around the city in a fake advertisement for erectile dysfunction."

I clenched my teeth to hide a smile. "You weren't supposed to know about that."

"You are loyal and kind, and you're a very lovable pain in my ass."

I chuckled in disagreement.

"My point is," she continued, "I have also watched you coast through life, avoiding real connection to save your heart. You can't do that with Annie—she knows you too well."

I sighed. "And that's what scares the shit out of me. The way she looks at me? She smiles at me like I'm actually worth something."

Kate shook her head. "She's *always* looked at you like that—for as long as I remember."

I swallowed hard. "I keep having all these"—I vaguely

gestured up and down toward my chest—"feelings. Forgotten memories that keep popping up. I keep thinking about Margo and what an idiot I was. How could I not see that Annie was right in front of me the whole time? I can't even trust my gut. How do you go through life like that?"

Kate shrugged. "Sometimes the heart sees what it wants to see. Annie and you have a deep and complicated past. You need to talk with *her* about it. Let her in."

I nodded, unsure but letting my sister's words sink in.

"One last piece of advice?" Her hand gently patted the middle of my back. "When she lets *you* in, hear her out. Really listen."

My brows furrowed. "What do you mean?"

"Whatever she tells you—listen with your whole heart. She's risking a lot here."

I looked at my sister, my jaw tight and brows pitched downward.

Kate sighed. "Look, I love you, but we all know you haven't been a commitment kind of guy. For as long as I've known her, Annie has wanted it all—a family, kids, *permanence*. Her own foster family up and left her. Have you ever thought about how that would feel?"

I frowned, hating to dwell on the sad upbringing Annie had suffered. "She has us."

Kate nodded. "She does, but if things go south with you two, how would that work out? She can't have a week where she isn't getting you out of some kind of mess—whether you're hiding from the Kings or some new girl has it out for you. All I'm saying is we're her family. *All of us*. If you're not sure about—"

"I get it." Frustrated, I crossed my arms.

Kate stepped closer. "I'm sorry. Okay? Just please be

careful here." My sister wrapped her arms around me in a side hug before letting out a deep, aggressively loud sigh. "Okay, I'm done offering sage advice. Want to get a beer?"

I ruffled my sister's brown hair, relieved to ignore the swell of raw emotions swirling inside me. "You're buying."

TWENTY-EIGHT
LEE

I WAS in love with Annie and, goddamn it, I was tired of hiding it. She made everything seem light. Happy.

There was no denying that Annie was having mixed emotions about the direction our relationship had taken, but I didn't care. I had finally realized how much I loved her—how I had *always* loved her—and that was where it all ended for me. Talking about our past was painful for the both of us, and I wanted nothing more than to forget about it and move forward.

With her.

I'd learned in the Army to let the past go and focus on the next mission. It was the only way to survive in one piece and stay sane. I found out myself that if you do it with a joke and a smile, no one ever questioned what was really going on inside your head.

Tonight was the last hurrah for the Matchmakers' Gala. All the auction dates got together for casual cocktails and appetizers. Final donations would trickle in for Remington County Child Protective Services, and the Top Couple would be awarded their winnings. I wanted that money for Annie so badly I could taste it.

Unable to trade shifts, I had promised to meet Annie at the Grudge, where the Bluebirds had overtaken the stage to make the announcements. Tourists gathered alongside townies to cheer on the couples before the house band took over for the evening.

Glancing around the bar, I laughed to myself at the visible divide between the Sullivans and Kings. Despite the crowd, we each stuck to our sides of the Grudge. I spotted Annie instantly, tucked into a corner with Lark and Wyatt. My brother saw me and gave a wave before gesturing for me to come over.

We greeted each other with handshakes, side hugs, and hellos. Like a magnet, I was drawn to Annie's side and smiled down at her. "You look gorgeous. You ready to accept your money for Outtatowner's Top Couple?"

She laughed softly, but her eyes cast downward. I couldn't read her expression, but I also couldn't deny that something was still a bit off with her. I placed my arm across her shoulder and pulled her into me. "It'll all be okay."

Her hand found my abs, and her other arm wrapped around my waist. She fit perfectly. "Hey," I whispered. "This is the best day of my life."

Before she could respond, Ms. Bug and Aunt Tootie walked onto the stage and up to the microphone. Bug cleared her throat and began. "Good evening, friends. We just want to take a moment of your time to announce our final totals for Outtatowner's Matchmakers' Gala. Through generous donations, incredible auction items, and our *famous* Matchmakers' dates, we have successfully raised a record-breaking thirty-two thousand, four hundred dollars, and fifty-eight cents!"

Cheers and polite applause rippled through the crowd at the impressive donation.

Annie sighed and clapped. "That's amazing. CPS can really use that money."

I leaned down to whisper to her. "And it'll be even sweeter when you deliver that big-ass check yourself."

"And now"—Aunt Tootie took her place in front of the microphone—"after weeks of neck-and-neck, *friendly* competition, the official Matchmakers' Gala Top Couple is . . ."

A pattering drumroll of hands tapping on tabletops rolled through the crowd as Tootie pulled a piece of paper from an envelope.

She cleared her throat, and my heartbeat ticked faster. I pinched my eyes closed.

Annie and Lee. Annie and Lee. Come on.

"Millie Reed and Royal King!"

My shoulders sagged as a mixture of whoops and boos rippled through the crowd.

"Bullshit!" Wyatt cupped his hand to yell above the crowd, prompting Lark to swat his arm.

In true Royal fashion, he made a show of tossing Millie over his shoulder like a caveman and stomping up the stage with her. When he hoisted the comically large cardboard check above his head, he reveled in the applause.

Taking the mic from Tootie, Royal took center stage, ignoring her scowl. "Thank you. Thank you. As you know, this was for charity, and I was glad to do my part. There was some hopeful competition, but, man, it's good to be the king."

I rolled my eyes. *Cocky motherfucker.*

"Well, you two are still *my* favorite!" Lark raised her glass and clinked it with Annie's, and I gave her shoulder a squeeze. I'd let her down and the slick, oily feeling in my gut was terrible.

"Are you disappointed?" I asked, searching her eyes.

She shrugged. "I would have taken my half of the money and given it to CPS anyway. So yeah, a little."

Shit. I'd planned on using the money to help her business and shut JP King up, while she was selflessly planning on helping more kids.

A stream of friends and neighbors filtered by the table to offer their condolences and let us know how wrong they thought the outcome was. Annie's tight smile was the only excuse I needed.

"Let's go for a walk." I grabbed her hand and lifted my chin to my brother. Wyatt offered a salute, silently letting me know he'd cover the tab and I could get him back later. With my hand at her lower back, I guided her through the crowd. When we hit the open air, she let out an audible sigh.

"Better?" I asked.

She finally smiled. "Much. Thanks."

"Walk with me." I guided her down Main Street toward the beach. The night air was warm, and the light breeze off the lake was perfect. When we hit the sand, Annie slipped off her shoes and tossed them in the bushes. I followed suit and let the sand sink between my toes as we headed toward the water.

We quietly walked down the beachfront, and cool waves lapped at our ankles. It was officially over. With the auction dates concluded, there was no more pretending. No showboating to try to win some money. We were the only thing left.

"Annette?" I stopped in the sand.

"Hmm?" Starlight reflected in her blue eyes.

"You're the worst fake girlfriend I've ever had."

Annie's eyes crinkled at the edges, and her familiar laughter rolled over me. "How dare you," she said, feigning shock. "I'm amazing."

I linked my fingers with hers. "You *are* amazing, but I need you to know . . . nothing about this was ever fake. Not for me. You're my girl."

Her smile spread—a true Annie smile—and my blood warmed. I ran a hand up her arm to ward off the slight breeze that floated off the lake. "You know, sometimes I think back on my time in the Army, and it's not the action or the high of a successful mission I think about. It's the quiet moments that get to me. My mind always drifts back to the times when I felt so *alone*. 'There is no distance between your heart and mine.' God, I thought I knew what that meant, but I am starting to realize I had no clue until I saw what was right in front of me."

Annie's eyes softened before she lifted onto her toes and kissed me. It started tender and slow, but morphed into pure need. Annie whimpered when my tongue invaded her mouth, and her thigh shifted against mine. I immediately went hard, and my hand closed around her hip. A deep, hungry male part of me wanted her to feel what her kiss did to me. To acknowledge the primal need that coursed through me from a simple kiss.

When she gasped for air, my mouth found her throat, and I dragged my tongue up her neck. My hands slipped around to grip her ass, and I held her against me. "Let's go home. Let me make love to you and *show* you how real this is."

"Lee, I need to—"

I swallowed her protest with another kiss. Our hands tangled as she gripped my shirt, pulling it up to gain access to my stomach. My hands moved up, slipping beneath the billowing fabric of her blouse. I needed to be closer to her, to feel more of her soft skin against me. My hand traveled up over her bra and kneaded her breast before thumbing over her hard nipple.

"You make me feel so good." My cock strained at her breathy words.

My need grew hotter, more desperate. I wanted to hear those words with my cock buried deep inside her. I backed her under the cover of a tree-lined sand dune.

I lifted her by her waist, holding her against me. The beach was quiet, save for the gentle rolling of the waves. I pressed her back into the tree, rocking her hips against my erection and loving how her eyes grew unfocused.

"What do you say, baby? Are you going to let me take care of you?"

On a whimper, Annie bucked her hips and raked her nails through my hair, then covered my mouth with hers. "I want you," she panted. "Right now."

My molars ground together as need threatened to overtake me. Risky public sex was hot as fuck, especially when Annie was breathless and begging for it. I didn't even hesitate. The small alcove of sand we'd hidden behind wouldn't keep us from view if someone wandered down the same stretch of beach, but it was secluded enough.

"*Fuck*, Annette." Need clawed at me. I lowered her feet to the sand. "Hands up."

Annie did as she was told, spinning from me and pressing her palms against the tree at our side. Her ass tipped up with a teasing grind into my cock. I was desperate for her. My nails raked up the smooth backs of her thighs and lifted her frilly little skirt. With an appreciative groan, I kneaded her ass as I took in her bare pussy.

My eyes flashed to hers as her teeth sunk into her bottom lip.

"I'm too worked up to go slow," I warned.

Her breaths sawed in and out as she brushed her fingertips over herself. "Good."

"Tell me. Tell me I can fuck you hard tonight, baby."

"Please, Lee. Yes."

One hand trailed up her thigh to find her pussy soaked and soft. I pushed in my ring and middle fingers, groaning at how easily they slipped into her tight cunt.

"You need to get fucked rough and dirty, don't you?"

She clenched around my fingers in response. My mouth worked on her neck and exposed shoulder as my fingers gently pumped in and out of her. I widened my stance, spreading her feet with mine. Working the button of my shorts, I lowered my zipper to free my cock. I slipped my fingers from her before dragging the head of my dick through her wetness. We moaned in unison. She was so soft and so wet. I dragged a teasing finger around her clit. When her hips started to shake, I knew she was already close.

As much as I wanted to pound into her, I needed more. If Annie came, I wouldn't be far behind her. Gripping her hips, I used the fallen tree trunk to prop her up, and in one powerful stroke, I filled her.

Annie's scream was muffled as she bit down on my shoulder. The strangled sound sent a flash of heat straight to my cock, and I throbbed inside her. I held her hips, giving three rough thrusts. As she cried out, I covered her mouth with mine, driving into her. The sound of my own primal grunts echoed in my ears as her tight pussy pulsed around me. Annie clung to me like a lifeline, her arms slung across my neck as I brought us both to the verge of release.

"You've been teasing me. Wearing these short little

skirts, knowing I get hard just thinking about you. Didn't you?"

"Yes," she panted, her pussy clenching and milking my cock. "It was for you."

My rhythm increased. Need drove my hips forward as I pounded into her. "Every time. Every time I see you I know just how fucking tight you are. How hot this cunt is when it's filled with my cum."

Against my chest, her hard nipples pressed through the fabric of her top. "I'm . . . *oh* . . ."

Her body shook as I kept up my punishing pace. "That's it, baby, come knowing I'm about to fill you up. You want that?"

"Yes," she cried through her orgasm, her heels digging into the small of my back. I hissed through the pulses of her orgasm, holding mine back, making sure she was completely satisfied before I finished. When she tightened one last time, I banded my arms around her and thrust deep, pressing my forehead against hers as I came.

Nothing and no one existed except for her in that moment.

After several long moments, the haze of postorgasmic bliss started to lift. "Lee?" Annie's hands gently moved down my face and neck.

I swallowed hard, breathing her in and wanting to freeze time while she was still wrapped around me and I was bottomed out inside her.

I lifted my head to find tears in Annie's eyes. Confused, I carefully slipped from her and set her feet on the ground. "What is it? Did I hurt you?"

She shook her head and swallowed. "No, I—it was incredible. I think I'm just feeling a little overwhelmed. Can you take me home?"

TWENTY-NINE
ANNIE

LEE WATCHED me carefully for the entire drive to the apartment above the barn at Highfield House.

Lee and I were friends, best friends, and we didn't keep secrets from each other—except for one tiny, life-altering, potentially relationship-ending secret that I had been holding for years.

Lee pulled his truck behind my car in the driveway. I climbed the stairs, gripping the railing until my knuckles turned white. I steadied my breath as I walked up to my temporary apartment.

Once they all find out what I've done, I'll probably have to search for a new apartment on top of everything else.

But a new apartment was the least of my worries. Once I told Lee the truth and the rest of the Sullivans found out I had been lying for years, I wouldn't blame them for completely disowning me.

They would leave like everyone else.

For one fleeting, hopeful moment, my thoughts flickered to Kate. She knew my secret and had kept it, not once alluding to Lee about the source of the letters he'd received during his time overseas.

There had been times over the years when she had encouraged me to tell him, but for one stupid reason or another, I had convinced myself that keeping the secret was protecting him—protecting the memory of Margo and the relationship he thought they shared. Keeping his heart safe had always been my intention.

But now that I had a glimpse of his true heart, I realized what a fool I had been. How my actions *added* to his pain. I would never forgive myself.

How many times had Lee lamented that the woman he'd dated and the woman he'd fallen in love with through the letters felt like two entirely different people?

How deeply had that flippant offhand comment cut?

I would find a way to tell him, to make him understand that everything I had done all those years ago had been done with the best of intentions.

Lee's hand traveled down the length of my spine as I fumbled to open the door above the barn.

"You okay, baby?" Worry laced through his deep voice, but a quiet nod was all I could muster.

"Just tired." I held back the tears that burned behind my eyelids.

As I pushed open the door, Lee pulled me into an embrace just inside the doorway. One hand wrapped around my middle, while the other tangled into my curls as he held me close.

When he pulled back, his eyes were searching mine. "Please tell me, Annette. Tell me if I was too rough with you or if it was too much."

The sheer protectiveness and gentleness of his expression was nearly enough to break me. "It's not that," I reassured. "To be honest, everything feels so perfect. I can't believe this is really happening."

"Well, believe it." He lowered his head to level his stare with mine. "There is nothing more real than this thing between us."

I swallowed hard and offered him a watery smile.

Once we stepped farther into my apartment, he eyed the small piles of messes littering the countertops and the pile of clean clothes lumped on the couch waiting for me to fold them. A fresh wave of embarrassment washed over me.

Let's be real.

I wouldn't be folding them, but more likely plucking clean items to wear straight from that laundry pile.

"I see moving in has gone well," he teased, trying to lighten the mood.

I swatted his hand as I gathered a pile of junk mail into my arms, then tried to shove it into an open drawer. Since moving into the apartment, I hadn't exactly unpacked everything, and there were boxes of my things strewn haphazardly around the apartment.

He laughed, toying with a rogue piece of mail. "Don't act all embarrassed now. I've seen the way you live and love you anyway."

My mind blanked at his flippant expression of love. Over the years those words had tumbled from his lips a time or two, and they never ceased to stop me dead in my tracks.

Only this time it was different.

Things between us had evolved. Intensified. Gotten complicated.

I stared at Lee's back, and my mind struggled to catch up. "I'm just going to wash up. I'll be back in five minutes. Just make yourself at home!" My voice squeaked out three octaves higher than what would be considered normal.

I hurried away and locked myself in the bathroom before he could respond. With my back against the door I sucked in a few breaths, willing my heartbeat to settle and for me to somehow find the courage to explain myself in a way he could possibly understand.

I piled my curls on top of my head and vowed to give them a thorough wash another day, then took the world's fastest shower as I scrubbed sand from my toes.

When I finished, I peeked from the doorway of the bathroom. Lee was sitting on the couch, so I silently slipped from the bathroom to the primary bedroom and quickly dressed in a pair of leggings and found a T-shirt with only a few splatters of pottery glaze on it.

Much like my chaotic apartment way of living, Lee had also seen me in my comfiest clothes. Gathering my courage, I plastered on a sunny smile and greeted him in the living room.

The smile slid from my face when I saw Lee resting his elbows on his knees, hunched over on my couch with a single piece of paper dangling from his fingertips. I stopped in the doorway and stared.

No, no, no, no, no, no, no. Please, no, not like this.

"Lee?" My voice was timid and small, and I hated myself for it.

"Why do you have this?" He held up the letter. "*How* do you have this?"

I exhaled and bit my lower lip to keep it from trembling. "Okay, so the letters—"

"Did her parents give you these?" He gestured toward the clear plastic shoebox full of paper. "Because I asked them after she died. I asked if I could keep those letters, but they claimed they had no idea what I was talking about. They said they couldn't find any letters."

My heart pounded against my ribs. I held up one hand, hoping he would let me finish without cutting me off. "Please don't blame them. They didn't give you the letters because they never had them. I did."

"What? She gave these to you? These were personal. Private." Emotion was building as each of his words grew more punctuated than the one before it.

"She didn't give them to me. They were *to* me . . . sort of." I stared at him, willing him to understand without me having to flay myself open and explain every sordid detail.

His brows pinched together and he shook his head. "What are you talking about? Why do you have the letters I wrote to Margo?"

I took one step forward and could feel the frustration simmering off him.

"Look, when you guys left, Margo and you were already on shaky footing, right? She told me the one thing you asked of her was that she would write to you while you were gone. Well, Margo was . . . you know . . . Margo. She asked me—" I shook my head, remembering that day with heartbreaking clarity. "No, she begged me to do it. She said that she wasn't the creative type, and I was. But I refused. I knew it wasn't right. But then she told me that you said it would be the one thing that would keep you going, knowing that there was someone here thinking about you and connecting you to your home. You were my friend, Lee. I didn't know what else to do. So I did it. I wrote that first letter and signed her name to it. She and I lived together, so the letters all came to our place. Anytime your letters came in the mail, she left them on the counter for me to open, and I would take them and read them and write you back. And it was me. Me who poured everything into those letters. Only I never once signed my name." Shame washed over me as tears streamed down my face. "I signed hers instead."

Lee stared at me as my voice cracked on those final words. His back was stiff and straight. His jaw tense.

My eyes pleaded with him. "Say something, please."

With a flick of his fingertips, he released the letter, and I watched it float to the floor in slow motion.

"I have to go." His voice was strangled and low.

I didn't have the courage to meet his eyes as he strode past me without looking back.

After the front door to the apartment clicked closed behind him, I sank to my knees, gathered the letter he had dropped, and sobbed.

THIRTY
LEE

THE OLD SCREEN door slammed behind me after I stomped out of Annie's apartment. The weight of her confession pressed heavily on my shoulders. Confusion, hurt, and betrayal swirled and collided like a raging storm. The revelation that Annie had written the letters—the letters that had captivated my heart and deceived my soul—was a cruel twist of fate. A war of emotions churned inside me, the hurt cutting deep as the truth settled in.

All this time it was her.

I knew it was true the moment the color drained from her face.

With a heavy foot on the gas pedal, I wound my truck through the looping country roads of Remington County. Music blared as I tried to drown out the flood of memories that fought their way to the forefront of my mind.

Every time Annie made a flippant comment and my head jumbled it with something I'd read in the letters. When Margo would ask a question and get pissy or defensive if I reminded her we had already talked about that in the letters.

It was Annie all along, and I was a fucking idiot. The two of them had probably laughed and laughed over what a moron I was.

I had always known my relationship with Margo had been superficial, marked by teenage drama and fleeting moments of happiness. We were young, caught up in the shallow facade of what we believed small-town love should be. What everyone around us told us *would* be.

But those letters—they painted a completely different picture. Through them, I found solace, depth, and the connection I had longed for. I fell for the woman in those letters. I had thought my being overseas would provide the space and clarity Margo needed to see the true connection we had.

But it was all bullshit.

Shaking my head and trying to quell my anger, I pulled down Kate's driveway and slammed my truck into park. Even in our darkest moments, Kate had always been a constant source of love and support. She knew Annie almost as well as I did. She could share my anger and confusion.

My fist pounded on the wooden door. Kate answered, immediately stepping aside so I could enter. As I stepped into her cozy living room, seeking refuge from the storm raging within me, I also hoped she could offer some clarity amid the chaos.

"Hey," Kate greeted me with a warm smile, unaware of the turmoil that consumed me. I sank into the familiar embrace of the worn-out armchair she'd gotten from the farmhouse, my gaze fixed on her as I struggled to find the right words.

"Kate," I began, my voice strained. "There's something I need to talk to you about. It's about Annie."

I watched as Kate's expression shifted, a flicker of guilt passing through her eyes like a fleeting shadow. The unspoken truth hung heavily in the air, thick with betrayal. It was in that moment, with the silence between us, that I realized she'd held the key to Annie's secret all along. My heart clenched with a fresh wave of hurt.

"You knew," I said, my voice barely a whisper, the words heavy with disappointment. I stood from the chair and Kate met my gaze, her own filled with remorse and sorrow.

Hot tears welled up in my eyes as a torrent of emotions threatened to engulf me. The weight of Annie's secret and Kate's complicity in keeping it was suffocating. My mind spun with questions, my heart aching for the truth to unravel.

How could the two people closest to me keep such a significant secret hidden for so long? How many wasted years had slipped through our fingers, swallowed by deception and missed opportunities for something real? How long had the guilt of my true feelings for Annie stopped me from telling her how I felt?

"Lee, wait." Kate stepped forward, but I stormed past her, then got in my truck and peeled out of her driveway without looking back. The weight of the truth was too much.

In need of solace and a momentary respite from the whirlwind of emotions that consumed me, I sought the company of the one person who also knew confusion and loss and hurt.

I entered the familiar surroundings of Haven Pines, and the scent of antiseptic and the faint hum of medical equipment filled the air. The sound of shuffled footsteps and distant murmurs formed a backdrop to my raging thoughts.

It was getting late, so the halls of the memory care neighborhood were quiet. I spotted Dad, sitting on his makeshift front porch with a cup of coffee.

"Hey, Dad," I greeted him with a soft smile, trying to hold back the weight of my troubles. His eyes met mine, his weathered face etched with both wisdom and confusion.

"Lee," he responded, his voice carrying the traces of the past. He held out his hand, and I shook it. "Heard there was a fire at Jennings Bakery." He shook his head. "Damn shame about the dog."

The Jennings Bakery fire was nearly twelve years ago, but I simply nodded. Lots of chatter was spreading through town after the Robinson house fire was ruled an arson, and it wasn't uncommon for Dad's timelines to get a bit confused. We'd learned years ago that it was better to let small slips like that go.

"I had a dog named Turkey when I was about your age . . . dumber than a box of rocks, but he was loyal. Someone stole him from the back of my truck when I was at a gas station. Took over a month, but that dumbass dog found his way back to me." Dad chuckled at the memory. "Maybe he wasn't so dumb after all. Hell, I don't know."

I chuckled lightly, appreciating the surface-level conversation that momentarily diverted my attention from the hurt and anger simmering just below the surface.

I sighed. "I could use some loyalty about now."

Dad nodded, his gaze drifting before returning to meet mine. "You know, your mother . . . she was as loyal as they come."

A pang of longing gripped my heart at the mention of my mother. Memories of her gentle touch and infectious laughter flooded my senses. The long-lost scent of her favorite perfume lingered in the air, intermingled with the faint aroma of the freshly brewed coffee that Dad held in his weathered hands.

"I miss her too, Dad," I replied, my voice thick with emotion. "I remember once I'd gotten in trouble with Principal Taylor over talking in class. He called Mom up, planning to get me in deeper trouble when I got home. Man, did that backfire on him."

I laughed, recalling how Principal Taylor's phone call had riled her up after he'd slipped and called me *no good*. She had stormed down to the school and walked straight into his office. Instead of taking his side and doling out a punishment for me, she had pointed a finger at him and given him a dressing down. She'd had my back, even when I was being a little shit, and told Principal Taylor he wouldn't know goodness if it crawled up his ass and laid an egg. It was the first time I'd ever heard my mother curse, and to this day I still got the urge to laugh whenever I saw Principal Taylor around town.

Dad's eyes glistened with a mix of melancholy and a flicker of remembrance. In that fleeting moment, I saw the depths of his love for Mom, an unwavering bond that surpassed the barriers of time and fading memories.

We sat in silence, and I couldn't help but contemplate the fragility of love and the complexities that now entangled my own heart. The weight of secrets and unspoken desires threatened to suffocate our connection, leaving me to question whether Annie and I could ever find our way back to each other.

"How did you know, Dad? With Mom?"

Dad sat back, looking out onto the faux neighborhood walkway, and I hated the fact this was his home.

Dad shrugged his strong shoulder. "Same way you know about your girl, I guess."

I turned to him, denial and deflection ready on my tongue, but I hesitated.

Dad's cool blue eyes bore into me, challenging me to disagree. "I may not remember much, but I remember that girl. And how you've always looked at her. Since you were kids, you were chasing around those bright-red curls, pretending like it was something else."

He scoffed like the only person I had been fooling was myself. I swallowed past the thick lump lodged in my throat.

"There's going to be plenty of times it feels hard." Dad leaned on his knees and looked into the black coffee. "You'll mess up, or maybe she will. It'll happen. But you gotta dig past the hurt. Go deep and remember how it feels when she looks at you like you're the best man in the room, because to her, you are."

My hand rubbed the tension building at the base of my skull. There was so much he didn't understand, but his words clung to me. "Thanks, Dad." I gave his knee a squeeze. "I'll be around later in the week."

Dad raised his cooled coffee in a silent salute, not realizing how his deep words burrowed into my chest.

Imagining a life without Annie felt wooden and hollow, despite the hurt and anger that still radiated in my chest.

Her steadfast heart had been an anchor, tethering me with friendship and family whenever life threatened to drown me. She had always found a way to see past the jokes and the one-night stands and the humor I used to deflect.

The reality that I didn't know Annie nearly as well as I'd thought nearly buckled my knees as I walked out of Haven Pines.

THIRTY-ONE
ANNIE

Not being above some mild stalking, I had driven past his apartment, the fire station, even Kate and Beckett's beach house. There was no sign of Lee.

I took a breath as I rolled through downtown and spotted his black truck. It was Friday night in Outtatowner, and I should have known Lee would be surrounding himself with friends and a few beers at the Grudge.

I took one last glance at myself in the mirror, satisfied with the subtly smoky eyeliner that enhanced my naturally blue eyes. I rarely wore more than just mascara, but if I was going to beg for forgiveness, I wanted to look damn good doing it.

In the height of tourist season, the Grudge was packed with people. Laughter, chattering voices, and music from the live band melded together to form the soundtrack of life in a coastal Michigan town.

My eyes moved over the King side to see Royal and Sylvie in a small group of their mutual friends.

Across the bar, a few Sullivan cousins and their friends

dotted the west side. When I glanced across the dance floor, my eyes paused. The familiar outline of Lee's strong shoulders stopped me.

Holding her at a respectable distance, Lee was with Mia Bradley, moving them around the dance floor. Despite years of seeing him dance with nearly every woman and tourist that came through this bar, I no longer had to stuff down the irrational feelings of jealousy. I knew him and I knew his heart. His hand didn't curl around hers and brush lightly around her wrist. And his arm didn't find the small of her back the way it always did mine.

In the back of the bar, Emma caught my eye and offered me a wave. I tipped up my chin and smiled at her, but turned and headed straight for the bar. The only open spot was between two tourists in board shorts and T-shirts, looking as though they had come straight from the beach.

I wedged myself in the opening between them as one turned toward me. "Well, hey there."

I only gave him a tight smile as I signaled to the bartender.

"Orphan Annie. What'll it be?" the bartender called over the demanding crowd.

I internally cringed at the nickname but plastered on a pretty smile. "I need a shot, something strong and something to chase it."

His look of surprise was fleeting, but he nodded. "Coming up."

I blew out a sigh of relief, and my shoulders sagged as I gathered my courage.

"Looking to cause some trouble tonight?" the surfer to my right asked with a smirk and tip of his eyebrow.

A little shotgun burst of laughter erupted from my chest

as the bartender slid an amber-colored shot toward me, followed by some greenish liquid.

I shook my head and looked at the surfer. "You have no idea." I leaned forward on the bar and gestured toward the shot glasses. "What is it?"

The bartender laughed. "Does it matter?" he asked, but then added, "It's a pickleback. A shot of whiskey and a pickle juice chaser."

My face twisted as I swallowed and stared down at the liquid. I needed something—*anything*—to give me the courage to walk up to Lee tonight.

I slapped my palm on the worn bar top. "Let's do it." In one quick motion, I threw back the shot and immediately followed it with the pickle juice. I was hit with the smoky, woody flavor of the whiskey, but the tang of pickle juice immediately counteracted the burn of the alcohol.

I swiped the back of my hand across my mouth. "Oh, man."

The guy to my left shot both arms into the air. "Took it like a champ!" he shouted above the crowd, and his buddy laughed. "Hey, next round's on me."

I shook my head and sucked in a deep breath. "Not this time, guys."

Instead, I headed in the direction of Lee and Mia, just as the song they were dancing to was coming to a close. I wound through the crowd, bumping into shoulders and politely maneuvering around the people crowding the dance floor.

Lee laughed as Mia said something funny, and nerves jumped in my belly, seeing them engaged in a casual conversation.

His eyes shot to mine over her shoulder, and I lifted my chin. "Mind if I cut in for the next one?"

Mia turned at the sound of my voice, and a polite smile graced her pretty face. "I know better than to get between you two when you're cutting it up on the dance floor." She opened her arm in a sweeping gesture. "He's all yours."

He's all yours.

God, I hope so.

Mia left the dance floor, and Lee was stiff as I took a tentative step toward him. I opened my arms. "Just gonna leave a girl hanging?"

With a low growl, Lee stepped forward, closing the distance between us. He wrapped his arms around me in a move he had done a thousand times before. While I would have preferred the moody romantic ebb and flow of a sad country song, I wasn't that lucky. The band kicked into an upbeat song, and Lee began to move me in a quick, familiar two-step.

I closed my eyes, letting the music move through me and feeling the strong support of his arm beneath mine. His hands were steady and his feet were confident as we moved through the crowd.

Dancing with Lee had always been special. They were the only moments I had allowed myself to be truly lost in him and experience the feelings I had always harbored but fought so hard to keep from the surface.

As we moved apart and came together again, my eyes were searching his. "Thanks for dancing with me."

His eyes barely flicked down to mine. "Yup."

"I was hoping maybe after this we could talk? That I might be able to explain a few things."

Lee's arms dropped and he took two steps away before stopping in his tracks. He turned toward me. "Explain a few things?" He lifted his palms up. "Now you want to talk?"

Shaking his head, he turned away from me and stormed toward the back exit. Feeling completely helpless and embarrassed, I looked around to see sad, knowing faces and a few pitiful shakes of the head from several couples on the dance floor.

Hurrying, I followed the path Lee had made as he cut through the crowd and pushed open the heavy back door of the Grudge to find him pacing in the dimly lit parking lot behind the bar.

"Lee. Hey, come on. I'm sorry!" I called out.

Anger flashed over his features as his steps ate up the distance between us and he stood right before me. I had to tip my chin up to look him in the eyes.

"You're sorry? You're fucking sorry? What are you sorry for, Annie? Please tell me. I'd love to know."

I had seen all versions of Lee over the years. I'd seen him sad or distracted or hung up on a girl or disappointed. I'd even seen him angry, but that anger had never once been directed toward me. I wasn't afraid of him but was deeply saddened at the pain I had caused, evident in his stormy green-gray eyes.

"Yes, Lee." My voice cracked. "I need you to know that I am so sorry for not telling you. For writing the letters in the first place."

Lee pointed a finger in my direction. "Don't. Don't you do that. God . . ." He let out a frustrated breath and turned to walk a few steps before turning back to me. "Do you know what? Yeah, I am angry. But do you even know why I'm so pissed off?"

Tears burned behind my eyelids. "I know. I know I should have never let Margo talk me into that. Into writing the letters for her."

"That's not even it!" he roared. Harsh breaths sawed in and out of him as he was struggling to remain in control of his emotions.

Tears streamed down my face. "I should have told you—"

"You're goddamn right you should have told me." Emotion was strong in his voice, and it nearly broke me. "You, of all people, know how much guilt I carried about the night Margo died. Knowing that I was the last person to talk with her. That I was the reason she stormed out of that wedding and was walking down that dark country road. But I never told you what we argued about. What the last thing I said to her was."

Confusion was evident on my face as I stood there, stunned, and shook my head. "What did you say?"

"I said she wasn't *you*! She was jealous that you and I were always cutting up and having a good time. She wanted to know why it couldn't be like that between us. So, yeah, I'm pissed you didn't tell me you wrote the letters." He tugged at his hair. "How many fucking years did we waste?"

Stunned, I could only blink up at him.

"Yeah, Annie, I'm fucking pissed at you. You don't even get it. You *don't*. You think this is about some fucking Matchmakers' Gala or winning some pathetic prize money or catching a break from desperate women at bars. You think I fell for you because we were put in romantic situations and I couldn't help myself? You're so goddamn wrong. What you don't realize is that I have been in love with you for the better part of my entire life. It was *always* you, Annette. We were cheated out of years of this." His arm gestured between us. "Of feeling known and seen and being fucking *loved*. You did that."

His hand scrubbed at the back of his neck.

"I know." When I could no longer hold back my sob, it consumed me. "I know. I made that choice, and it was all my fault. I thought I was doing the right thing. But then the auction happened and then our dates and I couldn't hide it anymore. I know we said it was fake when we started. I thought I could keep my emotions buried and hold on to that secret for your sake. But you never said anything! Not once in all of our time being friends."

Hurt and embarrassment mixed with anger and sadness.

Lee scoffed. "What if I had told you, and we couldn't be best friends anymore? You don't think that scared the shit out of me? Because typical Lee couldn't help himself but want to see you naked and hold you and be with you. I took you however I could have you."

Tears streamed down my face. "I didn't know. I didn't know how you felt. Then it all started to feel so *real*. I wasn't sure what to think. By the time the dates were happening, I was in so deep I couldn't figure out how to get myself out anymore."

Lee surged forward, his hands diving into my hair and his fingers pressed into the base of my skull. "You want to know how I feel? I love you. Do you need me to say it again? I fucking love you. I loved you every time I watched you date some asshole who didn't deserve you. I loved you every time I took a woman home and wished it was you. I loved you. I convinced myself you could never love me in the same way, so I loved you the only way I could. But watching Charles string you around and toy with your emotions, I couldn't stand it. Once I gave in, there was no holding back. So, yeah, I'm fucking pissed at you." Lee pointed over my shoulder at the bar. "So I'm gonna go back in there and finish my beer and go home. *Alone.* I need time to figure out how the hell we are going to get over this."

Lee moved past me without another word, and I jumped as the heavy metal door slammed behind him.

I sank to my knees, hugging them close as I let my sobs echo into the dark, lonely parking lot.

THIRTY-TWO
LEE

AVOIDING the woman you love in a small town proved to be damn near impossible. Annie Crane had left her mark on the town in more ways than I'd ever imagined. I couldn't walk down the street without seeing bits and pieces of her, the beach she loved so much, knowing how Huck's pastry of the week would make her smile and hum as she took her first bite, listening to Big Barb tell me how she had always known we were meant to be together.

The CLOSED sign on the door to Sand Dune Studio only deepened the pit in my stomach. I had, quite literally, screamed in her face that I loved her and then walked away.

Again.

Thankfully, a shift at the fire station would be the distraction I needed to not think about how *scared* Annie looked to admit the truth. How shocked she was at the depth of my love for her. I lost myself in the routine of cleaning and checking my equipment and a punishing workout.

When the ache in my chest never let up, I went for

another round, slamming my fists into the bag with punishing blows.

"Who pissed in your Cheerios?" Whip's smug face was the last thing I needed.

I punched the bag again, this time imagining his stupid smile on the end of it.

He pulled free weights from the rack and started his own workout. "Little Orphan Annie finally get tired of being the flavor of the month? Maybe send her my way and I'll—"

I didn't let him finish his sentence before I was in his face. "What did I tell you? Don't fucking call her that. In fact, you can keep her name out of your fucking mouth."

Whip's strong chest swelled. He wasn't about to back down, and a fistfight at the station would have some serious repercussions for the both of us.

My entire world is already on fire. Fuck it.

I stepped forward. "You or any other King so much as *looks* at her? Your family's money won't be able to protect you from me. I can guaran-fucking-tee that."

"Fucking try it, dickbag." Whip's eyes blazed with challenge, and my fist ached to connect with his smug jaw.

"Whoa. Hey. Enough!" Brooklyn was inches shorter than either of us, but she wedged her way between us, planting her hands on our chests and prying us apart. "Back the fuck up!"

We each took a step back but continued to stare the other down.

"You both know better than to bring that petty rivalry shit in here."

We did, but I couldn't find it in me to care. There was a gaping hole in the center of my chest where Annie had ripped my heart out, and getting into a scrap with Whip felt like a damn good way to ignore it.

Brooklyn raised her chin. "Shut it down before Chief comes in here and slaps a suspension on both your asses."

Whip shook his head and turned his back to me to leave. Keyed up, I continued to stare at him.

"Hey," Brooklyn said, her voice lowering for only me to hear. "What the hell, Lee?"

"He pushed my buttons. One of these days I'm not going to hold back."

She shook her head, my chest still heaving with rapid breaths and her hand grounding me. "You've always been able to ignore his overinflated ego. What is going on with you?"

My jaw clenched. How could I possibly explain that the bottom had dropped out of my entire world, and despite the fact that my best friend and the woman I was in love with had completely eviscerated my heart, all I could think about was how much I missed her?

"I'm fine," I ground out.

She scoffed. "Well, go be fine over there. I have shit to do and can't spend my shift babysitting you two idiots."

With one last petty glare at the back of Whip's retreating head, I snagged my towel and strode out of the station's workout room. I walked down the hallway and realized I'd taken a wrong turn somewhere. Instead of heading to the showers, I found myself at the end of a corridor outside my lieutenant's office and bunk. A large window overlooked the truck bay, where our trucks and ambulances waited at the ready.

Truck thirty-eight was my favorite, and on the dash was a small hula girl figurine. I had found it in my freezer, and the best part was that she was poorly made, with only three fingers on each hand and her painted eyes pointed in different directions. After she joined us on a call for a five-car pileup on the interstate outside of town, the crew had dubbed her a lucky charm, and she'd sat proudly on the dash for years. The sun had faded her green grass skirt, but her wonky eyes still stared you down when she bobbled.

I looked at the tiny figurine. The past few weeks had been perfect, like the misshapen pieces of my life had finally started to fit together. No more shoving them into place or cutting off different parts to make it fit. With Annie, it just clicked.

I braced my hands on the window frame and let my head hang. Flashes of the past few months assaulted me. Painful reminders of how Annie's laughter turned into moans as I kissed her. The feel of her skin as I committed every inch to memory. Whispering tender words in the safety of my darkened bedroom.

"Hey, man. You okay?" Connor's concerned voice came up behind me, and I straightened.

Blowing out a breath, I shook my head. "I don't know."

"Brooklyn said you blew up at Whip."

"He's a prick."

Connor laughed. "You two are worse than an old married couple. Don't let him get under your skin. Is it about Annie?"

My chest ached at the sound of her name. "Yeah, it's . . . complicated."

He scoffed. "Of course it is. Every relationship is complicated. But, come on, you're Lee Sullivan. Nothing gets to you, man."

I turned to him and leaned against the window, crossing my ankles, his words sinking in and deepening my frustrations. *Let it roll off your back. Lee Sullivan doesn't give a shit about anything. He never takes life too seriously.*

My friend had no idea of the man I was. I'd never let him or anyone else in this town see below the surface. But she knew. Annie would always hold space for me and all my moods, while everyone else just wanted me to be the happy-go-lucky guy. The man with the jokes. The life of the party.

It was fucking exhausting.

I shook my head and took a chance on opening up to my friend. "This is different. We've got some old, painful history, and some things came to light that she'd been keeping from me. Big things."

He let my words soak in and leaned against the wall. "That's rough, man. Why do you think she didn't tell you?"

Annie had brought up Margo more in the last few weeks than she had in a decade. Every time I'd found a way to stop her—to ignore the pang of guilt I felt. She'd tried to tell me, several times, in fact. With painful clarity I could see the uncertainty swirling in her blue eyes, and I did what I always did. I *chose* to ignore it. I didn't want to see what I already knew . . . I took advantage of the fact that Annie was mine for the auction dates and used it as an excuse to break the rules of our friendship. Whenever she had tried to open herself to me, I had shut it down.

Pressure built in my skull. "She tried. I kind of . . . shut down on her."

Connor shook his head like a disappointed father, and though I thought I couldn't feel any lower, somehow that silent gesture did it.

"You two have a history." He scoffed. "I've watched her clean up your messes more than once, and she always did it with humor and a smile on her face. You can't tell me you're giving up on her just because she made a mistake."

Giving up?

The more his words rattled around inside my brain, the more it didn't feel right. Not at all. There was no *giving up* on Annie. In my mind that wasn't even an option.

Annie had been my steadfast friend since childhood, my *best* friend for a decade. She constantly tried to remind me of my worth beyond my humor, and I'd gloss over it with another joke. Every second of my friendship with Annie came to life, and I let it play out in a painful, endless loop.

Finally I let out a frustrated breath. "I gave her the out she deserved."

His face screwed up before he shook his head and turned around. "If you really believe that, you're dumber than you look."

I watched yet another friend walk away from me. As I stared at his back, self-loathing threatened to consume me. Because in the end, I was right.

I loved Annie, but I also knew I was far too broken to deserve her love in return.

THIRTY-THREE
ANNIE

"He really just . . . said nothing?" Kate's sad eyes searched mine, and I could only shrug. The ache in my chest was a permanent fixture now that I had royally fucked up with my best friend. He said a lot more than *nothing* when he confessed his love in the back parking lot of the Grudge, but right now Kate and Lark were focused on me telling Lee about the letters.

The only silver lining in the whole thing was that they hadn't totally turned their backs on me once I'd come clean about the letters.

Lark stared out onto the water, watching Penny giggle as she kicked at the waves. "And you . . . couldn't just blurt it out or something?"

I knew it was hard for Lark to understand why I had let so much time pass without telling Lee I had written the letters. Saying it out loud was bad enough. "I wanted to," I admitted. "So many times. Then, after a while, it was just something that felt too big to admit to. I was afraid."

Kate's hand sliced through the beachy air. "You also have to understand Margo and Lee's role in all of this." She turned to Lark. "Margo was special around here. The kind of girl who people would say lit up a room, or 'That girl's going places.' She was practically Outtatowner royalty. But she was also *always* in the middle of some kind of drama. She had a way about her that sucked you in and made it impossible to say no to her, even when you *knew* that TP-ing the principal's house in the middle of the day was probably a bad idea. When it came to Margo, no one ever said no to her."

Lark nodded as Kate continued, "Lee and Margo were on and off *forever*. They were both young and dumb, and neither could get their shit together. It didn't matter that I was younger. Even then I could see it for the disaster it was. They'd break up and make up so many times I lost count."

Kate sighed. "When Lee joined the Army, we were all shocked." I recalled the dread that pooled in my stomach when I had heard the news. "Before we knew it, he was gone and his Army unit was shipped overseas."

"We were all so worried," I added, remembering the nights I cried myself to sleep, wondering where he was and whether he was alive.

An unladylike snort came from Kate. "*Most* of us were worried. Margo seemed unfazed and could bask in the attention of Outtatowner's male population without worrying about Lee's jealousy getting in the way."

"Why didn't she just break up with him?" Lark asked.

Kate's face twisted. "And not get to revel in the attention of living a heartbreaking sob story of an Army girlfriend? Please."

"Lee had asked her to write, but months went by and she didn't. When I'd asked her about it, she said, *Why don't you do it?* I thought she was joking. Only the idea rooted, and she wouldn't let it go. She convinced me that it was the right thing to do. For *him.*" I shook my head. Even saying it out loud sounded stupid and childish.

"Okay, wait." Lark popped a Twizzler in her mouth and considered. "Let's just say . . . you exchange these letters and share a connection. Why not tell him after he gets home?"

"I know." My heart sank. I knew all this, and talking about it made me feel only worse. "Margo and I got into a huge fight about it. She had sworn me to secrecy, but I was determined to tell him. She was *pissed* because the Lee who came back had changed, and she was worried I would mess things up for her."

Kate snagged her own Twizzler from the bag. "Plus, it was only two months before she was gone. After she died, Lee went off the deep end. He clung to those letters like a lifeline and convinced himself Margo was the love of his life." She scoffed and shook her head.

I looked out onto the water. "He was so *sad*. Her death was tragic and sudden, and he would say over and over how much her letters meant to him. How they were the only piece of her that he had left. It broke my heart, but I couldn't bring myself to tell him and take that away from him."

"Jesus." Lark shook her head.

We all sat in silence as the dumpster fire of my story hung between us. Deep shame washed over me, and I swallowed back tears.

"Okay, one more thing." Lark's brows were pinched in concentration. "Wouldn't he have recognized your handwriting or something?"

I let out a sad, watery scoff. "I tried. For a while I had purposely left notes or handwritten things around, and he never said anything."

"Do you really think Wyatt would recognize your handwriting?" Kate asked. "I know for sure that Beckett probably wouldn't."

Lark picked up her phone. "Well, let's find out."

I looked over her shoulder. "What are you doing?"

"Texting Wyatt and asking if he thinks he would know my handwriting if he saw it."

Kate's eyes brightened. "Excellent idea."

She also grabbed her phone, and my head sank into my hands. "You two are ridiculous."

"Shh." Lark grinned. "This is for science."

A few moments passed before Lark frowned at her phone. "Well, that's bullshit. Wyatt said, *and I quote*, 'Probably a ten percent chance if I'm lucky.'"

Kate laughed and tipped her phone toward us. "Beckett is coming in at an underwhelming forty percent."

"So it's possible Lee is just stupid like the rest of our men," Lark teased and pulled a sad laugh from me.

"Who's stupid?" Penny kicked sand toward us as she barreled back to her beach towel.

I let out a frustrated exhale and willed the constant threat of tears to go away. "Me, unfortunately."

Penny wrapped herself in a towel and plunked down onto the sand. Her hand dug into the bag of Twizzlers, coating them with a layer of grit.

"You should tell the lake to go fuck itself." Penny bit into her Twizzler.

"Pickle!" Lark scolded as Kate and I let out dual shocked laughs.

"What?" she said around a mouthful of candy. "Dad said the only time I could swear is if I stood with my feet in the water when no one else was around and yelled it at the lake." Realization washed over her cute features, and she looked sheepishly at Lark. "Oh. Sorry."

Lark ran a loving hand down her hair and winked at her before pulling her into a side hug. "You're a pretty great kid, you know that?"

Penny laughed and nodded. "Yeah. Uncle Lee told me I was his second favorite human."

Even hearing his name hurt, but I loved witnessing the bond between Lee and his niece. I smiled at her. "Number two's not so bad."

Penny scoffed and rolled her eyes. "Says the person who's his number one."

Her words were like a lance between my ribs. Kate reached over and squeezed my hand, and tears blurred my vision.

Not wanting to cry in front of everyone—*again*—I hopped up and dusted sand from my butt. "I'm going to head in." I looped my beach bag over my shoulder and managed a small smile. As soon as my back was turned, hot tears streamed down my cheeks.

You had this coming. What did you expect?

I swiped angrily at my tears. For now I had to focus on putting one foot in front of the other. Going through the motions was the only way I would survive, no matter how daunting a life absent of Lee would be.

THIRTY-FOUR
LEE

I MISSED HER.

Not only my quirky best friend who was a constant oversharer but the woman my soul craved.

How had I not seen it?

Now that I knew it had been Annie behind the letters, it all made sense—the deep bond we shared, how it always felt like I was tethered to her. It was as if my soul had found its mate in hers and was just waiting for me to wake up and see it.

I knew, in my bones, Annie was an honest person. I remembered how in third grade she'd cheated on a science test and ratted herself out to Mrs. Dockley when she received an A minus. I had always known her to be kind and caring for everyone in town. Hell, she'd taken care of me more times than I could count.

I needed to see her. I wanted to apologize for bailing on her before she could explain herself. Apologize for raising my voice at her and finally admitting aloud that I loved her.

I was still pissed, but we could work it out.

We had to.

She'd avoided my calls for the past two days, so showing up to her work was the next logical option. My eyes narrowed when I saw JP King standing outside of Sand Dune Studio, hanging a For Rent sign in the window.

I parked my truck and stormed toward him. "What the hell is this?"

JP looked me over but turned back to the building. "Sullivan."

I gestured toward the sign and repeated, *"What the hell is this?"*

JP turned toward me, a bored expression on his smug face. "Are you looking to rent a downtown storefront or are you just wasting my time?"

"Fuck off. Where's Annie?"

JP had the audacity to look bored as I fumed in front of him. "Ms. Crane opted to break her lease." I started to argue, but he put a hand up in the air. "We came to a mutually beneficial agreement, only charging her half of what her contract clause originally stipulated for a premature exit." He leaned forward. "So you're welcome for that."

"Such an asshole," I muttered. I shook my head and stormed off in search of Annie.

Unable to track her down, I found myself sitting at Aunt Tootie's dining room table and scowling into a cold glass of lemonade. Looking around the space, I couldn't help but feel happiness for my aunt. The farmhouse was old, but Kate and Beckett had managed to completely renovate it while keeping the integrity of our old home. My eyes moved to a framed board. During construction, Beckett had unearthed a section of wall where our mother had marked our heights over the years. Instead of demolishing it, he'd preserved a piece of her. I absently rubbed the tattoo of my mom's handwriting.

Tootie came up behind me, placing her hand between my shoulder blades, and sighed. "It's a great house."

I nodded. "A lot of memories here."

She rubbed small circles on my back. "Some good, some bad, but these walls have lived through it all."

I sank into her maternal touch. Tootie had stepped in to be the matriarch of our family after Mom died and even more so after Dad got sick. She'd watched us grow and make mistakes and loved us through it all.

A tiny peck sounded by the door. Just beyond the screen, Henrietta was tilting her head and poking the frame with her beak. I stood, opened the screen door and scooped her in my arms. With a low, contented cluck, Henrietta nestled into my embrace.

With a sigh, I sat back at the dining room table, gently petting Henrietta's soft feathers. "Do you ever get tired of it?" My voice came out small, and I ground my teeth against the swell of emotions rising in my chest.

When she didn't answer, I continued: "Tired of how people look at you and see only one part of you?"

Tootie took the seat next to mine. "What do you think when people see you?"

I scoffed. "They see a Sullivan or the son of a man losing his mind. A bachelor who will never commit. The poor guy who should be lamenting his perfect dead girlfriend."

She shook her head, but I didn't have the balls to look her in the eye.

"Have you ever considered that you are seeing their looks through the lens of how you view yourself? Because when I look around, all I see are people who love you. People who see a man who always helps his friends and neighbors without being asked. A man who takes care of the people around him. A man who knows the value of a life and lives his to the fullest. A man *worthy* of great love."

Emotion clogged my throat. "I don't know that man you're talking about."

She smiled. "Sure you do. You see him every day in the mirror."

"What if I already lost my chance at great love?"

My aunt was quiet before she set her glass down onto the wood table with a clink. "What you had with Margo was not great love. It was *young* love. Usually young love is intense and cleverly disguised as great love. But the lucky ones learn that great love isn't the explosive drama and all-consuming passion of young love. It's subtler. It's a deep, cavernous ache that won't *ever* let you go. That, dear boy, is great love."

I shook my head and stood, angry that everyone always associated me with a tragic love story that happened so damn long ago. "I wasn't talking about Margo."

Tootie smiled up at me with loving eyes. "I know you weren't."

I sighed, defeated. "I messed up. Annie tried to open herself up to me, and instead of listening, I shut her out. Then she found me and I dumped all my frustrations on her. I messed up."

"When a door shuts, great love finds a window." Tootie smiled at me one last time before taking her lemonade outside to visit her chickens.

My pulse pounded in my neck. *Great love finds a window.*

Annie had been loyal to Margo, even in death. Even

when that meant sacrificing her own heart to save me the pain of knowing Margo never loved me the way I thought. For years I had been angry at how my life had turned out when I came home. How *unfair* it all seemed, and Annie had loved me through it.

For me, that said a whole lot more about her character than the lie she carried. If roles were reversed and I thought the person I loved was hanging on to the memory of someone else, and that the one thing that brought my love peace meant holding back my own heart? I'm not sure what I would have done. It sure as hell wouldn't have been an easy choice, that much I knew.

Besides, hadn't I been lying too? Every time someone joked about Annie and me being together or asked why I would never shoot my shot with her. We'd both been lying for years. Sure, I was angry for all the wasted years between us, but when it came down to it, I never had the balls to tell her how I felt either.

I was just as complicit as she was.

I stood, knowing exactly what I needed to do.

I stomped toward the door, setting Henrietta down and gripping the doorframe to look back at my aunt. With renewed energy, I flashed her a smile and tore out of her house and leaped off the porch stairs as I raced toward my truck.

"Heading home?" Tootie called out across the yard, and little Henrietta ran toward me.

Hopeful excitement raced through me. "Going to make things right for my girl!"

THIRTY-FIVE
ANNIE

SITTING on the rickety stairs to the barn apartment, I let the bright summer sun wash over me. Closing my eyes, I felt its warmth seep into my skin. The crunch of tires on gravel had me peeking through one eye.

Surprised to see Beckett's work truck rolling down the driveway, I opened both eyes and sat a little straighter. He came to a stop and climbed out, but instead of heading toward Highfield House like I'd imagined he would, he walked toward me.

"Morning!" I called out. "Helping with the move?" Lark and Wyatt had finally finished their home build and had spent the last few days packing up and moving everything over to the new custom home Beckett had helped them build.

Beckett shook his head as he stopped in front of me. He tipped his head toward the barn. "Came to check out my new jobsite."

My nose crinkled. "Jobsite? I thought you and Kate were taking a break between filming?"

He smirked. "Something came up."

I looked over at the creepy-ass barn below my temporary apartment. For as long as I could remember, it had been mostly vacant, save for random Sullivan storage. "Did Tootie finally decide to fix it up?"

Beckett's eyes narrowed at me. "Something like that. I just need to get in there and start taking a few measurements."

I stood, slapping my hands against my thighs. "Well, don't let me keep you."

I had taken a few steps up toward my apartment when Beckett stopped me. "Hey, Annie?"

I turned to face him as he continued: "You love him, right?"

I swallowed thickly and nodded.

"It'll be worth the heartache in the end. I promise."

A surge of affection for Kate's grumpy, sweet man flowed through me as I rushed down the steps and threw my arms around his neck. He stood stiffly and awkwardly patted my back as I sniffled. "Thank you."

"Okay." Beckett turned and disappeared into the barn, and I couldn't help but laugh. Buried beneath his grumpy exterior was a heart of gold, and I was so happy he and Kate had found each other.

It'll be worth the heartache in the end.

God, how I hoped there was a shred of truth in those words.

ANOTHER MISERABLE WEEK passed as I hid in the barn apartment and contemplated what to do with my life. After dodging Lee's initial calls in an effort to give him space and to clear my own head, they stopped, and that cut deeper than I had expected.

I was surrounded by boxes of unsold pottery—another shining example of how I had epically failed at life. The only comfort I had was that the construction noise below me drowned out my own thoughts as Beckett and his crew got to work on cleaning up the barn. The sawing and hammering noises became the perfect distraction as I set up an online storefront, hoping to sell a few pieces while I figured out what to do next. Maybe Huck could hire me at the Sugar Bowl for a while. At this point I'd happily take payment in the form of carbs.

My hand hovered over my phone, but I stopped myself from picking it up and texting some snarky comment to Lee. It was something that had happened a thousand times since I'd last seen him, and each time I'd stopped myself. It was clear to me that Lee was deeply hurt when he discovered it was me who had written the letters, and he was *very* clear that he wanted to be alone and needed time to process.

I didn't blame him.

I deserved the cold shoulder and his silent treatment. I deserved the pain that made breathing feel like a chore.

I gritted my teeth to keep from crying.

Again.

Do I beg for forgiveness? Scream at him for all the times he stopped me from telling him? Wait it out and hope he forgives me one day? Move away and give him the space he needs?

Every option seemed worse than the last, and I could feel my thoughts spiraling. I needed to get out—go for a walk or *something* to stop obsessing over how epically I had fucked up my relationship with the greatest man I'd ever known.

I turned to open a kitchen cabinet and grab my water bottle. Staring at me was a tiny resin duck. One of what felt like a thousand I'd found tucked away in the apartment. Constant, googly-eyed reminders of Lee. I swiped the green duck and dropped it into the small ceramic bowl I'd used to collect them all. Its vacant eyes stared back at me as a hollowness opened in my chest.

Even if I had ruined any chance of things working out with Lee, he deserved to know how I felt. That I loved him too. I needed to make him see himself the way I had *always* seen him. He was so much more than a playboy or the comic relief.

Lee was *everything*.

Determined to seek him out, I left the water bottle and barreled out of the apartment, bounding down the wooden stairs two at a time. As I hurried across the lawn toward my car, my feet came up short.

Lee was standing with his arms crossed and a deep furrow in his brow, talking with Beckett and gesturing toward the barn. Beckett pointed at something on a set of large architectural plans.

I stared, unable to move. Unable to *breathe*. It had been only a week, but it felt like I hadn't seen him in months.

He sensed me, and his back stiffened as he looked my way. I wanted to look down, look away and not let him see the shame and regret in my eyes, but I was locked in his stare.

A muscle in his jaw flexed, and I thought I saw the tiniest smirk lift at the corner of his mouth. He said something to Beckett and started walking toward me.

My feet were rooted to the ground.

"Annette." The ripple of his deep voice moved over me. I sucked in a breath, pulling in his familiar scent.

When I didn't respond, he tipped his head toward the barn. "I need to show you something."

A tiny "okay" was all I could manage as he walked away. I followed, my eyes never leaving Lee as he walked into the construction zone.

"Can I get a few minutes, guys?" he asked the construction crew. One by one they nodded and cleared out until we were alone in the expanse of the empty barn.

"Wow. The guys moved fast." I scanned the barn, empty except for a few ladders, power tools, and a whole lot of dust the crew had left behind.

My fingers itched to lace with Lee's and to bury my face in his chest and beg for forgiveness. It felt like I was at the edge of a cliff, my breaths shallow as I waited to see if Lee would shove me off or grab my hand and jump with me.

"So here's what I'm thinking . . ." Lee left my side and moved through the dusty barn. "Tables, big ones that seat at least eight, lined up in the middle. Along that wall, there will be custom shelving strong enough to support the weight of finished pieces that need to get picked up."

I stared at Lee, still trying to wrap my brain around what he was talking about. He gestured for me to follow. "Come on. Over here I think there's enough space for the raw, unfinished pottery. People can shop around and decide what pieces they're going to paint. The register will be over there. We'll convert the upstairs apartment into an office space, but then through here . . ." Lee pushed open a creaky door that led to a small room with a wall of ancient-looking windows. "New windows, walls, flooring." He shrugged. "Well, new everything pretty much, and I think this makes a perfect studio."

Studio? I could only stare at him as his body radiated with excitement.

"Around the back and sides of the barn there's room for outdoor seating or classes. Whatever you want to do."

"Lee, I . . ." I shook my head. "I don't understand."

Lee's handsome grin spread as he opened his arms wide. "Welcome to the Sand Dune Art Barn."

Through the dust and construction, I could see it with perfect clarity. The vision of blending art and community with tourism formed before my eyes. The dream I had shared with Lee in late-night whispers and flippant, offhand comments. He'd listened to every detail, and I could see it taking shape before my eyes.

I couldn't keep my voice from breaking when I turned to him. "What did you do?"

His eyes burned into me. "I'm doing whatever it takes. Whatever I need to do to show you that it was always you."

My heart thumped painfully against my ribs.

"It took me a little bit to wrap my head around the fact you wrote the letters, but once I did, it was painfully obvious. When I think back to my time in the Army, I don't think about the drills or the missions. Instead I think about the small, *human* moments—laughter with my unit to break up the tension and stress, the ripple of excitement when another letter came. Those letters saved my life. *You* saved my life. And then when I got home and everything fell apart, you saved me again. Your friendship and loyalty held me up when I was self-destructing. Not my brothers, not Kate, not Margo. *You*."

Lee's voice was thick in a way I'd never heard before, and I fought back my own tears as he continued: "I know what the hell I'm fighting for. I found myself and I will work for you and this love. What you did—keeping Margo's secret —isn't who you are."

Lee reached forward to grab my hand. He planted it on

his chest, his heart hammering beneath my palm. "Feel this." He tapped his fingers against the back of my hand to the rhythm of his heartbeat. "There is no distance between your heart and mine. Every single day with you is the best day of my life."

Finally my tears broke free, and I crumbled at his words. My eyes searched his. "Isn't it the person who messed up who should be doing the big, romantic gestures?"

He shook his head and smiled. "I know you. You are too good and too kind to be selfish. You would never take more than anyone asked, but that's what I'm asking. Take me—all of me. The jokes and the pranks and the sadness I keep buried too. Just like you've always done. Annette, will you take me?"

THIRTY-SIX
LEE

My question hung in the air, and a ripple of panic coursed through me. *Was I too late? Had she finally come to her senses and realized I really wasn't worth all the trouble?* Now that she was free of her secret, maybe she'd decided that moving on was the best option.

A tear slipped down her cheek and I caught it, then brushed it aside with my thumb.

"I will take you. All parts of you." Annie's whispered words broke me. I gathered her in my arms, and relief washed over me as she clung to me. "I love you and you're my best friend, but we have to think about growing up. You don't get to be an idiot all the time anymore. Silly pranks are one thing, but you can't be reckless. When it's time to talk about things, we actually need to talk about them."

Bundling her in my arms, I clutched her closer as she sobbed into my chest. As much as I hated to see her cry, my heart was soaring. Annie was mine, and I'd stop at nothing to give her everything she deserved—every part of me. She needed comfort and stability, and I would be the man to give it to her. "You're right. I shut you out because I was afraid too. Afraid that this was all too good to be true and that you would realize that I'm a fuckup."

Annie swiped at her eyes. "You're not—"

"I was. I wanted to have fun, fuck around, play pranks on the Kings, and not think about the consequences of giving in to all the feelings I'd bottled up for so long. At any point I could have told you, but I let fear win out. I won't do that again." I cupped her face in my hands. "I swear to you."

Fresh tears spilled over her lashes and down her cheeks before she clutched me close and wiped her face on me, quickly trying to hide the wet spots with a swipe of her hand. "I'm blubbering all over you." She wiped again. "I think I got snot on your shirt."

A laugh shot out of me, and I held her at arm's distance to give her a disgusted look. "Gross."

Her gentle laughter was a balm for my soul. We were going to be all right—better than all right. I had plans for us, and it was going to be fucking epic. My hands tangled in her hair, and I took one step closer, fusing her body to mine. Her hands found my hips, and heat spread between us.

"Annette Crane, I am so fucking gone for you." My mouth moved over hers as I swallowed her whimper. "I love you. I love you." I said it over and over as I peppered kisses everywhere—her lips, her face, her hair.

"I love you, Lee. I have been in love with you my whole life. I'm so sorry I was too afraid to tell you before." Annie stopped my kisses, placing her hands on the sides of my face. Her crystal-blue eyes bore into me. "I will make up for every moment we missed out on. I will fight for you and for this love, because it is everything. *You* are everything."

I had never been more seen. More wanted. More loved.

"I will fight for you." I reiterated her words, setting her fears to rest and knowing I would die before I let another wasted moment fall between us.

Bending down, I gripped Annie under her thighs and hoisted her up so she could wrap her legs around my waist. She squealed in delight, and I held her close, kissing her neck.

Sure, we may have had countless missed opportunities over the years, but what we got instead was a rock-solid friendship that would be the foundation of a perfect life together.

I had missed her every second of every day we had been apart, and I was damn sure going to make certain that would never happen again. I gently placed her on her feet. "So what do you say? Are you ready to make all your dreams come true?"

She shook her head and looked around. "It's too much. This is too much."

I smirked. "Well, if you think this is too much, buckle up, because there's more." I loved the bewildered expression she wore as I flicked the tip of her nose and grabbed her hand to lead her outside. Still holding her tightly, I smiled at the crew. "Thanks, guys, it's all yours."

As they filed back into the barn to continue their work, I dragged Annie into the sunlight. She stopped, and her hand squeezed mine as she looked up at me. "Wait. I have something for you."

Annie took a few steps toward the barn. "Wait here." She ran up a few stairs before stopping to turn back to me. "I'll be right back! Please, just one second."

Annie ran into the apartment. It was only a few moments before she was pushing open the door and running down the stairs. She stopped in front of me. "Here."

She shoved a slim envelope in my hands. Turning it over, I recognized the overseas address. There was a stamp in the corner, and the edges of the envelope had been bent and crinkled with time. "I should have mailed this. It's been sitting at the bottom of the box for years. I should have given it to you, but I was so afraid. Only I'm not afraid anymore. I want you to have it."

I turned the old envelope over in my hands before slipping a finger under the seal. A letter, written on familiar lined paper. I looked from the letter to Annie.

"I wanted to tell you. *So many times.* I tried but couldn't do it. I can't give us back those years, but I wanted you to know that I always wanted to tell you. I was afraid—of losing you, losing your whole incredible family. They had no reason to take me in and love me the way they do. I couldn't bear that heartbreak, and I would take you however I could have you. Eventually, I had convinced myself that us being friends would be enough."

My eyes scanned the pages. Right there, in black ink, Annie had spilled her secret and exposed her heart. My fingers moved over the words on the page as I read them. My best friend's words were raw and honest, and the last pieces of my broken heart clicked into place. I didn't need this letter to feel complete with Annie, but simply knowing her words were genuine and unfiltered soothed my soul.

I looked down into her hopeful blue eyes. "Thank you." I lowered my head to kiss my girl, soft and slow. Her breath hitched. "Please don't cry."

"I'm so mad at myself," she whispered. "All this time it could have been like this. I tried to tell you."

I smoothed her wild hair away from her face. "I know you did. And I'm sorry I didn't let you. But we have a lifetime of new memories to make. Right here, you and me."

"Here?"

My grin widened as I tipped my head toward Highfield House. "You've always loved this house, and I've always loved you. I made a deal with Aunt Tootie, and it's yours if you want it. We can redo it however you want to."

Fresh tears swam in her eyes as I painted a picture of a new life together. "I want laughter and babies and lazy Sundays. I want it all with you—the passion, the laughter. I want to sit across a kitchen table and go over a grocery list with you. I don't know how to love small. Not when it comes to you."

She managed a tight nod as hope danced in her eyes.

"But I have one condition."

She blinked back tears. "What's that?"

"I'd like to build a coop. Bring over Horny Henrietta and maybe get her a few friends."

Her watery laugh lifted my spirits. "You are so weird about that bird."

I laughed. "I can't explain it. Henrietta and I share a bond."

Annie gripped onto me, pulling her face to my chest. "I want that life, and I want it all with you."

Our mouths fused as a sense of urgency moved through me. I had never been so certain about anything in my entire life than I was with Annie. "Come on," I growled as I lifted her into my arms and stomped up the porch steps to the house. *Our house.* The home where I would build a life with the woman who was my entire universe. I knew in time she would forgive herself, and I would use that time to prove to her that everything in our past had laid the foundation for a solid future. I would show her every day that she and I were meant for each other. That every day with her was the best day of my life.

All I needed was one chance.

EPILOGUE

Annie

THE WARM COASTAL breeze carried the familiar scent of blueberry fields as I stood outside the Sand Dune Art Barn, my heart overflowing with gratitude. It had been a remarkable year—a year of growth, love, and fulfillment. The once-rundown, probably haunted barn had transformed into a thriving sanctuary of creativity, where locals and tourists alike flocked to unleash their artistic talents. The community events we hosted were always filled with laughter, joy, and the sense of connection that came from shared artistic expression.

I glanced over at Lee, my anchor, my love, my best friend. He stood beside me, his eyes filled with pride. His commitment to his role as a firefighter was unwavering, and his dedication to our relationship was unmatched. Together we had built a home at Highfield House, a place where laughter echoed through the rooms, lazy Sundays were spent in each other's arms, and dreams found their safe haven.

As the sun cast a golden glow over the distant fields, I marveled at the beauty of the life we had created together. Lee's hand found mine, and a surge of warmth spread through me, reminding me that every moment of heartache and missed opportunity had led us to this place of unwavering love and unbreakable bond.

The Sand Dune Art Barn had flourished beyond my wildest dreams, becoming not only a creative haven but also a symbol of the vibrant community that surrounded us. Artists from near and far had come to share their expertise and stories, infusing the space with inspiration and passion. The barn was alive with color, echoing the kaleidoscope of emotions that art had the power to evoke.

I turned to Lee, my eyes shimmering with the certainty of our future. His smile was the reflection of my own happiness, and the love that radiated from him enveloped me in a cocoon of safety and belonging.

"Annette," he said, his voice a soothing melody. "You did the damn thing."

Tears of gratitude welled in my eyes as I surveyed the vibrant landscape before me, a testament to the strength of our love and the beauty of second chances. "I could never have done this without you. Your love and friendship have surpassed anything I could have ever dreamed of."

He cupped my face in his hands, his touch a gentle caress that ignited a fire within me. "Annie Crane, you will always be my everything."

A soft breeze rustled through the blueberry field, whispering promises of a future filled with endless possibilities. With each passing day, I discovered new depths to our connection, a love that defied logic and boundaries. I had found my forever in Lee, and I vowed to cherish and protect our love with every breath I took.

As we stood there, hand in hand, I couldn't help but marvel at the irony of fate. The letter I had given Lee, finally revealing the truth that had been locked away for so long, had brought us closer than ever. The truth in its words had opened our hearts to a love that was unshakable, a love that had withstood the test of time.

"Take me home."

His eyes sparkled with a mixture of love and mischief. In a swift move, Lee tossed me over his shoulder, and we headed toward our front door.

Laughter bubbled between us as he smacked me on the ass. Barely inside the door, his hands moved over my legs, slipping between my thighs, his touch warm through my jeans. He set me on my feet, and his body covered mine. We fit together so seamlessly it was hard to know where he ended and I began.

"There are people right outside." My breath was needy and insistent as I tugged at his shirt.

"Good. Let them hear how well you take me when I stretch you open."

Every muscle inside me clenched at his filthy speech. No amount of time would ever dim the way his words made me feel. Sexy. Cherished. *His.*

Whatever was on the dining table clattered to the floor as Lee pressed me against it, his front to my back. His words were hot against my ear. "You are so beautiful, Annette. I'm going to show you just how pretty you are when you're dripping with my cum."

I moaned as his rough hands squeezed my butt. I pressed back into his lap, feeling how hard he was for me. A devilish thought crept through my mind, and I fought a smirk, glancing back at him.

"You're going to have to catch me first."

Without giving him a second to think, I shot out of his embrace and up the stairs. My squealing laughter filled our home as he bounded after me. Sure, he'd catch me, but I knew damn well Lee Sullivan would make it worth my while.

His arms captured me around my waist, and I squealed in surprise.

His chuckle tickled my ear and sent tingles racing down my back. "This is the best day of my life."

I leaned into him, nudging his shoulder, and he hugged me. "You always say that."

From behind me, he presented a small box, and my world spun. "Yeah," he said as I turned to face him. "But this time, I mean it."

Lowering to his knee, Lee opened the small velvet box. "When, one day, our son or daughter asks me about falling in love, I will tell them about the only woman I have ever loved. I won't even have to pull out a picture. Instead, I can point to you and simply say, 'She's right over there.' You were always meant to be a Sullivan. Meant to be mine. Annette Crane, will you marry me?"

My hand pressed into my lips, and my eyes filled with tears. The ring was a sparkling diamond, but something dark and red caught my eye. I leaned closer as Lee plucked the gorgeous, sparkling ring from my hand. "You mentioned once that diamonds could have other gemstones as inclusions. Like this one, the diamond and garnet formed and grew together. It reminded me of us. You've always been a part of me. Be my wife?"

Through a watery sob, I shook my head and sputtered, "Yes."

Lee slipped the ring onto my finger and wrapped me in his arms.

I was his and he was mine.

Always.

Need more of Lee & Annie? Check out this exclusive BONUS SCENE here: https://www.lenahendrix.com/get-lee-and-annies-bonus-scene/

SNEAK PEEK OF ONE NIGHT

Duke Sullivan is a broody, grumpy farmer—the oldest son of my family's rival. He also happens to be my *good morning* text, and the man I have no right to have a secret crush on. **Duke is strictly forbidden.**

Knowing our relationship could never be more than stolen glances and longing looks, we agree to stay secret friends. But after months of keeping our friendship hidden, the stars align, sparks ignite, and we *finally* give into temptation.

Every soft smirk, every brush of his calloused hand against my sensitive skin makes me want to burst into flames. **It become clear, despite the feud, Duke is relentlessly going after what he wants and I think that might be . . . *me*.**

I'm the quiet daughter with the wrong last name, but it's clear he wants so much more than just ***one night*.**

~

Preorder One Night here: https://geni.us/onenightduke

HENDRIX HEARTTHROBS

Want to connect? Come hang out with the Hendrix Heartthrobs on Facebook to laugh & chat with Lena! Special sneak peeks, announcements, exclusive content, & general shenanigans all happen there.

Come join us!

ACKNOWLEDGMENTS

Did you ever have a friend in junior high you were CERTAIN you'd eventually end up with? I did. Looking back, it really would have made for a beautiful and swoony romance if it wasn't mired in awkward glances, missed chances, teenage heartbreak, and one disastrous date as adults. I feel like Lee and Annie got the happy ending that he-who-shall-remain-nameless and I didn't get. Because really, the romance I'd concocted in my teenage mind was *so much better* than real life. (Isn't it always?) We each got our own happily ever after and it all worked out the way it was meant to.

Speaking of my own happily ever after, I always have the thank my husband. He puts up me with my constant daydreaming about fictional men and always offers his advice, even when I rarely take it. I liked to tease you that you're the lucky one, but we both know no one else would put up with my bullshit. I love you to the ends of the earth.

To my readers, thank you. Thank you for loving a town that means so much to me. Coastal Michigan is my safe space, my dream small town, and I am so grateful you love it as much as I do! Your excitement for each new book drives me to write the best stories I can for you. You're the reason I keep going.

To my assistant Stephanie, thank you for being the ultimate hype girl. You have a knack for knowing when I need a laugh and to tell me that something is in retrograde so that's why I'm feeling out of sorts. You've become a friend and for that I am more grateful of all!

To Elsie and Kandi, THANK YOU! You are so much more than my early morning sprint session. You're the ultimate cheerleaders and safe space. God help us all if anyone ever reads that text thread.

To my alpha reader and friend, Nicole. Your attention to detail and dedication to this series has been overwhelming. I trust you more than you know. I love that we can laugh about bedhead, gardening, kitchen remodels, and books all in one ridiculous conversation. If I had a sister, I'd want her to be just like you. I love you!

To my friend Jenn, I value our writing/plotting conversations more than you know. You always offer a fresh perspective when I'm stuck and I look forward to seeing your smile every day!

To my beta readers Trinity and Anna, I made a mistake allowing y'all to comment *together* while beta reading! I don't think I ever laughed so hard while going through feedback and for that, I thank you. I appreciate you pointing out things that hit and areas that don't. I'm so glad you love how dirty Lee is!

Finally, to my ARC readers and Content Creator team, THANK YOU! Whether you've been with me from the beginning or are recent additions, I wouldn't be here without you. I am always so honored to see the amazing content you bring to life and how much you fall for the characters I write. I could never have imagined that I would have a team of strong, creative, POWERFUL women in my corner and I am so grateful. Every time I'm tagged, I am humbled and honored. You're the girl gang that little Lena never thought she'd have. 🤍

ABOUT THE AUTHOR

Lena Hendrix is an Amazon Top 10 bestselling contemporary romance author living in the Midwest. Her love for romance stared with sneaking racy Harlequin paperbacks and now she writes her own hot-as-sin small town romance novels. Lena has a soft spot for strong alphas with marshmallow insides, heroines who clap back, and sizzling tension. Her novels pack in small town heart with a whole lotta heat.

When she's not writing or devouring new novels, you can find her hiking, camping, fishing, and sipping a spicy margarita!

Want to hang out? Find Lena on Tiktok or IG!

ALSO BY LENA HENDRIX

Chikalu Falls

Finding You

Keeping You

Protecting You

Choosing You (origin novella)

Redemption Ranch

The Badge

The Alias

The Rebel

The Target

The Sullivans

One Look

One Touch

One Chance

One Night (Jan 2024)

One Taste (charity novella)

Printed in the USA
CPSIA information can be obtained
at www.ICGtesting.com
LVHW041143261023
762208LV00052B/882